New Casebooks

TONI MORRISON

NEW CASEBOOKS

Further titles are in preparation

New Casebooks Series
Series Standing Order
ISBN 0–333–71702–3 hardcover
ISBN 0–333–69345–0 paperback
(outside North America only)

You can receive future titles in this series as they are published by placing a standing order. Please contact your bookseller or, in case of difficulty, write to us at the address below with your name and address, the title of the series and the ISBN quoted above.

Customer Services Department, Macmillan Distribution Ltd
Houndmills, Basingstoke, Hampshire RG21 6XS, England

New Casebooks

TONI MORRISON

Edited by
LINDEN PEACH

St. Martin's Press
New York

TONI MORRISON
Introduction, selection and editorial matter copyright © 1998
by Linden Peach

St. Martin's Press, Scholarly and Reference Division,
175 Fifth Avenue, New York, N.Y. 10010

First published in the United States of America in 1998

This book is printed on paper suitable for recycling and
made from fully managed and sustained forest sources.

Printed in Hong Kong

ISBN 0–312–21121–X (clothbound)
ISBN 0–312–21123–6 (paperback)

Library of Congress Cataloging-in-Publication Data
Toni Morrison / edited by Linden Peach.
p.   cm. — (New casebooks)
Includes bibliographical references and index.
ISBN 0–312–21121–X (cloth). — ISBN 0–312–21123–6 (pbk.)
1. Morrison, Toni—Criticism and interpretation.   2. Women and
literature—United States—History—20th century.   3. Afro-American
women in literature.   4. Afro-Americans in literature.   I. Peach,
Linden, 1951–   .   II. Series.
PS3563.O8749Z893 1998
813'.54—dc21   97–37238
                                                                        CIP

Contents

Acknowledgements

The editor and publishers wish to thank the following for permission to use copyright material:

Houston A. Baker, Jr, for 'Knowing Our Places: Psychoanalysis and Sula' from *Workings of the Spirit: The Poetics of Afro-American Women's Writing* (1991), by permission of The University of Chicago Press; Angela Burton, for 'Signifyin(g) Abjection: Narrative Strategies in Toni Morrison's *Jazz*' (1997). Copyright © 1997 Angela Burton and the University of Leeds, by permission of the author; Cynthia A. Davis, for material from 'Self, Society, and Myth in Toni Morrison's Fiction', *Contemporary Literature*, 23:3 (1982), by permission of the University of Wisconsin Press; Madhu Dubey, for material from '"No Bottom and No Top": Oppositions in *Sula*' from *Black Women Novelists and the Nationalist Aesthetic*, Indiana University Press (1994), by permission of the author; Jennifer FitzGerald, for material from 'Selfhood and Community: Psychoanalysis and Discourse in *Beloved*', *Modern Fiction Studies*, 38:3–4 (1993), by permission of the Johns Hopkins University Press; Doreatha Drummond Mbalia, for '*Tar Baby*: A Reflection of Morrison's Developed Class Consciousness' from *Toni Morrison's Developing Class Consciousness*, Susquehanna/Associated University Presses (1991), by permission of Associated University Presses; Terry Otten, for 'The Crime of Innocence: *Tar Baby* and the Fall of Myth' from *The Crime of Innocence in the Fiction of Toni Morrison*, University of Missouri Press (1989), by permission of the author; Rafael Pérez-Torres, for material from 'Knitting and Knotting the Narrative Thread – *Beloved* as Postmodern Novel', *Modern Fiction Studies*, 39:3–4 (1993), by permission of the Johns Hopkins University Press; Barbara Hill Rigney, for 'Hagar's Mirror:

Self and Identity in Morrison's Fiction' from *The Voices of Toni Morrison* (1991). Copyright © 1991 by the Ohio State University Press, by permission of the Ohio State University Press; Eusebio Rodrigues, for material from 'Experiencing *Jazz*', *Modern Fiction Studies*, 39:3–4 (1993). Copyright © 1993 by the Johns Hopkins University Press, by permission of the Johns Hopkins University Press; Ashraf H. A. Rushdy, for excerpts from 'Daughters Signifyin(g) History: The Example of Toni Morrison's *Beloved*', *American Literature*, 64:3 (1992). Copyright © 1992 by Duke University Press, by permission of Duke University Press.

Every effort has been made to trace the copyright holders but if any have been inadvertently overlooked the publishers will be pleased to make the necessary arrangement at the first opportunity.

General Editors' Preface

The purpose of this series of New Casebooks is to reveal some of the ways in which contemporary criticism has changed our understanding of commonly studied texts and writers and, indeed, of the nature of criticism itself. Central to the series is a concern with modern critical theory and its effect on current approaches to the study of literature. Each New Casebook editor has been asked to select a sequence of essays which will introduce the reader to the new critical approaches to the text or texts being discussed in the volume and also illuminate the rich interchange between critical theory and critical practice that characterises so much current writing about literature.

In this focus on modern critical thinking and practice New Casebooks aim not only to inform but also to stimulate, with volumes seeking to reflect both the controversy and the excitement of current criticism. Because much of this criticism is difficult and often employs an unfamiliar critical language, editors have been asked to give the reader as much help as they feel is appropriate, but without simplifying the essays or the issues they raise. Again, editors have been asked to supply a list of further reading which will enable readers to follow up issues raised by the essays in the volume.

The project of New Casebooks, then, is to bring together in an illuminating way those critics who best illustrate the ways in which contemporary criticism has established new methods of analysing texts and who have reinvigorated the important debate about how we 'read' literature. The hope is, of course, that New Casebooks will not only open up this debate to a wider audience, but will also encourage students to extend their own ideas, and think afresh about their responses to the texts they are studying.

John Peck and Martin Coyle
University of Wales, Cardiff

Introduction

LINDEN PEACH

I

Toni Morrison, the first African-American writer to win the Nobel Prize for Literature, has published six novels to date: *The Bluest Eye* (1970), *Sula* (1973), *Song of Solomon* (1977), *Tar Baby* (1981), *Beloved* (1987) and *Jazz* (1992). Apart from a play, *Dreaming Emmett* (1985) – based on the brutal killing of a 14-year old black boy, Emmett Louis 'Bobo' Till, for allegedly whistling after a white woman – she has also published an important critical work, *Playing in the Dark: Whiteness and the Literary Imagination* (1992) and edited *Race-ing Justice; En-Gendering Power: Essays on Anita Hill, Clarence Thomas, and the Construction of Social Reality* (1993), a discussion of the ramifications of the United States Senate hearings in 1991 on the controversial nomination of Clarence Thomas to the Supreme Court, and the accusations of sexual harassment brought by Anita Hill.

Critics should always be cautious of making definitive judgements about the work of a living writer at the height of her powers, and in Toni Morrison's case the difficulties are compounded by the diversity and, in some respects, the unpredictable nature of her output. With each novel, Morrison has retained the capacity to take us by surprise. However, a collection of essays which are representative of the different approaches which have been taken to her work and which reviews and historicises these different critical perspectives is timely. It is also made necessary by the status and popularity which Morrison has achieved as a writer, the extent to which she is studied and the sheer volume of published critical work on her fiction.

In the wake of her Nobel Prize, the plethora of published critical writing on Morrison should not surprise us. But, although she has courted controversy, as the debates which followed her award of the Nobel Prize testify, Morrison's fiction has won such critical acclaim that the Nobel Prize was only the icing on the cake. The road to the Glittering Prize can be said to have begun when *Sula* was nominated for the National Book Award, but before the publication of *Beloved*, it was *Song of Solomon* which brought her considerable recognition in the form of the Fiction Award of the National Book Critics' Circle. In 1977, she also received the American Academy and Institute of Arts and Letters Award and in 1986 the New York State Governor's Art Award. Black writers and critics protested nationally when *Beloved* failed to win the National Book Award, but it did secure the Pulitzer Prize for fiction.

Morrison's novels have a complex relationship to history. Her life spans the last two-thirds of a century which has seen significant changes in civil rights for black people in America and wider public recognition of African-American women writers. All her novels are in a sense 'historical novels' in which characters, as Barbara Rigney has said, are 'both subjects *of* and subject *to* history, events in "real time", that succession of antagonistic movements that includes slavery, reconstruction, depression, and war'. But even though they may appear to be 'quasi documentaries that bear historical witness' they posit history as narrative, sometimes deliberately distorted or half-remembered, as fantasy or even as brutal nightmare.[1]

Morrison is not an autobiographical writer in the strict sense of the term. She admitted to Claudia Tate: 'My life is uneventful. Writing has to do with the imagination'.[2] Nevertheless, her up-bringing is clearly important as a piece in the jig-saw of her fiction. Lorain, Ohio – a small mid-western steel-mill town, 25 miles west of Cleveland – where she was born Chloe Anthony Wofford, the second of four children, on 18 February 1931, seems to have been especially significant. She thought of the small, black community there as a village in the traditional African sense, but the nature of Ohio itself is not irrelevant to many of her novels. In an interview with Claudia Tate, Morrison herself recalls:

> Ohio is an interesting and complex state. It has both a southern and a northern disposition. The Ohio River has historically represented

freedom ... The northern part of the state has underground railway stations and a history of black people escaping into Canada, but the southern part of the state is as much Kentucky as there is, complete with cross burnings. Ohio is a curious juxtaposition of what was ideal in this country and what was base.[3]

In fact, Morrison's novels not only reflect this kind of cultural schizophrenia, but often deconstruct it in favour of greater complexities.

Morrison's parents and grandparents, too, later proved to be important formative influences upon her imagination. George and Rahmah Willis, Southern migrants, had come to Lorain via Birmingham and Kentucky. Her mother, whose name had been plucked blindly from the Bible, was one of seven children born to John Solomon and Ardelia Willis. Perhaps theirs was the most obvious family influence to reveal itself in her fiction. While John was a skilled musician, Ardelia's magic book and the stories of ghosts and magic which they both told acquainted Morrison with black lore. These stories must have been at least partly responsible for the blurring of the boundaries between fantasy and reality and between fact and fiction in Morrison's novels, which some critics have taken, despite Morrison's own objection to the label, for 'magic realism'.

It was not until she had been through university, achieved a first degree and postgraduate degree, and had embarked upon a teaching career, however, that Morrison began work on her first novel. These years together with a subsequent period working in a prestigious publishing house are worth reflecting on in relation to Morrison's fiction. After graduating with honours from Lorain High School, Morrison attended Howard University, where she changed her name to Toni. Here she received a BA degree in English in 1953. She then obtained an MA degree from Cornell University for a thesis on suicide in the work of William Faulkner and Virginia Woolf and became an instructor in English at Texas Southern University. Eighteen months later she returned to the English Faculty at Howard University as an instructor where her students included Houston A. Baker and Stokely Carmichael, founder of the Black Power Movement. In 1958 while an instructor at Howard she married Harold Morrison, a Jamaican architect, by whom she had two sons – Harold Ford and Slade Kevin. Her marriage ended in divorce in the mid-1960s whereupon she returned to

Lorain for a short while, but in 1965 she became editor for a text-book subsidiary of Random House, L. W. Singer Publishing Company, in Syracuse, New York. After a few years, she was promoted to Senior Editor at the headquarters in New York City where she became responsible for establishing an impressive black fiction list which included Toni Cade Bambara, Angela Davis and Gayl Jones. Meanwhile, she was encouraged by Alan Ricler, editor at Macmillan (USA), to expand a short story she had drafted about a little girl with blue eyes into a novel which he subsequently published when he joined Holt, Rinehart and Winston. From 1971 to 1972 she was Associate Professor of English at State University of New York at Purchase and subsequently taught at Yale University (1967–7) and Bard College (1986–8). In 1977, having won the Fiction Award of the National Book Critics' Circle and the American Academy and Institute of Arts and Letters Award, Morrison was appointed to the National Council on the Arts by President Carter. From 1984 to 1989, she was Schweitzer Professor of the Humanities at the State University of New York at Albany and from 1989, having won the Pulitzer Prize for fiction, Robert F. Goheen Professor of the Humanities at Princeton University.

II

The extent of the critical interest in Morrison's work, which is extraordinary by any standards, is much wider and more varied than can be reflected in any selection of 11 essays. However, I have tried to suggest some of the important areas of debate among critics over both the nature of Morrison's writing and the appropriateness of different critical methodologies. All these critics see themselves engaged in something wider, and sometimes more contentious, than a reading of her work. Each of the essays has been written in an atmosphere of debate – pertaining, especially, to the nature of a black aesthetic and to African-American critical paradigms.

Henry Louis Gates, Jr, was among the first of a group of literary scholars to question the predominance of sociological approaches to black literature. In arguing for wider critical paradigms, which as he later said respected the literary text as 'a rhetorical structure' with its own 'complex set of rules', he unleashed a long-running and fierce series of debates.[4] The result was that the death knell for a predominantly sociopolitical African-American critical canon, which the Black Aesthetic movement of the 1960s had posited, was being tolled by the 1970s.[5] Even so, the contested assumptions that black literature has a role in countering negative representations of black people and in promoting black consciousness informs much of the critical writing here and elsewhere on Toni Morrison.

There is also a pervasive unease in critical writing on Morrison's work about the appropriateness of contemporary European critical methodologies to African-American writing. This may be the result – at least in part – of the initial hostility created by the architects of the new African-American literary criticism, such as Robert B. Stepto and Henry Louis Gates, Jr. They were accused – as indeed have many of the new critics in Europe – of obscurantism and of burdening literary scholarship with jargon. But there was also scepticism as to whether poststructuralist literary theories and critical methodologies, developed in the old colonial centres, were not themselves another form of oppression. There was a danger of African and African-American literatures being marginalised within, and by them, at the very moment when they were reclaiming their own centres. The deployment of new critical methodologies, as Barbara Christian has noted, risked displacing the specific and historical contexts in which the black literary texts themselves originated.[6] But also important in the opposition to the new critical paradigms was the debate as to whether black writing constituted a separatist or syncretised literature. This issue has proved especially pertinent to criticism of Toni Morrison's work as the controversy which accompanied the award to her of the Nobel Prize testified. Some black writers objected to the award because they felt that her work was too Euro-American in structure and form.

There have been few attempts to apply a liberal humanist model to Toni Morrison's work or indeed to black literature in general. C. W. Bigsby offers the most interesting reading of African-American literature from this perspective, finding in black writers a refreshing moral assuredness which white liberal American writers had rejected in favour of cosmic conspiracies and fragmented layers of experience.[7] He argues that the moral assuredness of *Song of Solomon* derives from faith in the liberal presumption that behind illusion and falsehood there are available truths. However, his reading of the novel ignores the fact that liberal humanism is underpinned by concepts of self, identity and individuality which are not necessarily applicable to African-American culture and which are subjected to scrutiny in black literature. For example, the concept of moral responsibility in *Song of Solomon* is not the same as that normally found in white American fiction. The moral vision underpinning the narrative fuses the reclamation of a black cultural legacy with moral responsibility towards a wider black community. Indeed, at times the mythologising of the African-American legacy and of black culture in this novel appears to displace the social and economic realities of many black people's lives.

The difficulty of applying a liberal humanist model to African-American writing arises also from the fact that it has been developed within a structure privileging its concepts over an imaginary 'other' that includes Africans and African-Americans. When viewed from the perspective of that other the so-called universal values and archetypes of liberal humanism appear for what they really are, cultural and gender-specific assumptions.

It is hardly surprising that so little scholarship in African-American literature employs a white, ethnocentric critical paradigm which has rendered its own work invisible. Many critics of African-American literature prefer to work within critical models, even those originating in Europe, that subject Western literary and cultural assumptions to scrutiny. One of the methods constituting the complex theoretical base in much criticism of Morrison – including most of the essays in this book – is deconstruction.

In one respect, deconstruction, developed by the French philosopher Jacques Derrida, has an obvious appeal for critics of African-American literature. Its primary focus of attention, like that of the formalists and structuralists, is the way in which we tend to structure our thinking in terms of opposites such as conscious and unconscious or speech and writing. Unlike structuralism, however, its concern is with the ways in which one element in that binarism – African/American, white/black, male/female – is privileged over another. Deconstruction, like Anglo-American New Criticism, attends to close analysis of a text, but, unlike New Criticism, Franco-American deconstruction adopts a model of close reading which is highly sceptical. Closer to the original meaning of the word 'analysis', which etymologically means to 'undo', deconstruction emphasises the tensions, contradictions and oppositions within a text. It thereby enables critics of African-American writing to challenge the values and assumptions implicit in hierarchies of opposites.

Deconstruction also has an obvious relevance for critics of African-American literature because, as in formalism and structuralism, the language in a literary text is not self-contained but derives its meanings from a network of associations and relationships that can be found between the constituent parts. This is especially applicable to Toni Morrison's fiction which relies heavily on cross-currenting and a structure that is cyclical and repetitive rather than linear and progressive. However, deconstruction stresses the limitless possibilities of meaning that may be found in a text. This, too, has a particular relevance for Morrison's work which is ambivalent and open, usually eschewing fixation of meaning, closure and resolution. But an implication of this aspect of deconstruction is that political commitment becomes more difficult where meaning is endlessly deferred and contradicted. Hence, many critics of African-American literature employ deconstruction as a tool rather than as an absolute paradigm of critical thought.

Where deconstruction is employed in African-American criticism, it is often subject to further qualification. Deconstruction, like structuralism, in its purest sense is not concerned with the details of an author's life, historical events or cultural contexts. However, a number of the essays in this volume draw on anthropological/cultural criticism, the crux of which consists of seeing literary symbolism in the context of symbolic structures operating in society. Anthropological/cultural criticism eludes tight description and exemplification. It is not a methodology as such and many individual critics who are engaged in it are also deconstructionists, feminist critics or Marxists. While few critics writing on African-American literature are able to work within a liberal humanist framework for the reasons outlined above, the majority find themselves engaging with the social organisation, symbols, structures, rituals and behaviours of both black and white cultures.

The staple of the Black Aesthetic for over 50 years was the need to inscribe the positive racial self in literature and art. This in itself was premised on an African-American critical paradigm which saw race as the sole determinant of being, identity as coherent and knowable, and literature as having the power to unify and liberate the black race. The feminist reconfiguration of black historiography and literary criticism was a major feature of African-American scholarship in the mid/late 1980s. Previously, African-American criticism had eschewed gender in favour of race or at best, as Barbara Christian suggests, had conceived of them as separate. But writers from Frances Harper to Toni Morrison, concerned with the interrelatedness of race, gender and class, demand a differently theorised approach.[8] In her work on late nineteenth- and early twentieth-century African-American novelists, Hazel Carby goes much further than Christian in identifying four revisionist responses to contemporary feminist cultural politics: identification of race-specific responses to patriarchy; recognition that white women identified themselves with a racist patriarchal order; awareness of the late nineteenth- and early twentieth-century black women's intellectual renaissance; and recognition that black women intellectuals made political as well as literary interventions in the social formations in which they lived.[9] Within this reconfigured feminist perspective, blackness becomes, as it does for critics like Barbara Rigney, symbolic of the radical dissidence in which black women's art is produced – a dissidence which embraces both a state of female consciousness as well as racial identity and which lies beyond the laws of patriarchy.

Each of the essays in this book reflects the wider nature of critical work on Toni Morrison in their varied and complex theoretical bases and in their readiness to challenge and develop the theoretical perspectives to which they subscribe. The aim of this collection of essays is not simply to demonstrate the proliferation of critical positions on Morrison's work, but to illustrate how they have been appropriated, qualified and rewritten in African-American critical discourses.

III

Cynthia Davis's essay (1) is one of the most impressive early attempts to employ a deconstructionist methodology within a cultural framework. She combines an interest in the use of mythic structure – a popular concern in much African-American literary criticism – with feminist deconstruction. A number of critics at this time – most notably Jacqueline de Weever and Jane S. Bakerman – concerned themselves with the subject of female self-discovery in Morrison's fiction.[10] In this respect, the parameters of Davis's essay are typical of much late 1970s and early 1980s criticism of Morrison's novels, especially her emphasis upon the white American cultural domination of African-American communities – arising, of course, from the priority given it in Morrison's *The Bluest Eye* and *Song of Solomon*. But like Susan Willis's essay published in the same year,[11] Davis's essay employs feminist deconstruction as a way of clarifying *how* Morrison represents the problem of maintaining cultural heritage under great psychological and environmental stress. Through its Marxist-sociological perspective, derived from Fredric Jameson's *Marxism and Form* (1971), her essay advances our understanding of how the search for myth adequate to African-American experience in Morrison's work is complicated by a society based on coercive power relations.

Davis's essay reflects the shift in the meaning of the word 'myth' in European critical theory in the 1970s from myth as a traditional story transmitted from one generation to another to myth as a way of thinking – closer in meaning to ideology. The essay is an important contribution to the debate over the significance of myth in African-American writing in that it warns of the dangers of abstracting myth from the black context. Morrison, according to Davis, combines an interest in myth with a strong awareness of the concrete situation of the oppressed. In Morrison's novels, Davis argues, even Western classical myth is rewritten to serve a non-white ontology.

Myth has long been a contentious subject in African-American literary criticism. Susan Blake, for example, in a paper on Ralph Ellison, questions the appropriateness of traditional black myths to modern black experience.[12] She points out that myth and folklore can transform the acceptance of blackness as identity into the acceptance of blackness as limitation. This is a moot point in Morrison criticism for, as Katherine B. Payant points out, Morrison has been frequently accused of placing limitations on her women characters, 'of not allowing her women to "fly"'.[13]

Heeding warnings by critics such as Davis, others have expressed anxieties over abstracting African-American myth from its context. Craig Werner argues that myth when uprooted from its historical context simplifies history.[14] Worried by European notions of myth as an expression of universal values, he has extended the discussion to include similar debates among African critics. Whereas Davis's essay is a response to Susan Blake's reservations, Werner's work contributes to the debate between Sunday Anozie and Wole Soyinka. Questioning his country's overdependence on European critical theorists, especially Barthes, the Nigerian writer and critic Soyinka challenged the structuralists' claim for the universality of their work and attacked African structuralists, of whom Anozie is the key figure, who appear to elide differences within African languages and even between African and European cultures.[15]

This questioning of both myth and the appropriateness of European critical theory has important consequences for Morrison criticism in its attempt to position itself in a complex debate, as in the case of Terry Otten's essay (essay 2). Otten's examination of the mythic substructure of *Tar Baby* is an extract from his book-length study, *The Crime of Innocence in the Fiction of Toni Morrison*. In this book, a study of the trope of the biblical Fall in Morrison's work, Morrison is envisaged as reconfiguring the fall from innocence as a necessary gesture of freedom – a *felix culpa* adapted to the demands of contemporary America. Whereas *Tar Baby* is generally interpreted within the framework of the Brer Rabbit myth, to which he alludes towards the end of the essay, Otten interprets the novel within the biblical myth of Eden. However, like Davis in her discussion of the Icarus myth, Otten is careful not to abstract the mythical foundation of Morrison's work from its African-American context. Otten's essay is written, like Davis's, from a deconstructionist base but, drawing on the work of Bessie Jones, he brings a postcolonial perspective to bear on the notion of the enclosed Holy Garden in which imperialism and environmental destruction are linked. In effect, his essay reminds us that it is possible to interpret the Bible from different perspectives and that there are African-American as well as white versions. It puts into practice what Davis's essay recommends, observing how the novel adapts the biblical myth to the African-American context in a number of ways. Otten finds more ambiguity in the novel than Mbalia whose Marxist analysis of the book appears later in this volume (essay 5).

IV

Feminist deconstructionist approaches to Morrison's work, as illustrated in Barbara Rigney's essay (3), are normally based on developments in contemporary critical theory which occurred in the 1970s and 1980s and which complicated common assumptions about the self and about race as meaningful categories of literary study. As a result of these developments it has become difficult to conceive of the self as unified, coherent, stable and known, and to envisage black women writers as a homogeneous bloc.

Rigney's essay is an extract from her book, *The Voices of Toni Morrison*, in which she argues that Morrison's work is distinguished by reformulations of self, identity and history and by her radical use of language. Drawing explicitly on the work of European theorists such as Luce Irigaray, Toril Moi, Julia Kristeva and Hélène Cixous, who have undermined common assumptions about the self which they attribute to Western humanism, Rigney stresses the multiplicity of the self rather than concepts associated with the 'integrated self'. She applies recent thinking about the concept of the self to Morrison's work and emphasises those concepts in traditional Western thought – 'oneness', closure, autonomy, self-containment – which are not applicable to African-Americans because of their sense of division and fragmentation.

The strength of Rigney's essay is its acknowledgement that Morrison's fiction originates in a zone outside of Western literary criticism so that French feminist theory needs to be employed with deference to African-American cultural paradigms. Thus for Rigney, Morrison's language, in line with French feminist thinking, implies the primacy of the maternal and the semiotic, the world of the mother passed down to the daughters, repressed by the symbolic, the Law of the Father. But Rigney is careful to point out that in Morrison's novel the maternal space described by Kristeva and Cixous becomes ambiguous, fraught with danger as well as with desire. In her fiction, daughters, such as Beloved, can be the primary aggressor and there is concern with, even fear of, maternal aggression.

Rigney's essay includes useful suggestions as to how the application of French feminist theory to African-American literature, notwithstanding parallels between the European postmodern notion of self and the African-American condition, must be flexible enough to acknowledge ways in which Western ideas of self and other are transcended. She illustrates this with reference to three areas: the way names are allied to a culture and history rather than to individual personalities; the ambiguity of matriarchal power; and the merging of characters with the identity of the community as a whole or with the concept of blackness. In *The Voices of Toni Morrison*, Rigney argues that although Morrison herself romanticises the African past at times and employs the myth of the African

Great Mother as an ideal redemption, her ethical position in regard to lost Africa is always one of ironic qualification.

Several subsequent French feminist approaches have developed Rigney's reflections on the difficulties of applying white feminist philosophy to black writers. Katherine Payant, who takes up Rigney's argument that Morrison's fiction includes the linguistic disorder which is truly feminine, distinguishes Morrison from white feminists and black 'womanists' such as Alice Walker (writers who feel themselves committed to the survival of the black people, male and female).[16] While white male power is often given short shrift by white feminist writers, the uneasy alliance between black men and black women is a recurring subject in Morrison's fiction because of their common experience of white oppression. The abuse by black men is explained, if not excused, in Morrison's work by the way they have been emotionally and sexually crippled by institutionalised racialism. As Payant also points out, Morrison is more willing than many white feminist writers, too, to acknowledge wrongdoing by women.

For Madhu Dubey (essay 4), the black feminine difference from the Black Aesthetic is at the heart of *Sula*. Like Rigney's essay, Dubey's is an extract from a book-length study, *Black Women Novelists and the Nationalist Aesthetic*. Dubey employs feminist and deconstructionist criticism within a historical cultural framework. *Sula* is seen as challenging the binary oppositions that constitute Black Aesthetic discourse. It is argued that the novel employs a black feminist perspective to undo the masculinist bias of nationalist ideology. *Sula* is seen as rejecting the black nationalist view of the male as the prime victim of racialism – a role which assigns women a secondary role as healer of the black man's damaged masculinity – and in its critique of heterosexuality rejects one of the key principles of black aesthetic discourse to depict male–female relationships as complementary unions. While recognising that aspects of the novel, such as the victimisation of women within the roles society allows them and the depiction of black men, invite a feminist reading, Dubey argues that *Sula* plays 'feminism' and 'black nationalism' against each other. The notion of unresolved contradiction is proposed as the central designing principle of the novel, suggesting that even though it undermines hierarchical binary structuring by refusing to valorise any one term, it is complicit in the structural dualities of black nationalist discourse.

V

Doreatha Mbalia's essay (5) is a Marxist reading of *Tar Baby*. The essay is part of a chapter from Mbalia's book *Toni Morrison's Developing Class Consciousness*, which suggests that each of Morrison's novels explores some aspect of and/or solution to the oppression afflicting African people. For example, *The Bluest Eye* examines racism, *Sula* gender oppression, and *Tar Baby* the class contradictions that keep African people divided.

Karl Marx (1818–83) and Friedrich Engels (1820–95) concerned themselves with economic, political and philosophical issues of capitalist theory and mode of production. They did not develop an 'aesthetic' theory of literature and culture, but their ideas have been adapted in the development of Marxist approaches to literature. Although Marx gave his name to Marxism, what we broadly call Marxism is the developing cumulator of many people's ideas over about 150 years; it is not surprising, therefore, that there should be many debates and contradictory perspectives within it. These debates and different positions are reflected in the many different Marxist approaches to, and perspectives on, literature. However, although they may argue about the nature of the relationship, all Marxists agree that the infrastructure or 'base' of a society – for example, its social and economic structures and its mode of production – determines its 'superstructure' – that is, how people think and relate to each other and how families, education and religion are organised. One of the fundamental premises of classic Marxism is that social being determines consciousness; that is to say that we are 'constructed' by the society into which we are born and in which we live.

For the most part, Doreatha Mbalia follows a classic, deterministic Marxist line of argument pointing out that, from a materialist perspective, literature is a product of the society in which it is produced, arising from and dependent on the material conditions of that society. Taken to its logical conclusion, classic Marxism would suggest that the source of the meaning of the text lies in the society of which the author is a part and in which they are formed. Mbalia's thesis is more complex however. The superstructural elements do act back on the base to cause social change. In other words, literature can in turn shape the society in which one lives:

> Since literature is mainly born out of those ideas prevalent in society, it can either reflect a ruling-class perspective or a people-class perspective. When that literature reflects a ruling-class perspective under a capitalist economic system, it primarily focuses on the profit and well-being of only a small sector of the population. When that literature reflects a people-class perspective, it primarily focuses on the welfare of the exploited and oppressed majority. Toni Morrison's novels are people-class oriented. All of them are concerned with the exploited and oppressed condition of African people.[17]

In Mbalia's reading of *Tar Baby*, the fundamental cause of the African's oppression is the exploitative economic system of capitalism and its overseas extension, imperialism. Like Davis, Mbalia argues that Morrison's novels ask questions, but they are of a different kind and concerned with the implications of a Marxist reading of the African condition. These include identifying an alternative to the current suppression of an African way of life under neocolonialism and whether the African people can negate imperial history by returning to a precolonial existence. Identifying the principal enemies of the African-American as capitalism and imperialism, Mbalia's essay discovers positive Marxist principles in traditional African society: humanism, collectivism and egalitarianism.

VI

Concerned with the unconscious mind, Freud's theories brought about a paradigmatic shift in Western concepts of the self and identity. His model of the psyche emphasises duality and repression. The rational, conscious mind (the 'ego')which interacts with the world outside itself and is associated with order is envisaged as repressing the irrational, passional unconscious (the 'id'). Although there is a third element (the 'superego') concerned with moral judgements where parental influence in particular is contained, it is part of the ego and in many cases is indistinguishable from it. Even though much of Freud's work is contentious and is privileged on the authority of the phallus as master signifier, many of his basic concepts such as the ego, complexes, sexual repression, wish fulfilment, secret desire, however much they have been challenged and revised, often occur in our thinking and criticism.

The notion of the mind as divided between a rational and irrational part may not have begun with Freud, but psychoanalytic criticism of literature undoubtedly did. He saw literature as expressing the unconscious desires of its authors and although this characterised psychoanalytic criticism in the first half of the twentieth century, contemporary psychoanalytic criticism has shifted the focus from the neuroses of the author and the psychoanalysis of characters to a concentration on the text. The assumptions are that repressed wish fulfilment, psychic conflict, dream and fantasy, for example, are sufficiently universal that they can be written into the text in such a way that we will be aroused by them, will identify with them or at the very least become interested in them.

Much feminist psychoanalysis is a critique or revision of Freudian psychoanalysis or a reaction against it. According to Freud the child is fused with the mother in what he calls the pre-Oedipal stage. But it is in the Oedipal stage when the child re-enacts the desires expressed in the Oedipus myth that the child acquires its gender identity. At this stage, the child identifies with the father – a process by which the female accepts castration and a sense of lack because she is unable to identify fully with the father, and the male child, identifying with the father, fears castration. The female emerges from Freudian – and subsequently Lacanian – theory, as Patsy Stoneman says, 'doomed by the Oedipal structure, by language, the law, the name of the father, to less than masculine autonomy'.[18] According to much feminist psychoanalysis the construction of female identity occurs through the mother–daughter relationship within the pre-Oedipal stage, the importance of which Freud neglected. The first psychoanalyst to argue for greater understanding of women's relationship with the mother was Melanie Klein in her articulation of what she described as object relations theory.[19] According to object relations theory, an infant's identity is constructed through a process of projection and introjection learned at the mother's breast. Emotions are projected on the breasts which are then introjected back into the infant's psyche. For example, different emotions are associated with the offered and the withdrawn breast. The infant thus learns to project emotions on external 'objects', including people, with which it comes into contact. They then become phantasy objects. These 'imagos', as they are called, are then introjected back into the infant's psyche.

Houston A. Baker's essay (6) is a short but pithy extract from his book, *Workings of the Spirit: The Poetics of Afro-American Women's Writing*. In employing a Freudian psychoanalytic framework to discuss the significance of a particular scene in *Sula*, he demonstrates how Freudian psychoanalytic criticism has shifted from what Freud himself envisaged as psychoanalytic criticism – a concern with the author's neuroses – to a preoccupation with dream, psychic conflict and repressed wish fulfilment in the text. While Baker focuses initially on Sula and Nel's relationship with the phallus and the Law of the Father, his essay soon assumes a broader theoretical base, exemplifying the difficulties of approaching African-American texts from a traditional psychoanalytic perspective.

Jennifer FitzGerald's essay (7), too, is a psychoanalytic reading of a Morrison novel, *Beloved*, which criticises psychoanalytic criticism for having isolated psychic experience from the diversities of ethnicity and class. Psychoanalytic theory is based on a particular bourgeois model of family life – the nuclear family – that developed in the wake of the industrial revolution. The difficulty of approaching Toni Morrison's work through a classic psychoanalytic model was first suggested by Byerman's study of the grotesque in the work of Morrison and Gayl Jones.[20] In their work, Byerman argued, absurd distortions are employed to reach readers beneath the usual level of consciousness in order that they might become more aware of the non-rational nature of social values and norms which lead to schizophrenia, incest and murder. FitzGerald's essay is a considerable advance on Byerman's work; its psychoanalytic method is clearly stated from the outset and is applied within a carefully conceived framework. She reads the novel through various discourses, including pre-Oedipal discourse of object relations psychoanalysis (especially in relation to Beloved's obsession with Sethe), slavery, the good mother, masculinity, and black solidarity.

FitzGerald's essay was written before she had the opportunity to read Barbara Schapiro's psychoanalytic reading of *Beloved*, offered without FitzGerald's reservations about the appropriateness of European psychoanalytic theory to African-American writing. Schapiro extends the pre-Oedipal psychoanalytic model in interesting ways by drawing on Jessica Benjamin's *The Bonds of Love: Psychoanalysis, Feminism and the Problem of Domination* (1988).[21] Benjamin modifies object relations theory to form what she calls 'intersubjective theory' as a complement to intrapsychic theory. She maintains Klein's emphasis on primary relationships in self-development, but argues that the self develops through relationships with another subject rather than through object relations.

Schapiro's essay is particularly useful follow-up reading to FitzGerald's essay, discussing how *Beloved* explores the intersubjective and intrapsychic effects of growing up as black in an environment where intersubjectivity is severely curtailed. Benjamin's location of domination in the breakdown of the boundaries which maintain the attunement of self and other is especially appropriate to the psychoanalysis of white racialism and intraracialism among black people.

FitzGerald's essay offers a more specifically Kleinian reading of *Beloved* than Schapiro's paper. For example, Schapiro argues that 'the mother is made incapable of recognising the child, and the child cannot recognise the mother ... In the case of Beloved, the intense desire for recognition evolves into enraged narcissistic omnipotence and a terrifying, tyrannical domination.'[22] She sees the infantile range in the novel as 'a form of frustrated, murderous love'. FitzGerald, on the other hand, argues that Beloved's excessive dependence corresponds to the symbiosis of mother and infant which Klein describes. While Schapiro argues that the intense neediness of the infant's own love becomes dangerous when it fails to receive the affirmation it claims, FitzGerald's emphasis upon Beloved's ambivalent feelings is closer to the letter of Kleinian theory: 'the infant has from the beginning of post-natal life a relation to the mother (although focusing primarily on her breast) which is imbued with the fundamental elements of an object relation i.e. love, hatred, fantasies, anxieties and defences.'[23] Klein's thesis that the infant copes with internal conflicts by directing feelings of gratification toward a proffered breast and of frustration toward a withdrawn breast, provides the basis for FitzGerald's reading of the way Beloved projects emotions on Sethe and the woman on the ship, '... split into "good" feelings, such as love (when each woman is idealised) and "bad" feelings (when she believes each has abandoned her)'.[24]

FitzGerald's essay offers a number of interesting contrasts with some of those we have already considered. It places more emphasis than Rigney, for example, on the fact that mothering is not a private act, independent of the economic, political or social conditions which affect the circumstances of parenting. Her reliance on object relations theory – that the psyche is constructed within a wider system of relations than parent–child – inevitably provides a different perspective, too, on how social, cultural and political forces become internalised from Cynthia Davis's sociological reading of Morrison's early work. Like a number of the writers in this selection, FitzGerald stresses Morrison's interest in community, but her emphasis on 'communal mothering' offers not only an alternative to the more usual sociological or mythic readings of community, but a challenge to the individualism and autonomy privileged by classical psychoanalysis. Identity, FitzGerald argues, is not constructed within the narrow confines of the hegemonic nuclear family but in relation to the whole community.

FitzGerald's linking of the 'fissure of the masculine' as evidenced in the character of Paul D with psychic trauma is not as well developed in her essay as the object relations discourse. However, she is one of the few critics to link these two subjects in the way in which she has done. The novel seems to offer an example of a phenomenon that Kaja Silverman has discussed largely in relation to the Second World War and labelled 'historical trauma':

> a historically precipitated but psychoanalytically specific disruption, with ramifications extending far beyond the individual psyche. To state the case more precisely, I mean any historical event, whether socially engineered or of natural occurrence, which brings a large group of male subjects into such an intricate relationship with lack that they are at least for the moment unable to sustain an imaginary relation with the phallus, and so withdraw their belief from the dominant fiction.[25]

FitzGerald's essay, then, takes us beyond the idea of split identity in the self to the way in which *Beloved* dramatises a larger, more powerful sense of a schism in the black community as a whole created by the impact upon its needs and desires of a particular historicised context. Such a movement is an important development in the psychoanalytic discussion of African-American literature. It is a further example of how the application of even different psychoanalytic approaches to black writing, as in Baker's and FitzGerald's essays, inevitably involves the critic in a questioning of the specific historical contexts in which classic, psychoanalytic theory developed.

VII

Rafael Pérez-Torres (essay 8), in arguing that *Beloved* is a postmodern novel, is as concerned as FitzGerald that an essentially European critical concept is applied with deference to African-

American paradigms. Postmodernism is a fashionable but elusive concept employed across a vast range of artistic, intellectual and aesthetic fields including literature, art, music, photography, drawing, philosophy, geography, architecture. The family of terms associated with the concept would suggest that postmodernism has some relationship to modernism and to modernity. The prefix 'post' signifies a break or rupture, literally that which comes after something, and certainly postmodernism is sceptical of the 'grand narratives' – for example, the idea of history as linear and as 'progress'; the concept of the autonomous, humanist subject; and the notion of universal, transcendent truths independent of partial, historically specific discourses. However, there are as many approaches to the subject of postmodernism as theories about the assassination of President Kennedy. Postmodernism has been approached as a style, as a concept, and as the description of a new type of consumer, media-oriented society – the society of the spectacle or the simulacrum. At the philosophical level, it invariably challenges the way we have traditionally conceived of history, or rather it challenges the norm of disembodied objectivity to which history has traditionally aspired. Postmodernism encourages us to ask: Whose history are we talking about? From what perspective and in whose interests has it been written? What and whose experiences have been occluded in and by the traditional narratives of history? These are the kind of questions which preoccupy historians and writers who come from or assume the perspective of groups frequently marginalised by many of the traditional historical narratives such as women or ethnic minorities. Postmodernism posits a new type of human subject – as fluid and fragmented rather than fixed and knowable – and frequently talks of subjectivities rather than subjectivity. Most accounts of postmodernism blur the boundaries between, say, culture and society, high and low art, male and female, reason and imagination, history and fiction.

Pérez-Torres' starting point is that *Beloved* transforms what has been a significant absence in the narrative of American cultural history – the exploitation and denial of black cultural identity – into a powerful presence. In other words, Morrison is seen as rewriting American history from a black perspective; forging a voice and identity out of a confrontation with dominant, white American discourses. Although *Beloved* has many of the characteristics of a European postmodern novel – crossing of styles, genre and narrative perspectives alongside multiplicity, transformation and a general slipperiness of language – unlike many postmodern European texts, it does not value sophisticated linguistic play for its own sake. Pérez-Torres argues that because Morrison challenges the facelessness which dominant versions of American history have imposed upon black people, *Beloved*, despite its postmodern characteristics, evokes a premodern epic structure and sense of purpose. Creating an aesthetic identity out of absence, *Beloved* plays through but also against the cultural field of postmodernism.

Following Pérez-Torres' reading is Ashraf Rushdy's new historicist approach to *Beloved* (essay 9) which highlights Morrison's concern with the history of history. New historicism is one of the most recent developments in contemporary critical theory. Since individual practitioners of new historicism may employ different combinations of critical methodologies, like postmodernism, it is difficult to define exactly. However, although it is the subject of much debate and disagreement even within its own church, there are a number of key assumptions. H. Aram Veeser has suggested that the following tenets bind most new historicists together:

1. that every expressive act is embedded in a network of material practices;
2. that every act of unmasking, critique, and opposition uses the tools it condemns and risks falling prey to the practice it exposes;
3. that literary and non-literary 'texts' circulate inseparably;
4. that no discourse, imaginative or archival, gives access to unchanging truths nor expresses inalterable human nature;
5. finally ... that a critical method and a language adequate to describe culture under capitalism participate in the economy they describe.[26]

At its most fundamental level, then, new historicism is an attempt to reclaim the 'historical consciousness' that is fainter in, or even missing from, much contemporary theory such as deconstruction, feminist criticism and formalism. Whatever else they may disagree about, new historicists share the conviction that texts are not independent of historical contexts and influences. However, it is important to recognise the force of the words 'new' and 'historicist' for new historicism is not the same as historical criticism. Informed by new critical methodologies and principles, such as deconstruction and feminism, it acknowledges the sociology and history of history. As Veeser points out, new historicism challenges 'the norm of disembodied objectivity to which humanists have increasingly aspired'.[27] Historical criticism tends to be very much less aware of its own narratives than new historicism, to be much less questioning of its own preconceptions and bias, to employ theories of history transparently and to adhere to a view of history as linear and progressive.

Ashraf Rushdy's essay is based on a theory of African-American literature provided by Henry Louis Gates, Jr, in his book *The Signifying Monkey: A Theory of African-American Literary Criticism* (1988). Put simply, in Signifying, one text 'plays upon' another, usually repeating it but making significant changes or inverting it. As Angela Burton explains in her essay (11), Henry Louis Gates distinguishes the African-American usage of 'Signifyin(g)' from the European linguistic concept 'signifying' by using a capital letter and by placing the final consonant in parenthesis.[28] Rushdy sees *Beloved* as Signifyin(g) – invoking and reinterpreting – on the story of Margaret Garner, an escaped slave from Kentucky who in January 1856 made the decision to kill her daughter rather than have her taken into slavery. Morrison found the story, as Rushdy reminds us, in Camille Billops's *The Harlem Book of the Dead*, an album featuring James Van der Zee's photographs of Harlem funerals. The novel Signifies not just the story of Margaret Garner, which was well known, but a specific text in Billops's book. However, the extent of the Signifyin(g), in *Beloved* – that is the number of texts which are reinterpreted in the course of the novel – is wide ranging. Morrison probably drew also, for example, on *The Black Book*, a compendium of newscuttings and advertisements chronicling the life of African people in the United States. Indeed, its Signifyin(g) on the received texts of black history – that is its re-visioning of black history – is one of the most important aspects of *Beloved*. The history of slavery in *Beloved*, for example, is reclaimed from the point of view of the black female slave, simultaneously overturning the white myth of the compliant, child-like black salve – the 'Uncle Tom' figure who was complicit in his own slavery. Rushdy's view of the novel as 'an introjection into the fields of revisionist historiography and fiction' is an important contribution to the development of African-American literary theory in the face of the kind of anxieties expressed by Barbara Christian that theory might lead to an abstraction, and a devaluation and/or simplification of the political content of the black text.[29] The essay argues that Morrison's novels make an important contribution to establishing a form of literary theory which will accommodate African-American writing – 'a theory based on an inherited culture, an inherited "history", and the understanding of the ways that any given artistic work negotiates between those cultural/historical worlds it inhabits'.

Beloved is not the only novel which is based on Camille Billops's *The Harlem Book of the Dead. Jazz* is based on a Van der Zee photograph which Morrison describes in a published conversation with Gloria Naylor which is also cited by Ashraf Rushdy:

> In one picture, there was a young girl lying in a coffin and he [Van der Zee] says that that she was eighteen years old and she had gone to a party and that she was dancing and suddenly she slumped and they noticed there was blood on her and they said, 'What happened to you?' And she said, 'I'll tell you tomorrow. I'll tell you tomorrow'. That's all she would say. And apparently her ex-boyfriend or somebody who was jealous had come into the party with a gun and silencer and shot her. And she kept saying, 'I'll tell you tomorrow' because she wanted him to get away.[30]

In fact, not only are both novels based on photographs from Van der Zee's album, but it was the way in which this last photograph inspired Morrison to re-vision the Margaret Garner story that led her to connect both stories around the trope of obsessive love.[31]

The final essays in this volume by Eusebio Rodrigues (10) and Angela Burton are concerned with Morrison's *Jazz*. Both essays approach the novel from complex theoretical bases embracing anthropological/cultural criticism, narratology and deconstruction. Both critics interpret the narrative structure of *Jazz* in terms of the jazz aesthetic; and for both black migration from the South to the North and the Northern city are important in reconfiguring black identity in the 1920s. Both writers are concerned with the relevance of the past in the lives of the main protagonists, exemplified as Rodrigues suggests in the way in which Joe Trace, in hunting Dorcas, the girl who has abandoned him, moves in a space between his past and his present. Although there have been a number of critical essays approaching the novel from the perspective of the jazz aesthetic, Rodrigues' essay exemplifies a recent trend in Morrison criticism, a concern derived from postmodern geography with the sociopolitics of space. As Brian Jarvis has pointed out, in *Jazz* Morrison crosses-over with the canonical white prose tradition of the 'Great American City Novel', but she envisages the City, spelt in the novel with a capital C, which witnesses 'eruptions of funk and a vital connectivity between the members of their community and their pasts', differently from the white city.[32] Rodrigues suggests that in the novel the City itself is the key presence,[33] requiring the kind of narrator who can reflect its breadth and (jazz) breath. Morrison, then, is interested not simply in the impact of the city on the lives of the Traces or on Dorcas, but in depicting spatial stories in non-Cartesian ways; that is in ways in which the rationalist's distinction between the mind and the external world is blurred. For Rodrigues, the elusive nature of *Jazz* is itself as much a product of such non-Cartesian thinking as its jazz aesthetic; of thinking which is episodic, imaginative and intuitive.

Angela Burton's essay approaches *Jazz* from the perspective of those episodes in the novel which on a cursory reading may seem like digressions from the main story line. Employing a theoretical framework which combines Julia Kristeva's concept of abjection and Henry Louis Gates, Jr's concept of Signifyin(g), she argues that in *Jazz*, Morrison is Signifyin(g) on the 'abjection' – the breakdown of identity – generated by miscegination in order to reconfigure the mixed-race figure. Burton argues that Morrison sees abjection as a space both of disenfranchisement and of potential empowerment. The novel is seen as re-visioning the mixed-race figure in the person of Golden Gray, but in the fate that befalls Dorcas as following the conventional narrative of such figures. The text, however, places importance not only on the fact that Golden Gray must re-vision himself, but that communities, as 'readers' of mixed-race figures, must reconfigure the way they 'read' hybridity. Like Rodrigues, Burton stresses the importance of the novel's jazz framework but for a different reason. She argues that jazz itself is a mixed-race aesthetic. The significance of Morrison's concern with miscegination in the novel is highlighted, Burton argues, by her decision to frame *Jazz* around the themes and structures of jazz aesthetics.

Clearly, the essays in this volume demonstrate that Morrison is a writer for whom Salman Rushdie's definition of 'hybridity' is appropriate: 'people who root themselves in ideas rather than places, in memories as much as in material things; people who have been obliged to define themselves – because they are so defined by others

– by their otherness; people in whose deepest selves strange fusions occur, unprecedented unions between what they were and where they find themselves.'[34] However, this is only the point from which recent criticism of Morrison begins. While it recognises the importance of Morrison's fiction for an understanding of the subject in African-American culture, recent scholarship, building on complex and often cross-cultural theoretical bases, is as concerned with unveiling an increasingly rich body of work. It is this kind of rereading of Morrison and engagement with current debates in African-American literary scholarship that has shaped the direction of recent criticism of her work and determined the purpose of this volume.

NOTES

1. Barbara Rigney, *The Voices of Toni Morrison* (Columbus, OH, 1991), p. 61.

2. Claudia Tate, *Black Women Writers At Work* (New York, 1989), p. 127.

3. Ibid., p. 119.

4. Henry Louis Gates, Jr (ed.), *Black Literature and Literary Theory* (New York, 1984), p. 5.

5. Joe Weixlmann, 'Black Literary Criticism at the Juncture', *Contemporary Literature*, 27: 1(1986), 48–62.

6. Barbara Christian, 'The Race For Theory', *Cultural Critique*, 6 (1987), 74–5.

7. C. W. Bigsby, *The Second Black Renaissance: Essays in Black Literature* (London, 1980), p. 154ff.

8. Barbara Christian, *Black Feminist Criticism: Perspectives on Black Women Writers* (New York, 1985).

9. Hazel V. Carby, *Reconstructing Womanhood: The Emergence of the Afro-American Woman Novelist* (New York and Oxford, 1989).

10. Jacqueline de Weever, 'The Inverted World of Toni Morrison's *The Bluest Eye* and *Sula*', *CLA Journal*, 22 (1979), 402–14; Jane S. Bakerman, 'Failure of Love, Female Initiations in the Novels of Toni Morrison', *American Literature*, 52 (1981), 541–63.

11. Susan Willis, 'Eruptions of Funk: Historicizing Toni Morrison', *Black American Literature Forum*, 16 (1982), 34–41.

12. Susan L. Blake, 'Ritual and Rationalization: Black Folklore in the Works of Ralph Ellison', *PMLA*, 94 (1979), 123, 126.

13. Katherine B. Payant, *Becoming and Bonding: Contemporary Feminism and Popular Fiction by American Women Writers* (London and Westport, 1993), p. 202.

14. Craig H. Werner, 'The Briar Patch as Modernist Myth: Morrison, Barthes and *Tar Baby* As-Is', in Nellie Y. McKay (ed.), *Critical Essays on Toni Morrison* (Boston, MA, 1988).

15. For the Soyinka–Anozie debate, see Henry Louis Gates, Jr (ed.), *Black Literature and Literary Theory*, p. 5.

16. Payant, *Becoming and Bonding: Contemporary Feminism and Popular Culture*, p. 202.

17. Doreatha Drummond Mbalia, *Toni Morrison's Developing Class Consciousness* (Selinsgrove, London and Toronto, 1991), p. 16.

18. Patsy Stoneman, *Wuthering Heights*, New Casebook (London, 1993), p. 6.

19. Melanie Klein, *The Selected Melanie Klein*, ed. Juliet Mitchell (1986; rpt Harmondsworth, 1991).

20. Keith Byerman, 'Intense Behaviours: The Use of the Grotesque in The Bluest Eye and Eva's *Man*', *College Language Association Journal*, 25 (1982), 447–57.

21. Barbara Schapiro, 'The Bonds of Love and the Boundaries of Self in Toni Morrison's *Beloved*', *Contemporary Literature*, 32: 2 (1991), 194–210.

22. Ibid., 197.

23. Juliet Mitchell (ed.), *The Selected Melanie Klein* (1986; Harmondsworth, 1991), p. 203.

24. See p. 114 below.

25. Kaja Silverman, *Male Subjectivity at the Margins* (London and New York, 1992), p. 55.

26. H. Aram Veeser, *The New Historicism* (London and New York, 1989), p. xi.

27. Ibid.

28. See below, p. 171. See also pp. 133 and 138.

29. Barbara Christian, 'The Race For Theory', *Cultural Critique*, 6 (1987), 51–63.

30. 'A Conversation, Gloria Naylor and Toni Morrison', *The Southern Review*, 21: 3 (July, 1985), 584.

31. See below, p. 143 and headnote to Rushdy's essay (9).

32. Brian Jarvis, *Postmodern Cartographies*: the Geographical Imagination in Contemporary American Culture', unpublished PhD dissertation, University of Keele, 1996, pp. 247, 251.

33. For a further discussion of this subject, see Linden Peach, *Toni Morrison* (London, 1995), pp. 118–27.

34. Salman Rushdie, *Imaginary Homelands* (London, 1988), pp. 124–5.

1

Self, Society and Myth in Toni Morrison's Fiction

CYNTHIA A. DAVIS

Toni Morrison's novels have attracted both popular and critical attention for their inventive blend of realism and fantasy, unsparing social analysis, and passionate philosophical concerns. The combination of social observation with broadening and allusive commentary gives her fictions the symbolic quality of myth, and in fact the search for a myth adequate to experience is one of Morrison's central themes. Because her world and characters are inescapably involved with problems of perception, definition, and meaning, they direct attention to Morrison's own ordering view and its implications.

All of Morrison's characters exist in a world defined by its blackness and by the surrounding white society that both violates and denies it. The destructive effect of the white society can take the form of outright physical violence, but oppression in Morrison's world is more often psychic violence. She rarely depicts white characters, for the brutality here is less a single act than the systematic denial of the reality of black lives. The theme of 'invisibility' is, of course, a common one in black American literature, but Morrison avoids the picture of the black person 'invisible' in white life (Ellison's Invisible Man trying to confront passersby). Instead, she immerses the reader in the black community; the white society's ignorance of that concrete, vivid, and diverse world is thus even more striking.

The constant censorship of and intrusion on black life from the surrounding society is emphasised not by specific events so much as by a consistent pattern of misnaming. Power for Morrison is largely the power to name, to define reality and perception. The world of all three novels[1] is distinguished by the discrepancy between name and reality. *The Bluest Eye* (1970), for example, opens with a primer description of a 'typical' American family: 'Here is the house. It is green and white. It has a red door. It is very pretty. Here is the family. Mother, Father, Dick, and Jane live in the green-and-white house.' And so on (*Eye*, p. 1). Portions of that description reappear as chapter headings for the story of black lives, all removed in various degrees from the textbook 'reality'.[2] *Sula* (1973) begins with a description of the black neighbourhood, 'called the Bottom in spite of the fact that it was up in the hills' (*Sula*, p. 4): another misnamed, even reversed situation, in this case the result of a white man's greedy joke. The same pattern is extended in *Song of Solomon* (1977): for example, the first pages describe 'Not Doctor Street, a name the post office did not recognise', and 'No Mercy Hospital' (*Song*, pp. 3, 4). Both names are unofficial; the black experience they represent is denied by the city fathers who named Mains Avenue and Mercy Hospital. And *Song of Solomon* is full of characters with ludicrous, multiple, or lost names, like the first Macon Dead, who received 'this heavy name scrawled in perfect thoughtlessness by a drunken Yankee in the Union Army' (*Song*, p. 18). In all these cases, the misnaming does not eliminate the reality of the black world; invisibility is not non-existence. But it does reflect a distortion. Blacks are visible to white culture only insofar as they fit its frame of reference and serve its needs. Thus they are consistently reduced and reified, losing their independent reality. Mrs Breedlove in *The Bluest Eye* has a nickname, 'Polly', that only whites use; it reduces her dignity and identifies her as 'the ideal servant' (*Eye*, p. 99). When the elegant Helene Wright becomes just 'gal' to a white conductor, she and her daughter Nel feel that she is 'flawed', 'really custard' under the elegant exterior (*Sula*, pp. 17–19).

To some extent this problem is an inescapable ontological experience. As Sartre has pointed out, human relations revolve around the experience of 'the Look', for being 'seen' by another both confirms one's reality and threatens one's sense of freedom: 'I grasp the Other's look at the very centre of my act as the solidification and alienation of my own possibilities.' Alone, I can see myself as pure consciousness in a world of possible projects; the Other's look makes me see myself as an object in another perception. 'The Other as a look is only that – my transcendence transcended.'[3] If I can make the other into an object in my world, I can 'transcend' him: 'Thus my project of recovering myself is fundamentally a project of absorbing the Other' (*BN*, p. 340). The result is a cycle of conflicting and shifting subject–object relationships in which both sides try simultaneously to remain in control of the relationship and to use the Other's look to confirm identity. The difficulty of such an attempt tempts human beings to Bad Faith, 'a vacillation between transcendence and facticity which refuses to recognise either one for what it really is or to synthesise them' (*BN*, p. 547). What that means can be seen in the many Morrison characters who try to define themselves through the eyes of others. Jude Greene, for example, marries Nel so that he can 'see himself taking shape in her eyes' (*Sula*, p. 71); and Milkman Dead finds that only when Guitar Bains shares his dream can he feel 'a self inside himself emerge, a clean-lined definite self' (*Song*, p. 184). Such characters are in Bad Faith not because they recognise other viewers, but because they use others to escape their own responsibility to define themselves. The woman who, like Mrs Breedlove, feels most powerful when most submerged in flesh, most like a *thing*, similarly falls into Bad Faith: 'I know that my flesh is all that be on his mind. That he couldn't stop if he had to ... . I feel a power, I be strong, I be pretty, I be young' (*Eye*, p. 101). Milkman complains that he feels 'used. Somehow everybody was using him for something or as something' (*Song*, p. 165). Many of Morrison's characters learn to like being used and using in return. They collaborate in their own reification so that they can feel that it is 'chosen'.

Such characters can fall into Bad Faith not only by dependence on one other, but also by internalising the 'Look' of the majority culture. The novels are full of characters who try to live up to an external image – Dick and Jane's family, or cosmopolitan society, or big business. This conformity is not just a disguise, but an attempt to gain power and control. There is always the hope that if one fits the prescribed pattern, one will be seen as human. Helene Wright puts on her velvet dress in hopes that it, with 'her manner and her bearing', will be 'protection' against the reductive gaze of the white other (*Sula*, p. 17). Light-skinned women, already closer to white models, aspire to a genteel ideal: green-eyed Frieda 'enchanted the entire school', and 'sugar-brown Mobile girls' like

Geraldine 'go to land-grant colleges, normal schools, and learn how to do the white man's work with refinement'. The problem with such internalisation is not that it is ambitious, but that it is life-denying, eliminating 'The dreadful funkiness of passion, the funkiness of nature, the funkiness of the wide range of human emotions' (*Eye*, pp. 48, 64). One who really accepts the external definition of the self gives up spontaneous feeling and choice.

Morrison makes it clear that this ontological problem is vastly complicated in the context of a society based on coercive power relations. The individual contest for 'transcendence' allows, in theory, for mutually satisfying resolutions, as Beauvoir points out: 'It is possible to rise above this conflict if each individual freely recognises the other, each regarding himself and the other simultaneously as object and as subject in a reciprocal manner.'[4] But that relation is unbalanced by social divisions of power. Helene cannot defy the white conductor; on at least the level of overt speech and action, his Look is unchallengeable. Thus she tries to accept the Look, and his power to give it, by becoming a more perfect object for his gaze: she gives him a 'dazzling smile' (*Sula*, p. 19). The temptation to Bad Faith is immensely greater in a society that forcibly assigns subject-power, the power to look and define, to one person over another. In such a context, even willed or spontaneous choices can be distorted to serve the powerful. Mrs Breedlove's channelling of her own need for order into the duties of 'the ideal servant' is a milder version of what happens to Cholly Breedlove, forced to turn his spontaneous copulation into performance before the flashlights of white hunters (*Eye*, pp. 114–17). Most perversely, even the attempt at rebellion can be shaped by the surrounding culture. The change from 'Doctor Street' (as blacks originally called Mains Avenue) to 'Not Doctor Street', for example, shows a lingering reluctance to accept white naming, but also a recognition of the loss of the original power to name. More profoundly, 'the Days', who take revenge for white violence, are also reactive, still achieving secondhand identity and initiative. [...]

The adoption of a rigid role, the withdrawal from life, is for Morrison as for Sartre a failure; but her condemnation is tempered by the recognition of the unnatural position of blacks in a racist society.

Power relations can have a similar effect on the community as a whole. The Look of white society, supported by all kinds of material domination, not only freezes the black individual but also classifies all blacks as alike, freezing the group. They become a 'we-object' before the gaze of a 'Third':

> It is only when I feel myself become an object along with someone else under the look of such a 'third' that I experience my being as a 'we-object'; for then, in our mutual interdependency, in our shame and rage, our beings are somehow mingled in the eyes of the on-looker, for whom we are both somehow 'the same': two representatives of a class or a species, two anonymous types of something ...[5]

Again, the basic problem may be ontological, but the institutionalisation of the relation, the coercive power of the Third, exacerbates it. This is the reason for all the misnaming: a whole group of people have been denied the right to create a recognisable public self – as individuals or as community. Given that combination of personal and communal vulnerability, it is hardly surprising that many characters choose the way of the least agony and the fewest surprises: they 'choose' their status as objects, even fiercely defend it. Helene and Geraldine increasingly become perfect images rather than free selves. In this retreat from life they are abetted by a community so dominated by white society as the Third that order and stability are its primary values. In *The Bluest Eye*, narrator Claudia comments that the worst fear is of being 'outdoors': 'Being a minority in both caste and class, we moved about anyway on the hem of life, struggling to consolidate our weaknesses and hang on, or to creep singly up into the major folds of the garment' (*Eye*, p. 11). Any 'excess' that might challenge the powerful Look and increase their isolation is terrifying. And so the images that caused the alienation, excluded them from the real world, are paradoxically received and imitated as confirmations of life. [...]

But the position of the black woman is doubly difficult. Black women in Morrison's fictions discover 'that they [are] neither white nor male, and that all freedom and triumph [are] forbidden to them' (*Sula*, p. 44). Womanhood, like blackness, is Other in this society, and the dilemma of woman in a patriarchal society is parallel to that of blacks in a racist one: they are made to feel most real when *seen*. Thus the adolescent Sula and Nel, parading before young males who label them 'pig meat' are 'thrilled' by the association of voyeurism with sexuality. But their role as image is complicated by their blackness. They are not just women in a society that reduces women to such cold and infantile images that Corinthians Dead can think that 'She didn't know any grown-up women. Every woman she knew was a doll baby' (*Song*, p. 197). They are also *black* women in a society whose female ideal is a *white* 'doll baby', blonde and blue-eyed Shirley Temple. Even if they accept their reification they will always be inadequate; the black woman is 'the antithesis of American beauty'.[6] No efforts at disguise will make them into the images they learn to admire. Defined as the Other, made to be looked at, they can never satisfy the gaze of society.

Because they are doubly defined as failures and outsiders, they are natural scapegoats for those seeking symbols of displaced emotions. Morrison shows the Look taking on monstrous proportions as the humiliated black male allies himself with the Third by making the black woman the object of his displaced fury. So Cholly Breedlove, in his sexual humiliation, looks not at his tormentors, but at his partner, with hatred. [...]

Prevented from looking outward at the oppressor, he displaces blame onto the Other who 'saw'. That she too is image in the white man's eye is so much worse, for he had counted (as Jude did with Nel) on her existing only for him, seeing him as he wanted her to, being *his* object and *his* subject. The desire to 'protect' her was the desire to create himself as her protector. All he can do to restore his selfhood is to deny hers further. In the recurring scene of black male resentment at black women's submission to oppression (the soldiers' stony stares at Helene and the conductor, Guitar's hatred of his mother's smile and of Pilate's 'Aunt Jemima act'), Morrison shows the displacement of male humiliation onto the only person left that a black man can 'own' – the black woman. Beauvoir remarks that woman in a patriarchal society is 'the inessential who never goes back to being the essential, ... the absolute Other, without reciprocity'.[7] The black woman – doubly Other – is the perfect scapegoat.

It is not only men who look for scapegoats. Barbara Smith points out that not only 'the politics of sex' but also 'the politics of race and class are crucially interlocking factors in the works of Black women writers'.[8] Morrison shows the subject–object pair and the triad created by the Third operating within a society so dependent on exclusion and reification that it creates 'interlocking' systems to define individuals in multiple ways. So even black women can find scapegoats. The prime example is Pecola, black and young and ugly. Claudia says,

All of us – all who knew her – felt so wholesome after we cleaned ourselves on her. We were so beautiful when we stood astride her ugliness... . And she let us, and thereby deserved our contempt. We honed our egos on her, padded our characters with her frailty, and yawned in the fantasy of our strength.

(*Eye*, p. 163)

Pecola is the epitome of the victim in a world that reduces persons to objects and then makes them feel inferior as objects. In this world, light-skinned women can feel superior to dark ones, married women to whores, and on and on. The temptations to Bad Faith are enormously increased, since one's own reification can be 'escaped' in the interlocking hierarchies that allow most to feel superior to someone. Only the very unlucky, or the truly free, are outside this system.

Pecola is so far 'outside' the centre of the system – excluded from 'reality' by race, gender, class, age, and personal history – that she goes mad, fantasising that her eyes have turned blue and so fitted her for the world. But not all outsiders go mad or otherwise surrender. There are Morrison characters who refuse to become images, to submerge themselves in a role. These characters are clearly existential heroes, 'free' in the Sartrean sense of being their own creators. But Morrison's treatment and development of this type in the social context she has staked out raise important questions about the nature of heroism and the place of external 'definitions' in it.

The characters who are 'outdoors', cut off from reassuring connection and definition, are profoundly frightening to the community, especially to a community dispossessed and 'peripheral'; it responds by treating the free person as another kind of scapegoat, using that 'excess' to define its own life. For example, Sula's neighbours fear and condemn her refusal to fit a conventional role, but her shapelessness gives them shape:

Their conviction of Sula's evil changed them in accountable yet mysterious ways. Once the source of their personal misfortune was identified, they had leave to protect and love one another. They began to cherish their husbands and wives, protect their children, repair their homes and in general band together against the devil in their midst.

(*Sula*, p. 102)

Displacing their fear and anger onto Sula, as onto Pecola, they can define themselves as 'better'. Sula, unlike Pecola, can bear that role, having chosen to be 'outside'; it is then tempting to argue that this kind of hero is 'a catalyst for good in the society'.[9] But Morrison has clear reservations about this situation. In a sick and power-obsessed society, even freedom can become distorted. For one thing, these characters are 'freed' by traumatic experiences. Cholly goes through abandonment, sexual humiliation, desertion and rejection: 'Abandoned in a junk heap by his mother, rejected for a crap game by his father, there was nothing more to lose. He was alone with his own perceptions and appetites, and they alone interested him' (*Eye*, p. 126). Similarly, Sula is 'freed' by her mother's expressed dislike of her and her own part in Chicken Little's drowning: 'hers was an experimental life – ever since her mother's remarks sent her flying up those stairs, ever since her one major feeling of responsibility had been exorcised on the bank of a river with a closed place in the middle' (*Sula*, p. 102). The whores in *The Bluest Eye* are also freed by exclusion from society; Morrison's suggestion that such freedom is more deprivation than fulfilment helps to explain their link with Pecola.[10] [...] Freedom defined as total transcendence lacks the intention and significance that can come from commitment; 'freedom', as Sartre comments, 'is meaningful only as engaged by its free choice of ends' (*BN*, p. 549).

Milkman Dead, in Morrison's third novel, finally completes the heroic mission. Morrison makes his status clear by depicting him in clearly mythic terms. Milkman's life follows the pattern of the classic hero, from miraculous birth (he is the first black baby born in Mercy Hospital, on a day marked by song, rose petals in the snow, and human 'flight') through quest-journey to final reunion with his double. And Milkman largely resolves the conflict between freedom and connection. At first the familiar cold hero, he comes to ask the cost of heroic quest – 'Who'd he leave behind?' (*Song*, p. 336). He learns not only that the hero serves a function for society, the exploration of limits it cannot reach, but also that it serves him: his great-grandfather Shalimar left his children, but 'it was the children who sang about it and kept the story of his leaving alive' (*Song*, p. 336). More, he finds that his quest is his culture's; he can only discover what he is by discovering what his family is. By undertaking the quest, he combines subjective freedom with objective fact and defines himself in both spheres. Sartre says that one may respond to the gaze of the Third not by scapegoating and identifying with the Third, but by 'solidarity' with the Other, which can allow for common transcendence of the outside definition

(*BN*, p. 394). By conceiving himself as both free individual and member of the social group, the hero unites his free and factitious natures and becomes part of the historical process by which the struggle for self-definition is both complicated and fulfilled. Thus at the end of *Song of Solomon*, Milkman has restored the names of his family, recovered their song; and he can 'fly'. But he does not fly away; he flies toward Guitar, his wounded 'brother': 'For now he knew what Shalimar knew: If you surrendered to the air, you could '*ride* it' (*Song*, p. 341). Only in the recognition of his condition can he act in it, only in commitment is he free.

Roger Rosenblatt has remarked that such Afro-American fiction tends toward myth because of its 'acknowledgment of external limitation and the anticipation of it'.[11] Morrison has always offered mythic possibilities in her emphasis on natural cycle, bizarre events, and narrative echoes. The mythic sensibility does seem to fit her view of the difficulties of freedom. But there are dangers in the use of myth that are especially acute for writers trying to combine the mythic sense of meaning with the concrete situation of the oppressed. Susan L. Blake has pointed out some of those problems in Ralph Ellison's combination of myth with black folklore. She suggests that the myth and the social situation described in the folklore 'do not have compatible meanings', that in fact the correlation to 'universal' Western myth 'transforms acceptance of blackness as identity into acceptance of blackness as limitation. It substitutes the white culture's definition of blackness for self-definition of folklore.'[12] This question is obviously crucial for Morrison, whose fictions try to combine existential concerns compatible with a mythic presentation with an analysis of American society. But her work resolves some of the problems Blake sees in Ellison's use of myth. [...]

Morrison's version of the Icarus story shows her approach. The Icarus tale offers a tempting pattern for a black writer interested in myth and folklore, since it ties in with folk tales of blacks flying back to the homeland; but its limitation, as Blake points out, is that it seems to carry a 'moral' incompatible with the concrete situation of blacks, suggesting the failure of the son to be the result of *hubris* rather than oppression.[13] Morrison plays variations on the story that correct that perspective. One version of it has Shalimar flying away and trying to take his son, as did Daedalus. But Shalimar's son is a baby, and Shalimar drops him, unable to soar with him. That version emphasises, first, that the son's 'fall' is the result of a situation beyond his control; second, that the father's desire for freedom and his family ties are in conflict. That second aspect is central to Morrison's analysis and reconstruction of the myth. In the Icarus tale, freedom is available to the characters – they can fly. If they fail, it is because they want an impossible kind of freedom. To transfer that pattern to the black situation would be to suggest that blacks must accept an inferior social position. Morrison's version of the tale shifts the emphasis to divided loyalties. Shalimar is free to return to Africa – totally free. But that kind of freedom is problematic, not because in itself it is wrong, but because in the particular context he is in – family and children – it involves denial of social and personal bonds. He does not destroy himself by soaring, but he wounds others because not everyone can take that way. The conflict is not between *hubris* and common sense, but between 'absolute' freedom and social responsibility. Milkman resolves the conflict when he leaps, flying *toward* his 'brother', finding freedom in 'surrender' to the air – not in acceptance of his situation as right or as eternal, but in acceptance of it as real. Morrison rewrites myth so that it carries the power of natural ties and psychic meaning but also speaks to a 'necessity' in the social order.

She is therefore very concerned with the sources of myth, with mythos and personal myth. All the novels try to show the machinery of myth, the ways that meaning can modify experience. Morrison distinguishes between false 'myths' that simply reduce, misinterpret, and distort reality – from Shirley Temple to the view of Sula as 'evil', from Smith's failed attempt at flight to Macon Dead's obsession with Pilate's hoard – and true myths that spring from and illuminate reality. She insistently raises questions about mythic or symbolic readings of life, often showing even the best-intentioned attempts at meaning going astray. She shifts point of view so often in her fictions that the limitation of the individual view is obvious, and the attempt to make one view into the myth, one person into the hero, is seen for the reductive act that it is.[14] For example, Milkman's early view of himself as the hero besieged by 'users' is partly confirmed by the possessiveness of others; his mother realises that 'Her son had never been a person to her, a separate real person. He had always been a passion' (*Song*, p. 131). But her need is explained by her personal history, and closely parallels Milkman's own selfishness. Thus the multiple perspectives not only qualify the myth by showing that any specific situation may be a different myth for each of the characters involved, since each sees himself at the centre of it; they also make the myth's relevance clear by showing the same problems manifested in many cases, so that Milkman's solution is for all. As the myth emerges from the multiplicity of daily lives, finally the mythic hero's estimate of his own significance is confirmed both by his centrality in other views and by his parallels to other lives. Morrison sees quite clearly the danger of myth as existentialist tract abstracted from real situations, and she adapts the myth to the black historical context, reconciling freedom with facticity on both individual and collective levels. But there is another area in which she does not adapt the myth so completely – the area of gender. She is quite able to show black women as victims, as understanding narrators, or even as 'free' in the sense of disconnection. But when the time comes to fulfil the myth, to show a hero who goes beyond the independence to engagement, she creates a male hero. Her own emphasis on the effect of particulars on meaning raises questions about that choice.

The use of a male hero does not, of course, necessarily imply the subjugation of women, and Morrison has the tools to correct the male slant. Her use of multiple perspectives has always allowed her to show a number of subjects as comments and variations on the central character. And her early alternation between male and female versions of the 'free' character shows that she does not exclude women from subjective life or choice. She even offers explicit commentaries on Milkman's sexism – from his sister Lena, for example (*Song*, pp. 213–18) – and parallels to women characters that make his quest a surrogate for theirs. That might seem sufficient: this is Milkman's story, so the other characters, male and female, are secondary. He is everyone's surrogate. To some extent, women are displaced because of the problem Morrison has studied all along – central versus peripheral perceptions – and she makes it clear that concentration on his life is not a denial of others'. But, as with the racial question, mere admission of multiple perspectives does not correct the mythic bias: the structure of the male-centred myth carries certain implications about gender that Morrison could disarm only by changing the story. Because she does not, her version of the hero-tale seems to allow only men as potential heroes. Thus Milkman is a surrogate for women in a very different way than for men. [...]

Milkman does have a female guide figure, his aunt Pilate, and she might further disarm the androcentric myth. She balances in her character the freedom and connection that Milkman must learn:

> when she realised what her situation in the world was and would probably always be she threw away every assumption she had learned and began at zero ... . Then she tackled the problem of trying to decide how she wanted to live and what was valuable to her. ... she knew there was nothing to fear. That plus her alien's compassion for troubled people ripened her and ... kept her just barely within the boundaries of the elaborately socialised world of black people.
>
> (*Song*, pp. 149–50)

Further, Pilate performs a social function by recognising the same balance in others. At Hagar's funeral, Pilate sings and speaks to each mourner, 'identifying Hagar, selecting her away from everybody else in the world who had died' (*Song*, p. 322). She pulls the individual into the group and recognises individuality at the same time. Later, she faces Milkman to face his responsibility for Hagar's death. Her own dying words are, 'I wish I'd a knowed more people. I would of loved 'em all. If I'd a knowed more, I would a loved more.' That free commitment to others is just what Milkman learns; it is no wonder that he answers by wishing for a mate like Pilate, saying, 'There's got to be at least one more woman like you' (*Song*, p. 340).

In these ways, Pilate too is like the hero, and the importance of her role should not be underestimated. But the terms of her life keep her from really fitting the heroic mould. It is important to the mythic conception that the hero understand what he is, and Pilate does not quite reach that point. She does have the independence and compassion of the hero, but her sense of mission is oddly garbled. She misinterprets her dead father's messages, mistakes his bones for someone else's, cannot complete her 'quest' without Milkman's explanation. She does the right thing, but from intuitive rather than conscious knowledge. Thus, while she embodies Morrison's values, she is not the complete hero that Milkman is, for she lacks his recognition of meaning. By contrast to his final state, she seems intuitive, personal, and rather passive.

This distinction is bothersome because it comes so close to the old active-man/passive-woman stereotype. It is quite clearly rooted in the myth structure. It seems fitting that Pilate dies and Milkman is left only with his *imagination* of a woman like her, for in the myth, woman gets meaning from or gives meaning to man; she does not both live and know the meaning as he does. Toni Morrison commented that *Song of Solomon* is about 'dominion', and about 'the way in which men do things or see things and relate to one another'.[15] What the novel shows is that the 'universal' myth of Western culture is just such a male story; and the parallels and discrepancies between Milkman and Pilate further show the difficulty of the heroic mode for a woman.

The heroic quest for identity achieved by conquest in and of the outer world embodies the human need for transcendence and self-definition; at the same time, the mythic sense of fate and necessity corresponds to the experience of facticity, both as irrevocable consequence and as concrete conditions for choice. Between those two poles – free heroism and determined role – move Morrison's characters. Further, mythic patterns are especially appropriate to her social concerns, since the mythic hero by his nature both embodies and transcends the values of his culture. These connections would be significant in most presentations of existential themes, but the special situations with which Morrison is concerned further complicate her use of myth. On the one hand, traditional myths claim to represent 'universal' values and experiences; on the other, they clearly exclude or distort minority experiences by offering inappropriate or impossible models (e.g., Shirley Temple). This contradiction produces the special treatment of myth that Chester J. Fontenot, Jr, sees in black American fiction, turning on 'the tension between the universal order and that produced by mankind for Black people'. The myth of what may seem the 'universal cosmos' in the majority view is so patently untrue to the black experience that from that perspective it is not mythic, but 'linear', demanding denial of past and present reality in favour of 'an obscure vision of some distant future'[16] (e.g., the struggle to become Shirley Temple). Meanwhile, the mythic consciousness adequate to the minority experience is in danger of becoming an imprisoning view of oppression as 'fated'. Morrison, then, must capture 'universal' aspirations without denying concrete reality, construct a myth that affirms community identity without accepting oppressive definitions. In the process, she must take the outline of the mythic structure already so well suited to the existentialist quest for freedom and identity, and adapt it to the historical circumstances that surround this version of the quest. She values the myth as a way to design, not confine, reality; it remains to be seen how much further she can carry that notion.[17]

From *Contemporary Literature*, 23: 3 (1982), 323–42.

NOTES

[As Cynthia Davis explains in her final note, this essay was written before the publication of *Tar Baby* which is discussed from the point of view of the Fall myth in the next essay and from a Marxist perspective later in this volume. Reading the novel confirmed for her that one of the salient characteristics of Morrison's fiction is that it provides more questions than answers, focusing on the choices with which black people are faced. What Davis does not say is that in this respect Morrison's fiction is redolent of the African dilemma tale, which as part of the continent's oral tradition, presented communities with moral dilemmas which they were then obliged to resolve.

Davis's essay pinpoints the origins of many of the debates and disagreements among the critics represented in this volume. For example, a central issue to which many critics return is the extent to which African-Americans are free to assume or abdicate responsibilities to their race, their communities, their families and themselves. Of course, terms such as 'community', 'individuality', even 'African-American' are difficult to define other than in a diverse range of particular and often contradictory contexts. But Davis stresses that the dilemma of self-identity for many black people is inseparable from the constrictive racialist society in which they have to make their choices.

For Davis, the principal characters in Morrison's first three novels internalise 'the Look' of the majority white culture and then try, often futilely, to live up to it. Subsequent criticism has gone further than Davis in exploring how differences in race and class create problems for characters and in relating content and form in Morrison's first two novels, especially, in this respect. Nevertheless, whereas Morrison demonstrates the interest of many writers in dislocation, alienation, contradictions and ellipses, these features in her earlier work seem to arise out of the distortion of self created by the imposition of Euro-American cultural ideals on black people, including the white concept of beauty. Beauty is as much a political as an aesthetic concept in the three novels which Davis discusses, whilst ugliness is not merely a matter of appearance: in Western thinking it is a manifestation of an inner ugliness, a spiritual failure. Jacqueline de Weever in *Mythmaking and Metaphor in Black Women's Fiction* (New York, 1991) points out that the (white) insistence on one standard of beauty contradicts the pluralistic nature of contemporary America (p. 107).

In critical terms, Davis is particularly indebted to the Marxist Fredric Jameson's idea of 'strategies of containment' – ideologies that allow society to provide an explanation of itself which suppresses the underlying contradictions of history (see note 5 below). This concept enables Davis to pursue Jameson's recognition of the sociological implications of Sartre's thesis that human relations revolve around the experience of the 'Look' where being seen by another both confirms one's sense of reality but threatens one's sense of freedom. Jameson argues that we become an object along with someone else under the 'Look' of a 'Third'. Whilst Davis is not alone in focusing on internalisation of the white 'Look' by African-Americans as the key issue in Morrison's early novels, she argues that a concomitant preoccupation is the institutionalising of the gaze of the (white) 'Third' and its coercive power.

Morrison, however, is engaged in a more exploratory and open project than an examination of characters who fall into Bad Faith by internalising the 'Look' of the majority culture. Her characters, Davis suggests, provide different perspectives on the struggle for personal freedom and individuation which often assumes mythic, heroic proportions. But the institutionalising of the gaze of the 'Third' provides an obstructive context for the search for mythic structures which reflect black experience. Morrison's novels are thus seen as exploring how myth offers universal values but distorts the experiences of minorities. The use of multiple perspectives and of constantly shifting points of view are ways in which Morrison seeks to resist the closure of inherited mythical structures. Davis, however, is critical of *The Song of Solomon* for its male-centred myth. Even though the importance of Pilate cannot be overestimated, the novel risks confirming the active male–passive female divide of the mythic structure which Morrison deploys. Ed.]

1. Editions of Morrison's novels used here are *The Bluest Eye* (New York, 1970), hereafter cited as *Eye; Sula* (New York, 1975); *Song of Solomon* (New York, 1978), hereafter cited as *Song*. Dates given in the text are of the first hardcover editions.

2. For a careful analysis of the relation between primer and novel, see Phyllis Klotman, 'Dick-and-Jane and the Shirley Temple Sensibility in *The Bluest Eye*', *Black American Literature Forum*, 8: 4 (Winter 1979), 123–5.

3. Jean-Paul Sartre, *Being and Nothingness*, trans. Hazel E. Barnes (New York, 1966), p. 239. Subsequent references to this work (identified as *BN*) will be in the text.

4. Simone de Beauvoir, *The Second Sex*, trans. H. M. Parshley (New York, 1974), p. 158.

5. Fredric Jameson, *Marxism and Form: Twentieth-Century Dialectical Theories of Literature* (Princeton, NJ, 1971), p. 249. Most of ch. 4, 'Sartre and History', is relevant to this discussion.

6. William H. Grier and Price M. Cobbs, *Black Rage* (New York, 1968), p. 33. Despite their overvaluation of female 'narcissism', Grier and Cobbs offer a useful analysis of the image problem, and also of the difficulties in mother–daughter relations that Morrison shows.

7. Beauvoir, *Second Sex*, p. 159.

8. Barbara Smith, 'Toward a Black Feminist Criticism', *Women's Studies International Quarterly*, 2: 2 (1979), 185.

9. Chikwenye Okonjo Ogunyemi, '*Sula*: "A Nigger Joke"', *Black American Literature Forum*, 8: 4 (Winter 1979), 130.

10. Chikwenye Okonjo Ogunyemi, 'Order and Disorder in Toni Morrison's *The Bluest Eye*', *Critique*, 19: 1 (1977), 119.

11. Roger Rosenblatt, *Black Fiction* (Cambridge, MA, 1974), p. 9.

12. Susan L. Blake, 'Ritual and Rationalisation: Black Folklore in the Works of Ralph Ellison', *PMLA*, 94 (1979), 123, 126.

13. Ibid., pp. 124–6.

14. Barbara Lounsberry and Grace Ann Hovet, 'Principles of Perception in Toni Morrison's *Sula*', *Black American Literature Forum*, 8: 4 (Winter 1979), 129.

15. Jane Bakerman, 'The Seams Can't Show: An Interview with Toni Morrison', *Black American Literature Forum*, 7: 2 (Summer 1978), 60.

16. Chester J. Fontenot, Jr, 'Black Fiction: Apollo or Dionysus?' *Twentieth-Century Literature*, 25: 1 (Spring 1979), 75–6.

17. This essay was written before the publication of *Tar Baby* (1981). The new novel deserves detailed treatment, but here it may suffice to remark that the patterns observed in the earlier novels do recur in *Tar Baby*. Problems of identity are raised in similar terms of self/other, seer/seen, public/private; and they are clearly depicted as complicated by social divisions and pressures – even more so, since for the first time Morrison shows intersections between black and white worlds more closely. However, some of the unresolved issues also still linger. In particular, the nostalgic, isolating, and – again – male terms in which heroism and myth are finally presented seem even more troublesome.

2

The Crime of Innocence: *Tar Baby* and the Fall Myth

TERRY OTTEN

Although the fall pattern informs all Toni Morrison's novels, *Tar Baby* employs it more explicitly than any other narrative. The novel opens in a quintessential paradise, the lush Caribbean estate where a retired Philadelphia candy manufacturer, Valerian Street, lives with his much younger wife, Margaret, and his longtime black servants, Sydney and Ondine. Visiting is Jadine, Sydney and Ondine's beautiful niece, whom they have raised. A fashionable Paris model, she has been educated at the Sorbonne with Valerian's money and has spent most of her time in Paris and New York among aesthetes and the wealthy, including a rich European who wants to marry her. The lush setting initiates the fall motif, for as Keith Byerman concludes, 'Isle de Chevaliers is a perverse Eden',[1] an exotic example of the flawed 'garden'. In a departure from her earlier novels, Morrison seriously treats white characters in *Tar Baby* by incorporating Valerian and Margaret Street in an extensive adaptation of the fall myth. Ultimately, though, the focus falls on the young black couple, Jadine Childs and Son Green, who attempt to flee the physical and spiritual bondage of a white man's garden.

Though the picturesque setting portrays 'a remoteness and beauty analogous to the Garden of Eden', as Bessie W. Jones observes, 'through this near paradise there are reminders of the Fall', evidence that white society is destroying 'the natural beauty and uprooting fowl and animals from their natural habitat'.[2] The small community of expensive homes had been built by Haitian labourers and constructed above a swamp called Sein de Veilles (witch's tit) that was formed when the white invaders rerouted the river and displaced it to end twenty leagues from the sea. 'The world was altered' by wealthy whites: 'The men had gnawed the daisy trees until ... they broke in two and hit the ground. In the huge silence that followed their fall, orchids spiraled down to join them.'³ Though seemingly idyllic, the land is rotting, and haunted by demonic forces. [...]

Enter Son. Like Guitar Bains or Sula, he threatens the tenuous peace and harmony of an already flawed world. The serpent in paradise is a distinctly black outlaw, a fugitive who, similar to Leggett in Conrad's 'The Secret Sharer', first appears at night, emerging from the waters of the unconscious self. As a mysterious force reborn into the world, Son swims to the Seabird II (where Jadine and Margaret first appear), previously having been caught in 'a wide, empty tunnel' and having ritualistically 'turned three times' in the dark water (p. 4). After hiding out in the ship, Son follows the road where the jeep takes Jadine and Margaret to the house. He secretly enters the house, partly from hunger, partly because it looks 'cool and civilized' (p. 134). A stranger in paradise, he ventures upstairs 'out of curiosity', and is enraptured by the sleeping Jadine, a symbol of refinement and civilisation. The house becomes his 'nighttime possession' (p. 138), in which he roams as a shadow figure of each character's undiscovered self.

More than the conventional tempter in the garden, Son is the manifestation of the black pariah in Western culture, the terrorising black male, the supposed rapist of white women. To Margaret and the whitewashed blacks at the estate, he represents the 'swamp nigger', a black 'beast' who jeopardises a distinctly white Eden. He is the rebellious black who will not behave according to the rules or values of the system, and it is precisely on such grounds that all the characters except Valerian Street judge him.

It is no small irony that Valerian feels 'disappointment nudging contempt for the outrage Jade and Sydney and Ondine exhibit in defending property and personnel that did not belong to them from a black man who was one of their own' (p. 145). The morning after Son's appearance, Valerian recalls his son Michael derisively using the word 'bourgeois'. Valerian thought it meant 'unexciting' until the others condemned Son, and then 'he thought [it] meant Uncle Tom-ish' (p. 144). With a touch of whimsy, Valerian compares Son with Michael, who always promises to visit but never does for reasons that surface later. As some critics have noted, Son becomes something of a parody of the Christ figure, a man who, Bessie W. Jones points out, is wrapped in 'a fine pair of silk pajamas' in place of 'swaddling clothes', put in the 'manger' of the guest room, and welcomed as the white god's surrogate only son.[4] We might add that when Son first arrives he notices 'the sky holy with stars' (p. 134) and that 'here he [is] with the immediate plans of a new born baby' (p. 138). Like the suffering Christ figure who brings redemption, Son is rejected by those he possesses the power to transform.

Indeed, the arrival of the 'criminal' in the garden sends the characters scurrying to protect their innocence. Sydney, who prides himself on being 'a Phil-a-delphia Negro' (p. 163), wants to call the police and get the 'swamp nigger' out as soon as possible. And Ondine, too, rejects him: 'The man upstairs wasn't a Negro – meaning one of them. He is a stranger', 'a nasty and ignorant ... nigger' (p. 102). And Jadine is indignant at Margaret's question, 'You don't know him do you?' She protests, 'Know him? How would I know him?' (p. 128). She had not seen a 'black like him' for some ten years, not since she lived on Morgan Street in Baltimore before her mother died and she went to Philadelphia at age twelve to live with her Uncle Sydney and Aunt Ondine. Her subsequent prostitution of her blackness is illustrated in her 'seduction' by the expensive fur coat sent her by her European lover, Ryk. Just before Son enters her room the morning after he is discovered in Margaret's closet, Jadine 'lay spread-eagle on the fur, nestling herself into it. It made her tremble. She opened her lips and licked the fur. It made her tremble more. Ondine was right; there was something a little fearful about the coat. No, not fearful, seductive' (p. 112). And later Son suggestively defines her false identity by tracing her pictures in a fashion magazine with his finger as she talks about the expensive jewellry and earrings she is wearing in the layout. She assumes he is going to rape her, but he returns, 'Rape? Why do you little white girls think somebody's trying to rape you?' Condemned as white, Jadine feebly responds, 'White ... I am not ... you know I'm not white' (p. 121), but Son captures her in a truth. It is no wonder she fears him.

Jadine considers Son's hair symbolic of criminality: 'Wild, aggressive, vicious hair that needed to be put in jail. Uncivilized, reform school hair. Mau, Mau, Attica, chain-gang hair' (p. 113). Yet she finds in him that part of herself she has long denied. When he grabs her from behind and presses against her, she has to acknowledge her own culpability. 'He had jangled something in her that was so repulsive, so awful, and he had managed to make her feel that the thing that repelled her was not in him but in her. That was why she was ashamed' (p. 123). She had sworn at age twelve that she would 'never' let herself be victimised by a man mounting her like a dog in heat, yet she cannot deny that Son was drawn to her by her own animal nature, 'which she couldn't help but which was her fault just the same' (p. 124). It is not the criminality of desire but self-denial that he exposes. In short Son enters paradise like the biblical serpent, articulates Jadine's forbidden desires, muted by her counterfeit identity, and galvanises her into action. In his insistence that she acknowledge the 'darker' side of herself, the authentic black self obscured in the distorted mirror of her adopted Eden, Son forces Jadine to see the 'beast' in the glass.

Until now, conditioned by her sophisticated European education, Jadine is detached from her own blackness, much like Helene Wright or Geraldine or Macon Dead. Eight years earlier when she last saw Michael while on vacation with the Streets, he had accused her of abandoning her people. Though she knew his idealistic scheme of generating social reform by having black welfare mothers 'do crafts, pottery, clothing in their homes' was silly, she admitted that he 'did make me want to apologize for what I was doing, what I felt. For liking "Ave Maria" better than gospel music' (p. 74). Yet when they talk about Michael's hopeless plot, Jadine tells Valerian, 'Picasso *is* better than an Itumba mask' (p. 74), and she confesses her embarrassment at attending 'ludicrous' art shows put on by pretentious blacks in Europe. Michael had encouraged her to return to Morgan Street with Sydney and Ondine to do handicraft. 'Can you believe it?' she asks Valerian. 'He might have convinced me if we'd had that talk on Morgan Street. But in Orange County on a hundred and twenty acres of green velvet?' (p. 75). She had long since moved into a white society where 'the black people she knew wanted what she wanted' and where success required her 'only to be stunning ... Say the obvious, ask stupid questions, laugh with abandon, look interested, and light up at any display of their humanity if they showed it' (pp. 126–7). She simply tells Son, 'I belong here. You, motherfucker, do not ...' (p. 125).

Nonetheless, Son's presence restores something of her black awareness, just as Guitar Bains awakens Milkman's black consciousness in *Song of Solomon*. He prompts her to recall the guilt she felt two months before when a beautiful African woman in a canary yellow dress spat on her in disgust in a Paris street. The manifestation of Jadine's own black heritage, the woman floated through glass like a vision out of her self, an alter ego passing judgement.[5]

[...] Jadine temporarily finds something restorative in Son's impulsiveness and powerful black pride. 'He unorphaned her completely. Gave her a brand-new childhood' (p. 229). But clearly Son cannot live comfortably in Jadine's self-constructed paradise, and when Son takes her to his lost Eden in Eloe, it is apparent that she cannot live in his world either. With its apparent poverty and ignorance and isolation, Eloe defines all the 'blackness' Jadine has long struggled to escape. To Son it represents the opposite: self-worth, wholeness, and human values. Long separated from his father because he fled after his wife's death, Son carries with him the guilt of a prodigal son. Though he had written money orders to his father, he feels ashamed that he had never written a note. His father had cashed only a few of the cheques, in part because Son wrote his name on them, and he treasured Son's handwriting: 'Pretty. Like your mama' (p. 250). A returned prodigal suffering remorse, Son honours his father's moral judgement that Jadine should not stay in his house if she and Son are not married. Made morally sensitive, Son insists to Jadine that she stay at his Aunt Rosa's modest house.

Jadine, too, becomes morally alive. She experiences profound self-awareness when Aunt Rosa accidentally sees her naked in bed: 'No man made her feel that naked, that unclothed. Leerers, lovers, doctors, artists – none of them had made her feel exposed. More than exposed. Obscene' (p. 253). Here too she dreams of judgement. She sees all the black women in her life in the dark outside the door: 'The night women were not merely against her ... not merely looking superior over their sagging breasts and folded stomachs, they seemed somehow in agreement about her, and they were out to get her, tie her, bind her. Grab the person she had worked hard to become and choke it off with their soft loose tits' (p. 262). More than the conventional metaphysical or psychological ghosts that haunt characters in literature, these are racial ghosts, black women who stand in judgement of Jadine's abandonment of her racial being. Not Dawn, Aisha, Felicite, or Betty ('They were her friends. They were like her.' [p. 261]), these are the 'night women', who, like Son, demand recognition of her racial consciousness.

Even when he first sees her sleeping at Valerian's estate, Son yearns 'to press his dreams' into Jadine's consciousness, to will her out of the white man's house and into a world of 'fat black ladies in white dresses minding the pie table in the basement of the church and white wet sheets flapping on the line' (p. 119). Yet he fears that she might 'press her dreams of gold and cloisonné and honey-colored silk into him' (p. 120). Though Son devastates Valerian's white paradise, he cannot reclaim her. His failure becomes apparent when Jadine tells him that while he was playing criminal by driving his car into his wife's bed and hiding from the law, she was being educated with the help of a 'poor old white dude'. 'Stop loving your ignorance', she tells him; 'it isn't lovable' (p. 264). Nor can he himself deny his failure, his 'shame' at not looking into Cheyenne's face as she was dying, at not writing a note to his father, at his 'loving his ignorance'. He informs Jadine that what they taught her in college 'didn't include me' and so they kept her ignorant: 'because until you know about me, you don't know nothing about yourself' (p. 264). But he, too, is from the beginning a wanderer in search of self. Morrison concludes, 'One had a past, the other a future and each one bore the culture to save the race in his hands. Mama-spoiled black man, will you mature with me? Culture-bearing black woman, whose culture are you bearing?' (p. 269).

Like the conclusion to *Song of Solomon*, the ending of this novel has provoked considerable controversy. Some critics read it as optimistic and affirmative. Bessie W. Jones goes so far as to call it the attainment of a 'new Eden, a celestial paradise'. On the other hand, James W. Coleman concludes that Morrison pulls 'an escape act by imposing on the novel a superficial good ending that, under analysis, proves unsatisfactory'. Cynthia Dubin Edelberg complains that in Son's flight Morrison 'posits a kind of primitivism as an answer, as something that counters education and work, but this primitivism is rhetorical rather than convincing'.[6] Morrison herself has admitted to uncertainty. 'I may have some attitude which one is more right than the other [Son or Jadine], but in a funny sense that book was very unsettling to me because everybody was sort of wrong.' Yet in the same interview, she relates the novel, as she does her other fiction, to Greek drama and comments, 'There was probably ... catharsis in the sense of a combination of the restoration of order – order is restored at the end – and the character having a glimmer of some knowledge that he didn't have when the book began.'[7] Finally, though, the knowledge both characters gain seems to lead to an incomplete catharsis. Neither Jadine nor Son achieves a full victory in defeat.

Coming to a frightening awareness, naked after the fall, Jadine eludes the truth. Like Blake's Thel, who scurries back to the vales of Har, Jadine flees back to the elite society she considers her paradise. Incapable of committing a saving sin against her security, she will never integrate her other self. According to Susan Lydon, Jadine is caught between her sex and her race. To be true to her freedom as a woman, she must resist Son's male insistence that she play the subservient role of 'fat black ladies' serving pies in the church basement. To be true to her black heritage, however, she needs to sacrifice success in a white culture. Says Lydon, 'she is neither female enough nor black enough to make it in her culture'.[8] Viewed in this context, Jadine's 'fall' leads to no regeneration. Cast east of Eden she exists in unresolved duality, knowing 'good' and 'evil', black and white.

Nor can Son survive. Looking at the photographs from Eloe after Jadine has left him, he discovers a lost paradise. 'It all looked miserable ... sad, poor and even poor spirited' (p. 295). He cannot go home again. As his father remarks when Son tells him he could have lied about being married to Jadine, 'But you didn't lie. You told the truth and you got to live by the truth' (p. 249). When he returns to the island looking frantically for Jadine, the wise Thérèse, descendant of the blind horsemen, asks, 'If you cannot find her what will you do? Live in the garden of some other white people house?' (p. 305). She tells him to forget Jadine because 'she has forgotten her ancient properties' (p. 305). And finally she offers him the only possible escape – joining the legendary horsemen in the hills. 'They are waiting for you. They are naked and they are black too ... Go there. Choose them' (p. 306). Elizabeth House argues that Son is 'the rabbit' that escapes to the briars, 'that Jadine, the tar baby, will not successfully lure Son again'.[9] Perhaps so, but Morrison allows Son no victory separate from the timeless world of legend and darkness. Becoming an eternal night rider returning to the dark unconscious from which he emerged, Son retreats from a world where he can find no reconciliation and no solution to his own fallen humanity.

Jadine and Son, Valerian and Margaret, Sydney and Ondine, all bear the consequences of self-knowledge. The fall motif in *Tar Baby* makes Morrison's work considerably more substantial and meaningful than some critics have contended. To be sure, Morrison partly follows in the tradition of American literature by depicting the essential conflict between primitivity and civilisation, the rural and the urban – redskin and paleface. But beyond this conventional dialectic, *Tar Baby*, like her other novels, describes the passage from innocence to experience with biblical and theological over-tones – garden images, references to the serpent, expressions of guilt and lost innocence, a yearning to return to the garden.

From Terry Otten, *The Crime of Innocence in the Fiction of Toni Morrison* (Columbia, 1989), pp. 63–8; 76–80.

NOTES

[Although Terry Otten's essay is essentially a deconstructionist reading of the Fall myth in *Tar Baby* which brings a postcolonial perspective to bear on the trope of the Holy Garden, it is indebted to a notion of a flawed humanity more usually found in liberal humanist criticism. The novel is not read simply as an allegory for white exploitation of blacks. While some readers may feel that the essay privileges white myth over black myth – the myth of Brer Rabbit is only mentioned toward the end of the extract – one of the strengths of the piece is its appreciation of the way in which the bib-lical myth of the Fall in the novel is reconfigured from an African-American perspective. For example, although Son is compared to the serpent in the Garden of Eden, he is seen as redolent of the black nationalist male ac-tivists of the 1960s through a comparison with Guitar in *Song of Solomon* and is also compared to the terrorising black male stereotype of Western culture. There are, however, African-American dimensions to Son which Otten does not pursue. In challenging the blacks and whites on the island to face truths about themselves, for example, he is the trickster figure of the African dilemma tale. That the other characters have to face what they repress or deny gives a psychoanalytic dimension to Otten's essay. However, throughout the essay, the Garden myth keeps the postcolonial rather than the psychoanalytic dimension to the fore. The blacks on the island are not simply repressing an undiscovered self but are 'whitewashed', a concept with a stronger sociocultural than psychoanalytic bias. Thus, Jadine's 'counterfeit identity' is discussed as more a socioeconomic than psychoanalytic phenomenon. Indeed, what Otten sees as repressed – an 'au-thentic black self' – is a collective rather than personal sense of identity which Morrison's later work especially tends to challenge rather than affirm. Ed.]

1.   Keith Byerman, *Fingering the Jagged Grain: Tradition and Form in Recent Black Fiction* (Athens, GA, 1985), p. 208.

2. Bessie W. Jones, 'Garden Metaphor and Christian Symbolism in *Tar Baby*', in Bessie W. Jones and Audrey L. Vinson, *The World of Toni Morrison* (Dubuque, IA, 1985), pp. 116–17. Jones parallels the description of place with Milton's account of Eden after Eve eats the forbidden fruit.

3. Ibid., p. 119.

4. Ibid., pp. 115–24.

5. Morrison identifies the African woman as 'the original self – the self we betray when we lie, the one that is always there. And whatever that self looks like ... one measures oneself against it' (Nellie McKay, 'An Interview with Toni Morrison', *Contemporary Literature*, 24: 4 [1983], 422). See also Gloria Naylor and Toni Morrison, 'A Conversation', *Southern Review* 21: 3 (1985), 572.

6. Jones, 'Garden Metaphor and Christian Symbolism in *Tar Baby*', p. 124; James Coleman, 'The Quest for Wholeness in Morrison's *Tar Baby*', *Black American Literature Forum*, 20 (1986), 69; Cynthia Dubin Edelberg, 'Morrison's Voices: Formal Education, the Work Ethic and the Bible', *American Literature*, 58 (1986), 236.

7. Bessie W. Jones, 'An Interview with Toni Morrison', *The World of Toni Morrison*, p. 135.

8. Susan Lydon, 'What's an Intelligent Woman To Do?', *The Village Voice*, 1–7 (July, 1981), 41.

9. Elizabeth House, 'The "Sweet Life" in Toni Morrison's Fiction', *American Literature*, 56: 2 (1984), 201.

3

Hagar's Mirror: Self and Identity in Morrison's Fiction

BARBARA RIGNEY

> One day Pilate sat down on Hagar's bed and held a compact before
> her granddaughter's face. It was trimmed in a goldlike metal and had
> a pink plastic lid.
>
> 'Look, baby. See here?' Pilate turned it all around to show it off
> and pressed in the catch. The lid sprang open and Hagar saw a tiny
> part of her face reflected in the mirror. She took the compact then
> and stared into the mirror for a long while.
>
> 'No wonder', she said at last. 'Look at that. No wonder. No
> wonder.'
>
> *(Song of Solomon)*

Mirrors are dangerous objects in Morrison's fictions. What destroys
Hagar is not merely Pilate's oppressive love (her gift of the mirror
being evidence of this) nor Milkman's failure to love, but the vision
of herself as *self* that the mirror reflects. The mirror lies in telling
her that she is not beautiful, for mirrors represent only white standards of beauty;[1] but the greater lie is that illusion of unified selfhood which mirrors also perpetate, for the 'self' in Morrison's
fiction is always multiple, contradictory, and ambiguous – if, in
fact, a self can be said to exist at all.

An interesting parallel to Hagar's mirror-death exists early in the
same novel, at the point at which Milkman gazes at his own face in

the mirror with at least mild approval of the 'firm jaw line, splendid teeth' but largely unaware of what the narrator knows, that the image 'lacked coherence, a coming together of the features into a total self' (pp. 69–70). According to Cixous and Clément in *The Newly Born Woman*, when a man looks into a mirror, he 'identifies and constitutes himself with the mirror. It reflects his image to him, *fixes* it as a subject and subjects it to the law, to the symbolic order, to language, and does it in a way that is both inalienable and alienating'.[2] Milkman's 'self' analysis is juxtaposed, significantly, to the entrance of his father, who surely represents for Morrison an exaggerated and clearly parodic version of patriarchal inscriptions, including those of identity and selfhood, most particularly the fiction that 'You have to be a whole man. And if you want to be a whole man, you have to deal with the whole truth' (p. 70).

Clearly, there are no 'whole truths' or 'whole' men and women in Morrison's novels, at least not in any traditional fictional sense. Just as she challenges the dominant cultural view of language and signification, so Morrison also subverts traditional Western notions of identity and wholeness. Patricia Waugh, in *Feminine Fictions: Revisiting the Postmodern*, is not alone in her observation that the death of the self is characteristic of all postmodern fictions, which thus act to undermine traditional philosophies by contradicting 'the dualistic, objective posturing of western rationality'.[3] More central to the present concern is Waugh's argument that 'for those marginalised by the dominant culture, a sense of identity as constructed through impersonal and social relations of power (rather than a sense of identity as the reflection of an inner "essence") has been a major aspect of their self-concept long before post-structuralists and postmodernists began to assemble their cultural manifestos' (p. 3). If this is true particularly for women, as Waugh maintains, how much more radical might be the deconstruction of the self as a concept in fiction by those doubly marginalised by race as well as gender?

French theorists are among those who in recent years have radically undermined notions of the unitary self, notions they attribute directly to Western humanism, which they see as totally and unmitigatedly male in origin as well as in values. Irigaray, for example, condemns what she and many others term phallocentric literature as the 'endless litigation over identity with oneself'.[4]

She defines feminine language by contrast as inherently multiple, based on the complex biology of women:

> in that 'syntax' there would no longer be either subject or object, 'oneness' would no longer be privileged, there would no longer be proper meanings, proper names, 'proper' attributes. ... Instead, that 'syntax' would involve nearness, proximity, but in such an extreme form that it would preclude any distinction of identities, any establishment of ownership, thus any form of appropriation.[5]

Alice Jardine, whose theoretical focus is an interpretation of French feminisms, characterises their works as a 'whirlpool of decentring' in which 'The notion of the "Self" – so intrinsic to Anglo-American thought, becomes absurd. It is not something called the "Self" which speaks, but language, the unconscious, the "textuality of the text".'[6] Toril Moi also analyses French resistance to concepts of selfhood in terms of Lacan and Derrida, and writes:

> As Luce Irigaray or Hélène Cixous would argue, this integrated self is in fact a phallic self, constructed on the model of the self-contained, powerful phallus. Gloriously autonomous, it banishes from itself all conflict, contradiction and ambiguity. In this humanist ideology the self is the *sole author* of history and of the literary text: the humanist creator is potent, phallic and male – God in relation to his world, the author in relation to his text. History or the text become nothing but 'expression' of this unique individual: all art becomes autobiography, a mere window on to the self and the world, with no reality of its own.[7]

As she has made clear in a number of interviews, Morrison does not write autobiography.[8] As the author has no self that is manifested in her fiction, so also Morrison's narrators are most often unidentifiable, anonymous, vehicles to transmit information and convey emotion rather than to provide moral interpretations or represent a personality.[9] Often these narrators disappear completely as one character or another steps forward to tell the story from a different point of view. But even these speaking characters reflect multiple and fragmented selves, which are sometimes undefined, inevitably amorphous, always merging with the identity of a community as a whole or with the very concept of blackness. Henry Louis Gates, Jr, has commented on the irony of African-American writers attempting 'to posit a "black self" in the very Western languages in which blackness itself is a figure of absence, a negation'.[10]

For example, in *Sula*, that point at which Nel looks into the mirror and discovers her 'me-ness' is almost as fraught with premonition of disaster as when Hagar peers into the pink and gold compact in *Song of Solomon*. For Nel, the mirror reflects, not a concept called Nel, but something other: '"I'm not Nel. I'm me. Me." Each time she said the word *me* there was a gathering in her like power, like joy, like fear' (pp. 24–5). Nel's assertion of self-hood, whether an indication of false pride or merely an adolescent delusion, ends in the reality of her common identity with other women of the community. For Sula, at least, Nel has become one of those unindividuated women: 'The narrower their lives, the wider their hips. Those with husbands had folded themselves into starched coffins, their sides bursting with other people's skinned dreams and bony regrets. Those without men were like sourtipped needles featuring one constant empty eye' (p. 105). In Morrison's fictions, identity is always provisional; there can be no isolated ego striving to define itself as separate from community, no matter how tragic or futile the operations of that community might be. Individual characters are inevitably formed by social constructions of both race and gender, and they are inseparable from those origins.

That early scene in *Sula* in which Shadrack attempts to discover an identity in the only mirror accessible to him, the water in a toilet bowl, confirms the idea that 'self' lies in blackness rather than in any subjectivity or uniqueness: 'There in the toilet water he saw a grave black face. A black so definite, so unequivocal, it astonished him. He had been harboring a skittish apprehension that he was not real – that he didn't exist at all. But when the blackness greeted him with its indisputable presence, he wanted nothing more' (p. 11). Interestingly, in this novel, blackness is a *presence* rather than an absence,[11] a key to an identity that is always multiple, shared, a form of membership in community.[12]

Even Sula, although the novel is named for her, is not, strictly speaking, a protagonist, for she shares the novel's focus as well as a black identity with Nel, Shadrack, Nel's mother, Eva, and the community itself. Her identity, multiple as it is, is a reflection of community identity; when she absents herself from that community for ten years, she ceases to exist within the text itself. Her much-quoted assertion, 'I don't want to make somebody else. I want to make myself' (p. 80), is almost demonic in Morrison's terms, one indication of many of the moral ambiguities Sula represents. To 'make'

one's self, or at least to make of one's self a single entity, is impossible, for all selves are multiple, divided, fragmented, and a part of a
greater whole.

Sula's birthmark, for example, interpreted by every other character in the novel as representing a variety of images, is not only a
reflection of the characters of those interpreting, but is also a valid
indication of Sula's own multiplicity.[13] Her mark is, in fact, a
stemmed rose, a tadpole, a snake, an ash from her mother's burning
body, all interacting to represent aspects of Sula's ambiguous
essence. As Deborah E. McDowell writes in 'The Self and the
Other: Reading Toni Morrison's *Sula* and the Black Female Text',
Sula's birthmark 'acts as a metaphor for her figurative "selves", her
multiple identity'. McDowell concludes, based on this argument,
that 'Morrison's reconceptualisation of character has clear and
direct implications for Afro-American literature and critical study,
for if the self is perceived as perpetually in process, rather than a
static entity always already formed, it is thereby difficult to posit its
ideal or "positive" representation'.[14]

Even beyond McDowell's conception of self-in-process, however,
lies the possibility of self as negation, as illusion, as contradiction,
as an aspect of 'the something else to be' (p. 44) which Nel and
Sula create for themselves.

Even Sula's birthmark, potentially a sign of an individual self
however fragmented and multiple, is rather an indication of relationship, being one of a series of marks, brands, or emblems that
Morrison employs in most of her novels, not to 'distinguish' individuals, but (as blackness itself is a mark) to symbolise their participation in a greater entity, whether that is community or race or
both. The marks are hieroglyphs, clues to a culture and a history
more than to individual personality. Whether the 'mark' is Pauline
Breedlove's crippled foot in *The Bluest Eye*, Eva's missing leg in
Sula, Pilate's navel-less stomach in *Song of Solomon*, Son's rastafar-
ian dreadlocks in *Tar Baby*, or the crossed circle mandala branded
beneath the breast of Sethe's mother in *Beloved*, or even the choke-
cherry tree scars on Sethe's own back, these represent membership
rather than separation. If these marks distinguish at all, they
distinguish a racial identity, for most are either chosen or inflicted
by the condition of blackness itself, by the poverty that has
historically accompanied blackness, or by the institution of slavery
which 'marked' its victims literally and figuratively, physically and
psychologically. 'If something happens to me and you can't tell me

by my face, you can know me by this mark', Sethe's African mother tells her. And the child Sethe answers, 'Mark me, too ... Mark the mark on me too' (*Beloved*, p. 61). Whether this is the mark of Cain or the bloodstain of a Passover, a curse or an anointment, it denotes a sisterhood (and sometimes a brotherhood as well) of Africa, which in itself is a political statement both subversive and confrontational.[15]

The verbal equivalent of such marks is the name, which, also like marks, does not necessarily designate an individual self so much as a segment of community, an identity larger than self. As Morrison has said in an interview with Thomas Le Clair: 'If you come from Africa, your name is gone. It is particularly problematic because it is not just *your* name but your family, your tribe. When you die, how can you connect with your ancestors if you have lost your name? That's a huge psychological scar.'[16] Of least importance in Morrison's novels are those names which are a part of the dominant signifying order, those denoting ownership, appropriation, those originating in slavery, those which deny group identity and African origins. In *Beloved*, Baby Suggs recalls her slave name as Jenny Whitlow; only as Mr Garner delivers her into freedom can she turn and ask him, 'why you all call me Jenny?' Her lack of a name – 'Nothing ... I don't call myself nothing' (p. 141) – is testament to the 'desolated center where the self that was no self made its home' (p. 140). Baby Suggs has no 'self' because she has no frame of reference by which to establish one, no family, no children, no context: 'Sad as it was that she did not know where her children were buried or what they looked like if alive, fact was she knew more about them than she knew about herself, having never had the map to discover what she was like' (p. 140).

Similarly, Paul D is one of a series of Pauls, identified alphabetically by some anonymous slaveholder, while Sixo is presumably the sixth of an analogous group.[17] Stamp Paid, born Joshua under slavery, has, however, chosen and devised his own symbolic name, which represents a rejection of a tradition of white naming as well as a celebration of freedom. His name is also and more specifically a symbol of freedom from debt; because he suffered under slavery and because he 'handed over his wife to his master's son' (p. 184), he has paid in misery any obligation to humanity, he believes, although his continued activity as a conductor on the Underground Railroad would indicate otherwise. All African-Americans are, in essence, 'Stamp Paid', Morrison implies.

Sethe's name is one of the few in this novel chosen by a mother, and that name is a mark of blackness and of acceptance into tribe and culture. As Nan tells the 'small girl Sethe', 'She threw them all away but you. The one from the crew she threw away on the island. The others from more whites she also threw away. Without names, she threw them. You she gave the name of the black man' (p. 62). Whether this name is derived from that of the Egyptian god, Seth, or from the biblical Seth, it represents, like most of the names that Morrison designates as chosen, a sense of heritage and a context of relational identity.

And, Beloved, whose birth name we never learn, takes her identity from the single word on her tombstone and from the love her mother bears her, the paradox of which is reflected in the novel's epigraph from *Romans*: 'I will call them my people, which were not my people; and her beloved, which was not beloved.' Finally, Beloved has no identity other than that merged with the 'Sixty million and more' of the dedication, all those who suffered the outrage of enslavement; her consciousness is a group consciousness, her memory a racial memory of the Middle Passage. All names in Morrison's fictions, finally, are, like that of Beloved, names of the 'Disremembered and unaccounted for, she cannot be lost because no one is looking for her, and even if they were, how can they call her if they don't know her name?' (p. 275).

Early in *Song of Solomon*, Macon Dead considers that he might have a better sense of the identity for which he futilely strives throughout the novel, mainly through an accumulation of wealth and an approximation of white bourgeois standards of living, if he could locate his ancestral context: 'Surely, he thought, he and his sister had some ancestor, some lithe young man with onyx skin and legs as straight as cane stalks, who had a name that was real. A name given to him at birth with love and seriousness. A name that was not a joke, nor a disguise, nor a brand name' (p. 17). For three generations, the Macon Deads have borne a name, the drunken mistake of a white bureaucrat, which is both a brand and a joke that continues throughout the novel: 'You can't kill me. I'm already Dead.' Although Milkman's nickname is so ignominiously earned, also a joke, and his character so ironically ambiguous, formed as it is by a parody of patriarchy, his ultimate dignity lies in his final realisation of the importance of 'Names that bore witness' (p. 333).

Morrison's epigraph to the novel reads, 'The fathers may soar/
And the children may know their names', but it is, finally, also the
names of the ancestral mothers which bear witness. Pilate's ambiguous name (inherently subversive in its anti-Christian intimations),
selected by that family custom of placing a finger on the first word
in an opened Bible (even though, in Pilate's case, the namer was
unable to read), is so critical to her that she places the written inscription of it in a box that she wears strung through her earlobe,
not because her identity as an individual is threatened, but because
the name itself is a connection with family, with tradition and
history. Even the young Milkman knows that Pilate's box contains
the magic knowledge of all names: 'Pilate knows. It's in that dumb-
ass box hanging from her ear. Her own name and everybody else's'
(p. 89).

Pilate carries her name with her, just as she carries a rock from
every state in which she has lived, to provide continuity in an otherwise random and dispossessed existence. Son in *Tar Baby* suffers a
similar dispossession and also attempts to protect the name that
will provide the only coherence he is capable of achieving:

> Oh, he had been alone so long, hiding and running so long. In eight
> years he'd had seven documented identities and before that a few un-
> documented ones, so he barely remembered his real original name
> himself. Actually the name most truly his wasn't on any of the Social
> Security cards, union dues cards, discharge papers, and everybody
> who knew it or remembered it in connection with him could very
> well be dead. Son. It was the name that called forth the true him. The
> him that he never lied to, the one he tucked in at night and the one
> he did not want to die. The other selves were like the words he spoke
> – fabrications of the moment, misinformation required to protect Son
> from harm and to secure that one reality at least.
>
> (p. 119)

The primary significance of the name Son is, again, not to denote an
individual self ('He did not always know who he was, but he
always knew what he was like' [p. 142]), but to place that self in a
context of relationship: Son is a son of Africa and also a son of the
American black male experience, the 'Nigger Jims ... Staggerlees
and John Henrys. Anarchic, wandering, they read about their
hometowns in the pages of out-of-town newspapers' (p. 143). Like
Pilate and any number of Morrison's other characters, Son is

dispossessed, permanently 'out-of-town', his name being his only connection with community and black tradition.

Most of the other characters in *Tar Baby* have at least two names, which Morrison indicates is symbolic of their fragmentation. Lost between the white and black worlds, Jadine is Jadine to her aunt and uncle but a more exotic Jade to the white Streets who have educated her and imbued her with their questionable values.[18] Ondine is Nanadine to Jadine, but Ondine to the Streets, just as Sydney is Sydney to the person he calls Mr Street, years of intimacy not being sufficient to challenge racial and class protocol. Thérèse and Gideon are the generic Mary and Yardman to the Streets and, ironically, even to Ondine and Sydney, whose 'superiority' as 'Philadelphia Negroes' depends on such distinctions. Son at one point ponders Gideon's identity: 'It bothered him that everybody called Gideon Yardman, as though he had not been mothered' (p. 138). There is some justice in the fact that Margaret Street, white but as powerless as anyone else in her relationship to Valerian (whose name is that of a Roman emperor), also has multiple names – Margaret Lenore/Margarette – wherein lies her essence, 'under the beauty, back down beneath it where her Margaret-hood lay in the same cup it had always lain in – faceless, silent and trying like hell to please' (p. 71).

Choosing one's own name, in certain tragic cases, can also represent a rejection of race and culture. Helen Wright in *Sula*, for example, abhors the circumstances of her own birth to a Creole prostitute; in order to 'be as far away from the Sundown House as possible' (p. 15), she exchanges her name, Helene Sabat, with its exotic associations with the witch's sabbath, for the prosaic Helen Wright, with its implications of both 'rightness' and 'whiteness'. Her recurrent advice to her daughter, 'Don't just sit there, honey. You could be pulling your nose' (p. 24), is further evidence of her discomfort with a racial identity she perceives as outside the limits of propriety and social acceptability by which she has defined (and thereby circumscribed) her life.

Pauline Breedlove in *The Bluest Eye* provides yet another example of Morrison's concern with the significance of naming. 'Mrs Breedlove' even to her husband and children, she is 'Polly' to the white family for whom she works, and the diminutive name is totally appropriate in this case, for Pauline has diminished herself through her obsequious dedication to whiteness just as surely as little Pecola is diminished by her desire for blue eyes. Thus nicknames are often appropriate in Morrison's novels, denoting truths about character, revealing secrets, determining how a person is viewed by a particular community. Elihue Micah Whitcomb, also in *The Bluest Eye*, is called Soaphead Church by the community, a name mysterious to him but nevertheless reflective of his perverted sexual preference for 'clean' little girls: 'His sexuality was anything but lewd; his patronage of little girls smacked of innocence and was associated in his mind with cleanliness. He was what one might call a very clean old man' (p. 132).

It is universal folklore that to know a person's name is to have power over that person, and this is the reason in Soaphead's mind that God refuses to name himself: in his letter to God, Soaphead challenges: 'Is that why to the simplest and friendliest of questions: "What is your name?" put to you by Moses, You would not say, and said instead "I am who I am." Like Popeye? I Yam What I Yam? Afraid you were, weren't you, to give out your name? Afraid they would know the name and then know you? Then they wouldn't fear you?' (p. 142).

But the power greater than knowing a name is bestowing it, for the act of naming another reflects a desire to regulate and therefore to control. This is true throughout Morrison's fictions, and it is a major point of contention for feminist theorists as well; to be female, as to be black, is most often to suffer the oppression of being named by another. Monique Wittig in *Les Guérillères* uses a master/slave metaphor (which, when applied to Morrison's texts, is ironically pertinent) to protest a male naming of women: 'unhappy one, men have expelled you from the world of symbols and yet they have given you names, they have called you slave, you unhappy slave. Masters, they have exercised their rights as masters. They write of their authority to accord names, that it goes back so far the origin of language itself may be considered an act of authority emanating from those who dominate' (p. 112). Kristeva, too, repeatedly counsels women writers to avoid nouns, meaning that they should resist the temptation to authority which naming represents and realise the extent to which subjectivity is constructed through the disposition of such power.

Matriarchal power, always ambiguous in Morrison's novels, includes the equally ambiguous power to name, and a primary example of this is Eva in *Sula*. That Eva murders her son is an extension of the symbolic fact that she has already emasculated and rendered him infantile by calling him 'Sweet Plum'. Tar Baby,

Morrison implies, might have lived more effectively if Eva had not ridiculed his white skin and infantilised him in the same stroke with her whimsical naming. And surely the Deweys would have been at least somewhat more individuated, perhaps even normal in stature, if Eva had not reduced them, truncated their potential, through her assignment of the same name for all three: 'What you need to tell them apart for? They's all deweys' (p. 32). Finally, the name is not even capitalised, and 'them deweys' become a 'trinity with a plural name' (p. 33), indistinguishable in their appearance as in their childlike behaviour. As Morrison has said in an interview with Bettye J. Parker, 'Eva is a triumphant figure, one-legged or not. She's playing God. She maims people. But she says all of the important things' (p. 255).

The African mothers, the ancestor figures as Morrison often refers to them, are the primary namers in Morrison's novels, just as they are the transmitters of culture and the inventors of language, itself the operative agency of culture. It is they who always 'say the important things'. However, the ancestor women are not themselves individuated any more than other characters; they represent a group consciousness, a history as well as a culture, what McKay refers to as the 'ineffable qualities of blackness'. McKay quotes Morrison as explaining that her characters have ancestors, not 'just parents ... but timeless people whose relationships to the characters are benevolent, instructive, and protective, ... [and who] provide a certain kind of wisdom'.[19] One aspect of that wisdom is that the self is a relative concept, decentred rather than alienated, relational rather than objectifying.

This relational self, which constitutes such an important pattern in Morrison's fictions, derives at least as much from the strong bonding among her female characters as it does from racial identification. The biological states of pregnancy and of motherhood itself, in Morrison's terms, are experienced as a splitting of the self; in *Beloved*, Sethe recounts her feelings to Beloved: 'You asleep on my back. Denver sleep in my stomach. Felt like I was split in two' (p. 202). No father, no man, can understand, according to Sethe, that this condition is less a splitting than a spreading, a dissolution of boundaries, an embrace of multiplicity. Of Paul D's reaction to the murder of her child, Sethe says, 'Too thick, he said. My love was too thick. What he know about it? ... when I tell you you mine, I also mean I'm yours. I wouldn't draw breath without my children' (p. 203). Perhaps the closest we can come in theoretical terms to understanding Morrison's rendering of motherhood is in Kristeva's argument in 'Women's Time':

> Pregnancy seems to be experienced as the radical ordeal of the splitting of the subject; redoubling up of the body, separation and co-existence of the self and of an other, of nature and consciousness, of physiology and speech. This fundamental challenge to identity is then accompanied by a fantasy of totality – narcissistic completeness – a sort of instituted, socialised, natural psychosis. The arrival of the child, on the other hand, leads the mother into the labyrinths of an experience that, without the child, she would only rarely encounter: love for an other. Not for herself, nor for an identical being, and still less for another person with whom 'I' fuse (love or sexual passion). But the slow, difficult and delightful apprenticeship in attentiveness, gentleness, forgetting oneself.[25]

Cixous, too, sees motherhood as the ultimate subversion of male-defined subjectivity; in 'The Laugh of the Medusa', she writes: 'The mother, too, is a metaphor. It is necessary and sufficient that the best of herself be given to woman by another woman for her to be able to love herself and return in love the body that was "born" to her. Touch me caress me, you the living no-name, give me my self as myself.'[21]

In Morrison's mother–daughter relationships, no Lacanian mirror (and the separation from the mother that mirror represents) interferes with the pre-Oedipal relationship, that sometimes destructive yet also potentially positive arrangement which occurs in each one of Morrison's novels and the discussion of which pervades each chapter of the present study. Most Western psychologists, including Chodorow in *The Reproduction of Mothering*, see a possible pathology in such an arrangement: Chodorow notes those cases in which 'mothers maintained their daughters in a non-individuated state through behaviour which grew out of their own ego and body-ego boundary blurring and their perception of their daughters as one with, and interchangeable with, themselves'.[22] While Morrison, too, sees such boundary confusion as problematic, she nevertheless renders her female family relationships as powerfully positive agents in the lives of black women.[23] 'Dread of the mother',[24] occurs in Morrison, too, but is always mitigated by a love that is virtually erotic, a merging of identities that transcends Western ideas about self and other, about subject and object.

Sula, for example, is primarily and inevitably one of 'those Peace women' (p. 35), linked inextricably to her mother and grand-mother, with both of whom she shares personality traits and behaviour patterns. Sula, like Hannah, 'went to bed with men as frequently as she could' (p. 105), and like Eva, Sula is also a mur-derer, her participation in the drowning of Chicken Little almost as damning as Eva's act of burning Plum. Sula's passive pleasure in watching her mother burn – 'not because she was paralyzed, but because she was interested' (p. 67) – is no less dispassionate than Eva's self-mutilation, her sacrifice of her leg for insurance money to feed her children. Even this mutilation, the use of one's own body as sacrifice and also as political statement, is echoed by Sula's act of cutting off the tip of her finger to protect herself and Nel and to threaten the abusive boys who terrorise them. Like Eva and because of Eva, Sula has 'no center, no speck around which to grow ... no ego. For that reason she felt no compulsion to verify herself – be consistent with herself' (p. 103). According to Cynthia Davis, it is Sula's rejection of her mother, and ultimately of Eva as well, which is that factor determining her lack of centre, her '"splitting of the self", a denial of facticity that can produce a centreless hero like Sula'.[25]

The same relationship characterised by ambiguity exists in *Song of Solomon* among Pilate, Reba, and Hagar. The daughter, Reba, like Hannah in *Sula*, is relatively inconsequential, content to live obscurely in her more powerful and protective mother's shadow; the more intense relationship and more obvious doubling occurs between grandmother and granddaughter. Pilate and Hagar form a continuum of 'wildness', each a 'wilderness girl', each manifesting the jungle of the female essence, like 'every witch that ever rode a broom straight through the night to a ceremonial infanticide as thrilled by the black wind as by the rod between her legs' (p. 28). Pilate's love for Hagar, finally, is more destructive and more tragic than Hagar's love for Milkman, and Hagar is 'My baby girl' (pp. 322–3) to the moment of her death, locked but secure in the matriarchal realm that is her existence.

The merging of identities in the pre-Oedipal bonding of the female triad is universal in Morrison's work but most pronounced in *Beloved*, the relationship among Baby Suggs, Sethe, and Denver giving way to that inverted trinity of Sethe, Denver, and Beloved, who become 'us three', the 'hand-holding shadows' on the road (p. 182). The first thing we learn of Beloved's manifested presence at 124 Bluestone Road is the shattered mirror (p. 3), highly significant as a prefiguration of the shattering and merging of identities that will occur throughout the novel. Even before Beloved's actual physical appearance, she is part of the trinity that represents both love and destruction, the empty white dress kneeling beside Sethe which Denver sees through the window: 'The dress and her mother together looked like two friendly grown-up women – one (the dress) helping out the other' (p. 29). But always the hands that begin with a caress end by attempting to strangle: 'Putting the thumbs at the nape, while the fingers pressed the sides. Harder, harder, the fingers moved slowly around toward her windpipe, making little circles on the way. Sethe was actually more surprised than frightened to find that she was being strangled' (p. 96). After Beloved arrives in the flesh, manifests herself on the tree stump outside 124, the three women live together, virtually at the end of the world, on the edge of consciousness and experience, sharing identity as they share the pair-and-a-half of ice skates on a mystical winter night when, repeatedly, 'Nobody saw them falling' (pp. 174–5). The pre-Oedipal bonding is also symbolised by Sethe's preparation of the 'hot sweet milk' (p. 175) they share on their return from skating.

Denver is the first to sense the melting of identity, the merging that is her love for Beloved, whose blood she has drunk 'right along with my mother's milk' (p. 205). Believing that Beloved has left her and returned to her otherworldly existence, Denver realises 'she has no self ... She can feel her thickness thinning, dissolving into nothing. She grabs the hair at her temples to get enough to uproot it and halt the melting for a while ... She doesn't move to open the door because there is no world out there' (p. 123). Beloved, too, finds herself melting, surrealistically disintegrating, as she surprises herself by pulling out one of her own teeth.

Beloved is, finally, 'exploded right before their eyes' (p. 263) according to community women, but not before there has occurred a merging of voices and minds as well as of bodies: 'I am Beloved and she is mine ... She smiles at me and it is my own face smiling ... Your face is mine ... Will we smile at me? ... She is the laugh; I am the laughter ... Beloved/You are my sister/You are my daughter/You are my face; you are me ... You are mine/You are mine/You are mine' (pp. 214–17). It requires all of Paul D's strength and all the power of a community of women to separate this triad, to disperse the ghost, to save Sethe's life, and to return Denver to a 'real' world. Paul D, with his male energy and his love, restores Sethe to at least a kind of subjectivity; but we wonder, at the end (such is the power of Morrison's ambiguity), whether or not he is more killer than healer, whether he lies when he says: 'You your best thing, Sethe. You are' (p. 273). The last word in the novel, after all, is 'Beloved', relegated though she is to the dreamworld, the realm of dark water, the unconscious where the self is always split and illusory, where 'the sound of one's own feet going seem to come from a far-off place' (p. 274).

From Barbara Rigney, *The Voices of Toni Morrison* (Columbus, OH, 1991), pp. 35–49.

NOTES

[Barbara Rigney begins by distinguishing between the concept of a multiple, contradictory and ambiguous self familiar in contemporary French theory and that of a unified, coherent self which has been posited in Euro-American literary humanism. For Rigney, Morrison is clearly a postmodern writer who challenges traditional Western views of wholeness and identity. This is also an approach taken later in this volume to Morrison's *Beloved* by Pérez-Torres (essay 8). However, Rigney's exploration of the postmodernism of Morrison's work is different in that it draws on a complex, French feminist theoretical base and emphasises the ways in which Morrison's characters seem to merge with the identity of a community as a whole or with the very concept of blackness. Rigney's own style of writing is to develop a molecular structure around her central thread – in this case that all selves are multiple and fragmented yet part of a larger whole. Thus the molecular structure of the essay embraces related subjects such as Sula's birthmark, naming (both the power of knowing a name and of bestowing it), the bonding of strong female characters, and female family relationships.

Deborah McDowell, to whose work Rigney refers (see note 14 below), also approaches Morrison's fiction from the point of view of its challenge to the commonplace assumption that the self is pre-existent, coherent and knowable. However, her line of argument is different from Rigney's. For McDowell, *Sula* opens up new literary and critical options for women, setting up new agendas for black women's social and narrative possibilities. Rigney argues that Sula, despite her multiple identity, is a reflection of community identity. However, McDowell and Dubey (in the next essay in this volume) follow Barbara Christian who, in her groundbreaking study *Black Feminist Criticism; Perspectives on Black Women Writers* (New York, 1985), recognises that community norms are often in conflict with individual desires and do not always work in black women's interests. McDowell maintains that *Sula* suggests that one cannot belong to the community and preserve the imagination since the orthodox vocations for women – marriage and motherhood – restrict if not preclude imaginative expression. Dubey argues that the novel provides a critique of the community's commitment to a reproductive definition of femininity. Admittedly, Rigney's reading seems much closer to the notion of individuality being realised within a community which Morrison has posited in interviews and is also closer to the importance of community in many African stories. Nevertheless, one of the strengths of Morrison's work is the way in which the tensions about which Christian, McDowell and Dubey write are presented and explored as a dilemma. This dilemma is certainly an issue in considering Mbalia's Marxist reading of *Tar Baby* which comes later in this volume (essay 5).

Rigney's page references are to the New York Knopf (1987) edition of *Beloved*, the New York Pocket Books (1970) edition of *The Bluest Eye*, the New York Bantam (1975) edition of *Sula*, and the New York Signet editions of the other novels. Ed.]

1. Susan Willis writes in 'I Shop Therefore I Am: Is There a Place for Afro-American Culture in Commodity Culture?', in Cheryl Wall (ed.), *Changing Our Own Words: Essays on Criticism, Theory, and Writing by Black Women* (New Brunswick, NJ, 1989), that Hagar has destroyed herself through her own and Milkman's rejection of blackness: Hagar 'decides that in order to hold on to her boyfriend she must make herself into a less-black woman. What Hagar does not grasp is that Milkman's uncaring regard for her is an expression of his primary sexism as well as his internalised acceptance of the larger society's racist measure of blacks in terms of how closely an individual's skin and hair approximate the white model' (p. 178).

2. Hélène Cixous and Catherine Clément, *The Newly Born Woman*, trans. Betsy Wing (Minneapolis, 1986), p. 137.

3. Patricia Waugh, *Feminine Fictions: Revisiting the Postmodern* (New York: Routledge, 1989), p. 22.

4. Luce Irigaray, *This Sex Which Is Not One*, trans. Catherine Porter (Ithaca NY, 1989), p. 118.

5. Ibid., p. 134.

6. Alice Jardine, 'Gynesis', in Hazard Adams and Leroy Searle (eds), *Critical Theory Since 1965* (Tallahassee, FL, 1986), p. 563.

7. Toril Moi, *Sexual/Textual Politics: Feminist Literary Theory* (New York, 1985), p. 8.

8. In an interview with Claudia Tate, for example, in *Black Women Writers at Work* (New York, 1989), Morrison stated 'I don't use

much autobiography in my writing. My life is uneventful. Writing has to do with the imagination. It's being able to open a door or think the unthinkable, no matter how silly it may appear' (p. 127).

9. Nellie Y. Mckay (ed.), in *Critical Essays on Toni Morrison* (Boston, 1988), quotes Morrison as saying, 'No author tells these stories. They are just told – meanderingly – as though they are going in several directions at the same time' (p. 417).

10. Henry Louis Gates, Jr (ed.), *Black Literature and Literary Theory* (New York, 1984), p. 7.

11. [Rigney's book from which this extract is taken includes a discussion of blackness as invisibility and absence in *The Bluest Eye*. Ed.]

12. In *Beloved*, whiteness rather than blackness becomes the signifier for absence, as Beloved recalls the slavers in the Middle Passage as 'men without skin' (p. 212).

13. Mae Gwendolyn Henderson in 'Speaking in Tongues: Dialogics, Dialectics, and Black Women Writers' Literary Tradition', in *Changing Our Own Words: Essays on Criticism, Theory, and Writing by Black Women*, argues that Sula's mark indicates as much about the sexism inherent in the black community as it does about her own identity: 'Sula is marked from birth. Hers is a mark of nativity – a biological rather than a cultural inscription, appropriate in this instance because it functions to mark her as a "naturally" inferior male within the black community' (p. 27).

14. Deborah E. McDowell, '"The Self and the Other": Reading Toni Morrison's *Sula* and the Black Female Text', in Nellie McKay (ed.), *Critical Essays on Toni Morrison*, p. 81.

15. Roberta Rubenstein interprets the significance of marking quite differently. She writes in *Boundaries of the Self: Gender, Culture, Fiction* (Urbana, IL, 1987): 'Whether self-created, imposed by others, or dictated by accident, each of the representations of physical or psychic mutililations or incompleteness expresses the characters' inner distress and social or cultural plight' (p. 233).

16. Thomas Le Clair, '"The Language Must Not Sweat": A Conversation with Toni Morrison', *New Republic* (March, 1981), 21–9.

17. As Trudier Harris has written in 'Reconnecting Fragments: Afro-American Folk Tradition in *The Bluest Eye*', in Nellie McKay (ed.), *Critical Essays on Toni Morrison*, 'To be called "out of one's name" ... can be just as negatively powerful as a nickname can be positive' (p. 72).

18. It is interesting that Margaret Street enjoys romanticising Jadine's blackness, at one point insisting on a comparison with Eurydice of

the film *Black Orpheus*. Jadine resists: 'She was uncomfortable with the way Margaret stirred her into blackening up or universalising out, always alluding to or ferreting out what she believed were racial characteristics' (p. 54). Morrison implies, however, that Jadine's resistance indicates a problem with her own self-image as well as with Margaret's patronising perceptions.

19. Nellie McKay (ed.), *Critical Essay on Toni Morrison*, p. 2.

20. Julia Kristeva, 'Women's Time', trans. Alice Jardine, *Signs* 7:1 (Autumn, 1981), 13–35.

21. Hélène Cixous, 'The Laugh of the Medusa', in Hazard Adams and Leroy Searle (eds), *Critical Theory Since 1965*, p. 313.

22. Nancy J. Chodorow, *Feminism and Psychoanalytic Theory* (New Haven, CT, 1989), p. 100.

23. In an interview with Sandi Russell in 'Conversations From Abroad', in Nellie McKay (ed.), *Critical Essays on Toni Morrison*, Morrison commented on the strong ties among the women of her family: 'I remember my grandmother and my great-grandmother. I had to answer to those women, had to know that whatever I did was easy in comparison with what they had to go through ... They taught me how to dream' (p. 45).

24. Chodorow, *Feminism*, p. 183.

25. Cynthia A. Davis, 'Self, Society and Myth in Toni Morrison's Fiction', in Harold Bloom (ed.), *Modern Critical Views: Toni Morrison* (New York, 1990), p. 22.

4

'No Bottom and No Top': Oppositions in *Sula*

MADHU DUBEY

While *The Bluest Eye* obliquely explores the black feminine difference from the Black Aesthetic, this difference occupies the centre
of Toni Morrison's second novel, *Sula* (1973). Sula embodies a
radically new black femininity that upsets all the oppositions
(between past and present, individual and community, absence
and presence) that structure Black Aesthetic discourse. In a contemporary review, Jerry Bryant wrote that in *Sula*, Morrison attempts to 'combine the aims of the Black Freedom Movement and
Women's Liberation'.[1] Rather than merely combining, *Sula* plays
feminism and nationalism against each other, staging the encounter
of these two ideologies as a dynamic contradiction. In a difficult
double move, the novel assumes a feminist perspective to clarify the
limits of nationalist ideology, but withdraws from a full development of its own feminist implications. The ideological ambivalence
thus produced should discourage any programmatic political
reading; *Sula* is, however, often read as a feminist novel. Barbara
Jean Varga-Coley, for example, argues that *Sula* advances 'the feminist argument that women are victimised in the roles society allows
them'.[2] Varga-Coley is right in that, unlike *The Bluest Eye*, *Sula*
emphasises the sexual rather than the racial constraints on black
women. Several other elements of the novel seem to invite a feminist reading, such as its depiction of black men and its critique of
the institutions of heterosexuality and reproduction. However, a
closer consideration of these elements reveals the counterpressure

exerted by black nationalist ideology on a feminist articulation of black femininity.

Predictably, black nationalist critics denounced the feminist elements of *Sula*, focusing their critique on the novel's extremely unflattering portrayal of black men. Addison Gayle argued that the novel's feminist intentions necessarily fail because

> You can't very well do a hatchet job on Black men without also doing a hatchet job on Black women. Therefore, if you read *Sula* ... , the images of both the men and the women are equally nauseating.[3]

Other critics, while not sharing Gayle's strongly censorious tone, emphasised that the novel's feminist focus involves a 'severe symbolic mutilation of the Black male psyche' and is 'psychologically devastating for the collective male ego'.[4] It is true that, with the exception of Ajax, all the black male characters in *Sula* fit the type that the Black Aestheticians wished to ban from black literature. The very names of characters like Chicken Little, Boy Boy, and the deweys evoke an image of black men as frozen in a state of perpetual, irresponsible childhood. The stunted physical growth of the deweys, who remain boys forever, is paralleled by Plum's psychological refusal of adulthood. The emasculation of black male characters in the novel seems to be counterbalanced by the strength of some of the novel's black women characters, such as Eva and Sula. Asked by Robert Stepto to respond to 'the feeling in certain literary circles' that black women should not be portrayed as emasculators, Toni Morrison remarked that 'everybody knows, deep down, that Black men were emasculated by white men, period. And that Black women didn't take any part in that'.[5] The presentation of Jude's character in *Sula* clearly pinpoints racial oppression rather than black female dominance as the cause of black male emasculation. Jude's failure to attain adult masculinity derives from his forced employment as a waiter, his inability to find any other meaningful work. As with Cholly in *The Bluest Eye*, Jude's humiliation in the white man's world directly colours his perception of black women. Jude's position as head of the household compensates for his humiliation in the workplace; only by viewing his wife as the hem of his garment is Jude able to reclaim 'some posture of adulthood' (pp. 82–3).

However, unlike the presentation of Cholly in *The Bluest Eye*, Jude's status as a victim of racism does not in any way extenuate his responsibility for his treatment of women. His narrative of himself as a pathetic victim of racism is mocked by the narrator as 'a whiney tale that peaked somewhere between anger and a lapping desire for comfort' (p. 103). Sula exposes Jude's complicity in his victimisation, and offers a startling perspective on the black man as 'the envy of the world' (p. 104), which defamiliarises the contemporary nationalist discourse on the black man initiated by the Moynihan Report. This discourse, constructing the black man as 'the number one object of racism',[6] assigned the black woman the subsidiary role of healing the black man's damaged masculinity. Unlike Nel, who willingly fulfils this prescribed feminine function, Sula refuses to offer 'milkwarm commiseration' (p. 103) for the woes of the black man. Rejecting the image of the black man as the prime victim of racism and its concomitant image of the black woman as nurturer, Sula brackets the issue of racism and opens the space for a new articulation of black masculinity and femininity. Sula's deliberate misreading of Jude's narrative is a double-edged gesture: her refusal to be the hem of the black man's garment displaces the masculinist emphasis of black nationalist discourse, but her negation of Jude's victim identity accords with the black nationalist goal of fashioning a new black identity free of the oppressive past. In this instance, the novel first employs a black feminist perspective to undo one element of black nationalist ideology (its masculine emphasis), and then aligns this feminist critique with another element of black nationalist ideology (its denial of the black victim type and its affirmation of a new black subject). This double move exposes the contradictory construction of the black male in black nationalist discourse, as both the helpless victim of racism and the new revolutionary subject.

The novel's treatment of black male–female relationships exhibits a similar uneasy adjustment to the terms of black nationalist discourse. All the major black male–female unions in *Sula* end with male desertion, and with a bleak vision of heterosexual femininity as characterised by loss and absence. For example, during his brief marriage with Eva, Boy Boy is rarely home, and when he ultimately abandons Eva, her attempt to rebuild her life without him mysteriously involves a lost leg. This pattern of desertion and loss is repeated in the narratives of Nel and Sula. Jude leaves Nel with 'no thighs and no heart' (p. 111), and Ajax leaves Sula with 'nothing but his stunning absence' (p. 134). Heterosexuality in the novel is insistently associated not just with loss, but with death. Reflecting upon the lives of the women in her community, Sula observes that 'those with husbands had folded themselves into starched coffins' (p. 122). Sula's own heterosexual experiences cause her to weep 'for the deaths of the littlest things' (p. 123). The description of Nel and Sula's adolescent erotic play powerfully establishes the symbolic connection between the vagina and the grave, between hetero-sexuality and defilement. [...]

Nel and Sula's union constitutes the novel's strongest challenge to Black Aesthetic discourse. As we have already seen, one of the func-tions of black women writers, as prescribed by the Black Aesthetic, was to depict black male–female relationships as necessary, com-plementary unions. *Sula* often summons the heterosexual cliché of men and women as the two halves of each others' equations. Sula's 'craving for the other half of her equation' (p. 121) is occasionally placed in a heterosexual context, as, for example, when she de-scribes herself through the traditional metaphor of the feminine as an empty space filled by a man: 'There was this space in front of me, behind me, in my head. Some space. And Jude filled it up' (p. 144). More frequently, it is a woman, Nel, who constitutes the other half of Sula's equation: for Sula, Nel is 'the closest thing to both an other and a self' (p. 119). The Nel–Sula union significantly but not entirely displaces the heterosexual formula of a man and a woman forming a complete person. Nel and Sula's first meeting is structured like a typical romantic, heterosexual encounter. The very fact that their fantasies are described as 'Technicolored visions' (p. 51) indicates their conventional nature. Nel imagines herself in a fairy-tale heroine's posture of waiting passively for a prince. Sula, as the active prince galloping on a horse, completes the hetero-sexual union of the active and the passive, the masculine and the feminine principles. This romantic fantasy is, however, disrupted by the simple fact that it is a female, Sula, who occupies the masculine place. Even more significantly, the heterosexual union of prince and princess yields primacy to the union of two female friends who can share the delight of the same dream. This scene certainly supports Barbara Smith's observation that, set within a heterosexual frame, Nel and Sula's erotic fantasies betray their hidden desire for a feminine rather than a masculine lover.[7]

In the first part of the novel, Nel and Sula's complementary union is explicitly distinguished from the oneness of the heterosexual couple, Nel and Jude. Whereas Sula helps Nel to define herself and to see old things with new eyes, Jude likes to 'see himself taking shape in her eyes' (p. 83). While the Nel–Sula union preserves the difference of each, in the Nel–Jude union, 'both of them together would make one Jude' (p. 83). The friendship of Nel and Sula is ruptured in the second part of the novel, which deals predominantly with the heterosexual conflicts between Nel and Jude, Sula and Ajax. Sula's affair with Ajax provides the most striking instance of the novel's capitulation to heterosexual conventions. With Ajax, Sula becomes 'like all of her sisters before her' and lapses into the expected role of the black woman as nurturer when she asks Ajax to lean on her (p. 133). The Ajax incident simply cannot be made to cohere with the presentation of Sula's character in the rest of the novel. Her affair with Ajax drastically reduces Sula's feminist difference from the heterosexual women of her community. Precisely because it lacks any plot preparation or psychological plausibility, the Ajax episode appears to be a compromise gesture that gives heterosexuality its due. The whole sequence of events from Sula's first meeting with Ajax to her death seems to square her down to size, to render her transgressive character readable according to an acceptable fictional code of feminine characterisation. The uncomfortable nature of this compromise is evident in the incoherent resolution of the Ajax incident. In an abruptly linked causal chain, Ajax's desertion of Sula leads to her awareness that there are no more new experiences in store for her, which leads to her death. Maureen Reddy remarks that Sula's death, of a mysterious wasting disease, is reminiscent of the deaths with which unconventional nineteenth-century fictional heroines were punished.[8] While evoking this conventional ending, however, the novel plays a significant variation on it. Sula does not feel the shame and contrition of her literary predecessors; she dies proudly, convinced that it is she rather than the conventional women of her community who is really 'good' (p. 146). In her conversation with Nel just before she dies, Sula herself points out the difference between the ending of her own unusual plot and the endings of most conventional black women's plots: 'I know what every Black woman in this country is doing. Dying. Just like me. But the difference is, they dying like a stump. Me, I'm going down like one of those redwoods' (p. 143).

Readings of *Sula* as a feminist novel emphasise that Sula's characterisation seems sharply discontinuous from earlier representations of the black woman in fiction.[9] Most of these readings are silent on the Ajax incident, for it seems to detract from the novel's presentation of Sula as the embodiment of a radically new black femininity.

That most readers are baffled by Sula's inconsistency is apparent from the strenuous critical attempts to translate her character into a familiar ideological format, whether feminist or nationalist. Roseann Bell, for example, turns to nationalist ideology to clarify the radical newness of Sula's characterisation: 'It should not be surprising that *Sula* is regarded as an important statement in contemporary discussions on the Black Aesthetic', for Sula's character 'suggests a positive way of freeing our fettered minds from the oppressive tentacles of a past which ... prevents us from progressing and projecting a new vision'.[10] Bell is partially right, in that the newness of Sula's character cannot be fully appreciated without reference to Black Aesthetic theories of the radical black subject. However, the contradictory newness of Sula is not fully readable within an exclusively nationalist or feminist ideological frame; instead it provides yet another example of the novel's selective and critical appropriation of both ideologies.

As Bell's comment indicates, Sula does share one central emphasis of black nationalist discourse: its affirmation of the newness of the ideal black subject. As we have already seen, Sula rejects the old image of blacks as victims and reaches for an identity free of the past of racial oppression. In fact, the temporal opposition of black nationalist discourse is enacted in the novel's opposition of Sula and the black community. While Sula perceives the present moment as pure possibility, the black community of the Bottom clings to an absolute, static vision of the past. In a contemporary review of *Sula*, Sara Blackburn observed that the setting of the novel 'seems somehow frozen, stylised' and 'refuses to invade our present'.[11] The novel's opening chapter, in particular, conveys this frozen impression by situating the Bottom in a remote, inaccessible past: 'In that place, where they tore the nightshade and blackberry patches from their roots to make room for the Medallion City Golf Course, there was once a neighborhood' (p. 3). This impression of temporal distance is strengthened by the 'nigger joke' that traces the origin of the Bottom all the way back to slavery. Encapsulating the folk philosophy of the Bottom community, the nigger joke perpetuates the history of racial exploitation, casting the white slavemaster as an omnipotent manipulator and blacks as his innocent dupes. The black community in *Sula* is deeply invested in this image of themselves, for the role of the victim offers them a way of safe resignation. Preserving their victim status protects them from the rigours of creating a new identity free of their oppressive past: 'They were merely victims and knew how to behave in that role. … But the free fall, oh no, that required – demanded – invention' (p. 120). The black community's tenacious attachment to a static past is perfectly expressed in Nel's statement, 'Hell is change' (p. 108).

Exactly contrary to her community's philosophy is Sula's conviction that 'the real hell of Hell is that it is forever' (p. 107). Sula's conception of time as a medium of ceaseless change gives rise to her sense of self as sheer risk and imaginative possibility; Sula dares 'the free fall', creates herself anew every moment. The temporal continuity valued by her community appears, through Sula's eyes, to be nothing but repetitive sameness: 'Nothing was ever different. They were all the same' (p. 147). Sula's entire life challenges this sense of sameness; even her death seems to result from her awareness that she has exhausted all new possibilities: 'There aren't any more new songs and I have sung all the ones there are' (p. 137). Shadrack, mistaking Sula for a typical member of her community, offers her the promising word '"always" to convince her, assure her, of permanency' (p. 157), but the only 'always' that Sula ultimately accepts is the finality of death (p. 149).

The opposition between Sula and the black folk community of the Bottom cannot, however, be read in staightforward Black Aesthetic terms as an opposition between a new present and an oppressive past. While privileging newness and change, Sula embodies a specifically feminine newness that cannot be easily assimilated into Black Aesthetic ideology. Sula rejects the reproductive function so valued by her community: when Eva advises her to become a mother, Sula replies, 'I don't want to make somebody else. I want to make myself' (p. 92). This emphasis on feminine self-creation at the expense of nurturance of children is crucial to a correct understanding of Sula's radical newness. In *Sula*, an important element of black nationalist discourse – its natural, reproductive definition of black femininity – is displaced from the 'new' Sula to the black community, which otherwise represents an ideology tied to the oppressive past and resistant to change. This incongruous yoking of the old and the new, of elements both essential and inimical to black nationalist ideology, exposes the limits of the newness valorised by this ideology. Employing a black feminist perspective on reproduction, the novel makes visible the point at which the 'new' black nationalist discourse regresses into the past.

Sula's refusal of reproduction is her greatest point of difference from her community; it is what renders her evil and unnatural to the people of the Bottom. Sula's return to the Bottom is heralded by an unnatural plague of robins, and her death is followed by an untimely frost in October and a false spring in January. These natural disorders symbolically parallel the disorder that Sula's 'unnatural' refusal to be a mother unleashes on her community. Barbara Christian persuasively argues that the problem of physical survival faced by the novel's black community determines their definition of women as mothers, as guarantors of temporal and natural continuity.[12] On the barren topsoil that the white slavemaster gives his slave, and where the Bottom is established, the black community daily confronts the malevolence of the natural elements. Their struggle for survival against natural disaster and their consequent, obsessive fear of death, explain the community's perception of Sula as an unnatural witch. Sula's subversion of motherhood and her commitment to temporal discontinuity cause the black community to construct her as a scapegoat and to defend with renewed vigour their conception of motherhood as the primary feminine function.

The novel's critique of reproductive ideology is accomplished not only through Sula's character, but also through several portraits of black women who live by their community's valuation of reproduction as the sole outlet for feminine creativity. Helene Wright, whose daughter, Nel, is her sole purpose for living, supervises Nel's upbringing so closely that she drives her daughter's imagination underground (p. 18). Her obsessive preoccupation with her children twists her maternal love into 'something so thick and monstrous she was afraid to show it lest it break loose and smother them with its heavy paw' (p. 138). Eva Peace, in the early part of the novel, is the stereotypical strong black mother whose life is entirely dictated by her concern for her children's survival. When Eva finds that her excessive maternal love has led her to a cold, dark, stinking outhouse, using her last piece of food to relieve her son's constipation, she abandons the role of mother altogether, leaves her children with a neighbour, and goes away to find a better life for herself. Upon her return, Eva maintains a careful distance from her children, and burns her son because he expects her to nurture him again. That Eva chooses to kill her son rather than play mother all her life powerfully dramatises the unhealthy consequences of the Bottom community's prescription that black women centre their lives around reproduction.

However, if the novel critiques the black community's commitment to a reproductive definition of femininity, it does not unreservedly endorse Sula's absolute rejection of motherhood.[13] To an extent, Sula's refusal to be a mother is a liberating feminist gesture that initiates a new exploration of black femininity outside reproductive parameters. But Sula's radical redefinition of herself also depends on her denial of her mother. It is her accidental discovery of the failure of the maternal bond (Hannah's remark that she does not like Sula) that motivates Sula's invention of herself: 'Hers was an experimental life – ever since her mother's remarks sent her flying up the stairs' (p. 118). This statement of a direct causality between Sula's rejection of her mother and her creation of a new self is reminiscent of the black nationalist discourse on the mother. While conceiving reproduction as the black woman's primary revolutionary contribution, black nationalist discourse constructed the mother as 'the undisputed enemy of all revolutionary ideas'.[14] Sula's rejection of reproduction is problematic precisely because it repeats the black nationalist gesture of constructing a new and free identity in explicit opposition to the mother. The novel's treatment of reproduction thus produces a contradictory interlocking of black feminist and nationalist ideologies. *Sula's* feminist critique of the institution of motherhood exposes the limits of black nationalist 'newness'; this feminist critique is then itself questioned because, when taken to its logical conclusion, it demands a denial of the mother that disturbingly recalls black nationalist discourse. Black nationalism and feminism are both distinguished from and folded back into each other, in a difficult dialectic that clarifies the troubling implications of both ideologies.

In a similar set of double moves, the novel questions both the black community's affirmation of reproduction as a means of ensuring temporal continuity, and the temporal discontinuity that results from Sula's rejection of reproduction. Sula's new identity entails a complete disregard for her ancestors, as, for example, when she enjoys watching her mother burn or when she shocks the sentiments of her community by sending her grandmother away to an old people's home. In her essay 'Rootedness: The Ancestor as Foundation', Toni Morrison writes:

> If we don't keep in touch with the ancestor, ... we are, in fact, lost. ... When you kill the ancestor, you kill yourself. I want to point out the dangers, to show that nice things don't happen to the totally self-reliant if there is no conscious historical connection.[15]

Morrison's remarks may be almost exactly applied to Sula, whose total self-reliance is suicidal because it lacks a historical connection with the ancestor. With no grounding roots in the past, Sula's radical difference proves to be meaningless and is ultimately reduced to the very sameness she tries to challenge: 'If I live a hundred years my urine will flow the same way, my armpits and breath will smell the same. My hair will grow from the same holes. I didn't mean anything. I never meant anything' (p. 147). Sula's newness so sharply departs from the past that it cannot revitalise her community's old ways; the encounter between the new (Sula) and the old (the community), far from producing a dynamic exchange, remains locked in a state of absolute contradiction. We are told that the black community's exposure to Sula 'changed them in accountable yet mysterious ways' (p. 117), but this change paradoxically works against change, only confirming the black community's adherence to their old, conservative ways.

The sterile confrontation between Sula and her community obliquely discloses the inadequacy of the nationalist conception of the radically new black subject. Showing that such a subject cannot be politically effective, the novel questions the absolute dichotomy between the oppressive past and the revolutionary future in black nationalist discourse. *Sula* elaborates but fails to choose between two antithetical views of historical change: the black community's passive fatalism and the black nationalists' belief in sudden, stark historical change. The narrator mocks the black community's hope that their condition will change on its own, a hope that keeps them mired in their oppression. The first time that the entire Bottom community joins Shadrack's Suicide Day procession, they are driven by 'the same hope that kept them picking beans for other farmers; ... kept them convinced that some magic "government" was going to lift them up' (p. 160). However, if this passive hope is suicidal, so is the black community's single act of rebellion against their oppression: their expression of anger at their exclusion from productive labour (the construction of the tunnel) results in collective suicide. The construction of the River Road in 1927 holds out the false promise of black employment, but is eventually built entirely by white labour. The same pattern is exactly repeated in 1937 with the construction of the tunnel. This presentation of history as circular repetition compels a critical reconsideration of the black nationalist vision of historical change as a clean, decisive break from the past cycle.

The novel directly engages the black nationalist conception of the 1960s as a period of unprecedented advancement for black Americans. The chapter '1965' opens with the lines, 'Things were so much better in 1965. Or so it seemed' (p. 164). The narrator concedes that some progress has taken place: more black Americans are integrated into white society and hold better jobs. This appearance of change is, however, thrown into doubt by the contradictory statement, 'The young people had a look about them that everybody said was new but which reminded Nel of the deweys' (p. 164). This puzzling comparison of the new young people of the 1960s with the deweys is not developed or explained. The only possible overlap between the two is that they both embody a 'plural name' (p. 68). Perhaps it would be overworking this brief, incidental comparison to suggest that the new people of the 1960s share the deweys' commitment to a plural, collective identity that erases all singularities and differences. The mention of the deweys in the context of the 1960s is even more startling because the deweys' stunted growth is utterly incongruous with the black nationalists' conception of the 1960s as a period of remarkable progress for blacks.

We must, of course, remember that the connection between the deweys and the new people of the 1960s is drawn by Nel, and we know that Nel is unlikely to appreciate even real changes, given her conviction that 'Hell is change'. Although the narrator's stance cannot be exactly identified with Nel's, the narrator unmistakably shares Nel's scepticism and regret about some of the changes that occurred in the 1960s.[16]

> The Black people, for all their new look, seemed awfully anxious to get to the valley, or leave town, and abandon the hills to whoever was interested. It was sad, because the Bottom had been a real place. These young ones kept talking about the community, but they left the hills to the poor, the old and the stubborn – and the rich white folks. Maybe it hadn't been a community, but it had been a place.
>
> (p. 166)

This passage brings into sharp focus the novel's interrogation of both the temporal and communal visions of black nationalist ideology. The value of community, which the black nationalists claimed as a distinctive feature of their new vision, is here displaced to the past, presented as one of the casualties of the changes of the 1960s. By means of this displacement, the novel suggests that temporal discontinuity, so strongly valorised in black nationalist discourse, inevitably produces a rupture of community.

By Black Aesthetic standards, the novel's inability to represent a new, revolutionary black community would certainly constitute an imaginative and political failure. The black community presented in the novel is moored to the oppressive past and is, therefore, problematic from a Black Aesthetic standpoint. When we are first introduced to the Bottom neighbourhood, in the beginning of the novel, it has already become a thing of the past. The narrator's description of the Time and a Half Pool Hall, Irene's Palace of Cosmetology, Reba's Grill, and singing and dancing in the streets, vividly conveys the sense of a 'real place' that Nel finds so lacking in the Bottom of the 1960s. Susan Willis argues that the social practices of the Bottom community 'have little or nothing to do with the economics of exchange and everything to do with the exchange of social life'. Willis seems to read the novel's presentation of the Bottom in entirely positive terms: 'for the Bottom, the impossibility of being a part of production and trade ... creates a space for the generation of community'.[17] The novel does make this connection between exclusion from economic production and development of a black community. In fact, racial and economic oppression appear to be the necessary conditions for the existence of a distinctive black folk culture. In the chapter '1965', the communal practices that characterised the earlier black neighbourhood have disappeared as a result of the increasing economic integration of blacks into the white US economic system. However, the novel does not uncritically affirm this kind of community contingent upon oppression and segregation. If the forced exclusion of blacks from labour and production generates a distinctive folk culture, it also precipitates their collective suicide at the end of the novel.

Moreover, the folk culture of the Bottom, like the folk culture presented in *The Bluest Eye*, keeps the black community trapped in its oppressed condition. The nigger joke, a folk survival mechanism, helps the community tolerate their difficult predicament but it does not offer any means of resistance or transformation. That the folk culture of the Bottom is geared toward survival rather than change is also apparent in the community's perception of evil as an uncontrollable natural phenomenon that must be allowed to run its course. This black folk philosophy, explicitly justified by the narrator as 'a full recognition of the legitimacy of forces other than good ones' (p. 90), can be read either positively, as resilience, or negatively, as slackness. The novel characteristically balances both interpretations in tension, and disallows our choosing between them. The black community's philosophy of evil results in an admirable acceptance of difference, evident in their treatment of Sula: they regard Sula's difference as evil, as a natural aberration, but they allow her to survive. The naturalistic philosophy of the Bottom folk, however, fails to discriminate between different kinds of evil, placing racial oppression in the same class of phenomena as floods and disease (p. 90). They greet all 'evil days' – whether caused by Sula, a natural disaster, or political factors – with 'an acceptance bordering on welcome' (p. 89). Such a world view inevitably keeps the community mired in its oppressive situation and obstructs the development of a new political creed directed at change and resistance.

If the black folk community of the Bottom is both celebrated and criticised, so is the radical, new identity of Sula. Kimberley Benston writes that the new black subject of the 1960s, based as it is on absolute temporal discontinuity, necessarily 'defaces communal reality'.[18] Sula's character clearly demonstrates that a wholesale rejection of the past can only produce a singular individual alienated from the community. Throughout the novel, Sula verbally constructs and satirises several collective 'they's', such as her discourses on black men (pp. 103–4), on the black community of the Bottom (p. 120), and on conventional black women (pp. 142–5). Sula's vision of her community as 'a drawn-out disease' (p. 96) is certainly liberating, in that it allows her to explore her own self outside all the constraining racial and sexual conditions that determine her community's construction of identity. However, Sula's denial of her community is countered by the novel's structure and mode of narration, which, beginning and ending with the Bottom community and intertwining the stories of Shadrack, Nel, and the Peace family, forces us to read Sula's story as part of the story of an entire community. Even if Sula sees herself as a distinctive individual pitted against her community, the reader is compelled to read her story 'sometimes against but always because of the group experience which provides the frame of reference'.[19] Sula's singular conception of herself also has been thematically criticised for its lack of social grounding. As Adrienne Munich asks, in her analysis of Sula's narrative about black men: 'Where is Sula in this story? Is she outside the world of which Jude is the envy? How would one analyse her voice?' That her story 'gives its teller no place'[20] is both Sula's strength and weakness. Her complete lack of social positioning allows her to defamiliarise and flout her community's conventions, but it also prohibits her from effective political intervention in the life of her community.

The opposition between Sula and her community thus plays havoc with the black nationalist articulation of the opposed terms of individual and community, past and present. In black nationalist discourse, the individual and the past are absolutely negated, while the community and the present are absolutely affirmed. In *Sula*, these oppositions refuse to remain in the places that black nationalist discourse allots them: the undesirable term 'past' is aligned with the valued term 'community', and the temporal discontinuity celebrated in black nationalist discourse is shown to produce the singular individuality decried by black nationalists.

The characterisation of Sula in opposition to her community also topples the one remaining opposition, between absence and presence, that structures Black Aesthetic discourse. While the black nationalists celebrated the new black subject as presence, *Sula* figures the new black subject as absence, and attaches the value of presence to the static world view of the novel's black community. The folk rituals of the Bottom are calculated to assuage the community's fear of process. An example of this is provided in Chicken Little's funeral, which is the community's resounding statement against the 'stupidity of loss' (p. 107). As Keith Byerman expresses it, the funeral 'transforms an absence into a presence' by asserting the permanence of communal structures and rituals.[21] This need for public rituals that confirm temporal and communal stability explains the black community's easy acceptance of National Suicide Day, a ritual that meets the community's need to control their fear of death. [...]

While it clearly derails a linear movement of time, the novel does not unreservedly endorse a cyclic temporal vision. If the oppressed condition of the Bottom community originates with the linear hierarchy of tops and bottoms, the circular repetition of history keeps them trapped in this condition. One example already cited is the River Road that raises and defeats hopes of black employment in 1927, followed by an exactly repetitive pattern in 1937, with the construction of the river tunnel. To give another example, the nigger joke of the beginning of the novel comes full circle by the end: the topsoil of the Bottom actually becomes more valuable than valley land, in an ironic fulfilment of the slavemaster's false promise. But this circular reversion of value works against the black community, for the value of Bottom land begins to increase just as the black residents of the Bottom begin to move down to the valley.

This circular repetition of history, which reinforces the economic and racial exploitation of the black community is not, however, identical to the circular movement of the novel's structure. Toni Morrison has suggestively characterised the structure of *Sula* as 'more spiral than circular'.[22] As opposed to the tightly closed circles that structure *The Bluest Eye*, the circular movement of *Sula* is accumulative rather than exactly repetitive. The beginning and closing points of the novel's spiral do not quite overlap, thus leaving open the possibility of transformation. The novel at first offers an incomplete rendering of an event, withholding its meaning from the reader. Later chapters curve back to the earlier event, filling out its implications. The reader is almost always refused interpretive access to the novel's major events the first time they are narrated. For example, Eva's burning of Plum is incomprehensible when it is first presented, in '1921'. We discover Eva's motivation two years later, in the chapter '1923'. Similarly, Sula's slashing her fingertip puzzles the reader in '1922', and is partially explained in '1937'. This circular movement, spiralling back to transform past incidents and to add new layers of meaning, resolves, at the level of narrative structure, the novel's thematic opposition between past and present. [...]

The collective construction of meaning elicited by *Sula*'s spiral structure is clearly contrasted with the authoritative transmission of meaning that the novel attributes to white American culture. The nigger joke illustrates the slaveowner's monopoly on meaning; the white master possesses the sole right to assign values in a dualistic, hierarchical scheme that bolsters his own politically powerful position. Perhaps less obviously, *Sula* suggests that the structural dualities of black nationalist discourse endorse a similar hierarchical construction of values. That the oppositions of black nationalist ideology are fundamentally top/ bottom opposition is clear in that each privileged term derives its value from an absolute negation of its other. *Sula* undermines this hierarchical binary structuring by refusing to valorise any one term of an opposition at the cost of devaluing its opposed other. Individuality and community, past and present, absence and presence: all these terms are both preserved and cancelled in *Sula*. The attempted synthesis of these terms, at the level of narrative structure, does not erase the novel's thematic contradictions. Instead, as I have tried to elaborate throughout this chapter, all the double meanings generated by *Sula* install unresolved contradiction as the central designing principle of the novel.

In this respect, *Sula* exhibits its own complicity with the binary structuring black nationalist discourse: even as it dislocates, the novel does depend on these very dualities to structure its own vision. Even the novel's central structuring device, the opposition of Nel and Sula, reflects and refigures the black nationalist opposition of community and individuality, past and present, absence and presence. That all these oppositions are subsumed in the Nel–Sula pair signals both the novel's containment within and transgression of the boundaries of black nationalist discourse. The gender construction of black nationalist discourse retains intact the white middle-class definitions of masculinity and femininity. The feminine pair of Nel and Sula unbalances, even as it cannot fully dismantle, the hierarchical gender opposition of black nationalist as well as white US middle-class ideology.

From Madhu Dubey, *Black Women Novelists and the Nationalist Aesthetic* (Bloomington and Indianapolis, IN, 1994), pp. 51–71.

NOTES

[Madhu Dubey's essay places Morrison's fiction in the context of ideas about a Black Aesthetic while most critics have concentrated on the relationship of her novels to works by other black writers. *Sula* is seen as having an uneasy relationship to Black Aesthetic discourse in Dubey's view. At one level, it rejects the masculinist emphasis of black nationalist ideology whilst at another level aligning with its denial of the black victim type and its affirmation of a new black discourse. This has implications for our reading of her other novels. The tension in *Tar Baby* between Son's black nationalist ideology and a feminist reading of the novel, for example, may be seen as a development of the oppositions which Dubey finds here in the earlier novel. Offering a more ambitious reading of *Sula* than that provided by critics who have seen Morrison as attempting to combine the aims of the Black Freedom Movement and Women's Liberation, Dubey's suggestion that *Sula* plays feminism and nationalism against each other is an important fresh perspective on the book. Since the two areas which the essay highlights as lending themselves to a feminist reading – its depiction of black men and its critique of institutions of heterosexuality and reproduction – are those which have attracted criticism from a black nationalist perspective, Dubey's essay helps us to understand why Morrison has attracted controversy as well as acclaim.

Since a key element in the Black Aesthetic was the positive promotion of black male–female relationships, Dubey's point that in *Sula* all the black male–female unions end with male desertion and with a bleak vision of heterosexual feminity deserves highlighting. Dubey concedes that, with the exception of Ajax, the black males in *Sula are* the types which exponents of Black Aesthetics wanted to ban from black literature. The suggestion that some of the names of characters evoke an image of black men as frozen in a state of childhood may be seen within a larger context of the emasculation of black men, as a result of slavery and racialism, which Dubey does not explore here. But the reading of *Sula* is an interesting one because it stresses the novel's rejection not only of the black man as the prime victim of racism but also of the black woman as nurturer. Dubey returns to what has become a key premise in feminist interpretations of *Sula*, that Sula affirms the black subject freed from victim stereotype. Feminist readings of the novel emphasise that Sula is different from earlier representations of the black woman in fiction in that she maintains a radical stance against heterosexuality. Dubey argues that on closer analysis Sula's responses to heterosexuality are contradictory. Although the novel offers a critique of the black community's commitment to a reproductive definition of feminity, it does not unreservedly endorse Sula's absolute rejection of motherhood. Viewed from this perspective, Jadine's reaction to the night women in Eloe in *Tar Baby* might be more complex than Mbalia (essay 5) and Otten (essay 2) allow, although Otten is more prepared to see Jadine as an ambiguously presented character. Moreover, within this framework, Barbara Smith's discussion (see note 7 below) of *Sula* as a lesbian novel is useful, despite its shortcomings, for pointing out how through its reversion to a conventional heterosexual plot *Sula* diverts attention from the subversive aspects of the Nel–Sula relationship.

References in parentheses in Dubey's text are to Toni Morrison, *Sula* (New York, 1973). Ed.]

1. Jerry Bryant, Review of *Sula, The Nation* (July 1974), 24.

2. Barbara Jean Varga-Coley, 'The Novels of Black American Women', PhD dissertation (State University of New York, 1981), p. 119.

3. Roseann Bell, 'Judgement: Addison Gayle', in Roseann Bell, Bettye J. Parker and Beverly Guy-Sheftall (eds), *Sturdy Black Bridges* (New York, 1979), p. 213.

4. The quoted phrases are from Richard Barksdale's essay 'Castration Symbolism in Recent Black American Fiction', *CLA Journal*, 29 (1986), 401, 408.

5. Robert Stepto, '"Intimate Things in Place": A Conversation with Toni Morrison', in Michael Harper and Robert Stepto (eds), *Chant of Saints* (Chicago, 1979), p. 219.

6. Alvin Poussaint described the black man as 'the number one object of racism', in 'White Manipulation and Black Oppression', *The Black Scholar*, 10: 8–9 (1979), 55.

7. Barbara Smith, 'Towards a Black Feminist Criticism', in Gloria T. Hull, Patricia Bell Scott and Barbara Smith (eds), *All the Women Are White, All the Men are Black, But Some of Us Are Brave* (1977; rpt New York, 1982), p. 165.

8. Maureen Reddy, 'The Tripled Plot and Center of *Sula*', *Black American Literature Forum*, 22 (1988), 43.

9. See Hortense Spillers, 'A Hateful Passion, a Lost Love', in Shari Benstock (ed.), *Feminist Issues in Literary Scholarship* (Bloomington, IN, 1987), p. 181; Jacqueline de Weever, 'The Inverted World of Toni Morrison's *The Bluest Eye* and *Sula*', *CLA Journal*, 22 (1979), 413; and Susan Willis, 'Black Women Writers: Taking a Critical Perspective', in Gayle Greene and Coppélia Kahn (eds), *Making A Difference* (New York, 1985), p. 213.

10. Roseann Bell, Review of *Sula*, *Obsidian*, 2:3 (1976), 95. Also see Odette Martin, '*Sula*', *First World*, 1: 4 (1977), 42.

11. Sara Blackburn, Review of *Sula*, *New York Times Book Review* (30 December 1973), 3.

12. Barbara Christian, *Black Feminist Criticism* (New York, 1985), p. 76.

13. For a balanced discussion of the novel's ambivalent treatment of the maternal, see Marianne Hirsch, 'Maternal Narratives: "Cruel Enough to Stop the Blood"', in Henry Louis Gates, Jr (ed.), *Reading Black, Reading Feminist* (New York, 1990), pp. 425–6.

14. Faith Ringgold, 'From Being My Own Woman', in Amina Baraka and Amiri Baraka (eds), *Confirmations* (New York, 1983), p. 301.

15. Toni Morrison, 'Rootedness: The Ancestor as Foundation', in Mari Evans (ed.), *Black Women Writers* (New York, 1984), p. 344.

16. Toni Morrison, too, shares Nel's and the narrator's regret about these changes: 'I felt a sense of loss, a void. Things were moving too fast in the early 1960s–70s … it was exciting but it left me bereft.' See Sandi Russell, 'It's OK to Say OK' (An Interview Essay), in Nellie Y. McKay (ed.), *Critical Essays on Toni Morrison* (Boston, 1988), p. 45.

17. Susan Willis, *Black Women Writers*, pp. 218, 219.

18. Kimberley Benston, 'I Yam What I Am: The Topos of (Un)naming in Afro-American Literature', in Henry Louis Gates, Jr (ed.), *Black Literature and Literary Theory* (New York, 1984), p. 162.

19. Quoted out of context from Sherley Anne Williams, *Give Birth to Brightness: A Thematic Study of Neo-Black Literature* (New York, 1972), p. 92. This statement forms an important part of Williams's argument that even when it pits the individual against the community, the black literature of the 1960s posits a communal vision.

20. Adrienne Munich, 'Notorious Signs, Feminist Criticism and Literary Tradition', in *Making a Difference*, p. 254.

21. Keith Byerman, *Fingering the Jagged Grain* (Athens, GA, 1985), p. 196.

22. Claudia Tate, *Black Women Writers at Work* (New York, 1983), p. 128.

5

Tar Baby: A Reflection of Morrison's Developed Class Consciousness

DOREATHA DRUMMOND MBALIA

Class struggle, the struggle between the ruling class and the subject class, is the thematic emphasis of Toni Morrison's fourth work, *Tar Baby*. Racism, the primary focus of *The Bluest Eye*, is discussed as a coequal but consequential cause of the African's oppression. The struggle between the sexes, having been explored in *Sula* and resolved in *Song of Solomon*, gets little of the author's attention, for Morrison has sufficiently matured to understand that the fundamental cause of the African's oppression is the exploitive economic system of capitalism and its overseas extension, imperialism.[1] Thus, racism and sexism, although equally oppressive, are treated as byproducts of capitalism. To eradicate the latter ensures the eradication of the former two. In *Tar Baby*, Morrison's increased consciousness is reflected in her ability and commitment to explore this cause-and-effect relationship between class, race, and sex.

Morrison's heightened class awareness creates qualitative changes in both the thematic and structural development of her fourth novel. Thematically, for the first time, the author chooses a setting outside the borders of the United States – Dominique and its surrounding islands. Place, then, in *Tar Baby*, is just as crucial to our understanding of the novel's dilemma and denouement, and to our understanding of the author's own consciousness, as it is in Joseph Conrad's *Heart of Darkness*. Place reveals both Morrison's

awareness of the innate viciousness of capitalism and her understanding that 'all peoples of African descent, whether they live in
North or South American, the Caribbean or any other part of the
world are African', have a common oppressor, wage a common
struggle, and need a common solution.[2] Then, too, the choice of the
Caribbean as setting allows Morrison and the reader to get a more
objective view of the United States, a view not dissimilar to that of
Gideon: 'The U.S. is a bad place to die in'.[3]

The second qualitative leap evidenced in Morrison's theme is her
use of European-Americans as major characters. In earlier works,
they serve as minor characters, usually invisible foes who are hinted
at, referred to, laughed about, or ignored altogether. In *Tar Baby*
their rise to prominence parallels Morrison's rise in consciousness,
for she now understands the dialectical role they play as the ruling
class in the African's oppression, a role that can be neither ignored
nor minimised. Significant, therefore, is the fact that she does not
choose Europeans of the lower or middle classes, but those of the
ruling class. Moreover, these Europeans have a direct connection
to the exploitation of African people in Dominique and in the
United States, revealing Morrison's unclouded understanding that
the capitalists and imperialists are one and the same.

The nature of the struggle of African people in the novel is an
additional piece of evidence that reflects the qualitative difference
between this work and earlier ones. Unlike Pecola Breedlove, who
struggles with the question of racial approbation, Sula, who struggles against the traditional role of African women, and Milkman,
who individually struggles with the issues of race and class, the two
protagonists in *Tar Baby* must struggle together to resolve their op-
posing class interests in order to unite. Symbolically, they reflect the
schism that exists in the African community, the class conflict that
African people must resolve in order to form an effective, unified
force against their primary enemy, capitalism/imperialism. What
Morrison does in *Tar Baby* is raise the question all Africans must
ask themselves: Do I identify with my oppressor or my people? In
light of this question, Morrison examines several other crucial ones:
First, if the African rejects the capitalist way of life, what is a viable
alternative? Second, can African people negate history by returning
to a pre-slave-trade, precolonial existence? Third, can there exist
'people's capitalism', 'enlightened capitalism', 'class peace' or 'class
harmony' between two groups of people whose interests are dia-
metrically opposed?[4] In other words, can Jadine and Son coexist in

harmony? The ending of *Tar Baby* provides answers to all three questions. It reveals Morrison's own clarity in regard to the irreconcilability of the interests of the ruling and subject classes. And while she clearly rejects vulturistic capitalism, she just as clearly rejects the naïve prescription of Kenneth Kaunda, President of Zambia, for an African communal socialism, a way of life that seeks to return to a glorified past without the benefit of modern technology, modern science, or modern consciousness. Unfortunately, however, she does not provide a viable alternative existence for African people. This is the thematic weakness of the novel.

Structurally, too, *Tar Baby* reflects Toni Morrison's heightened consciousness. She produces a work that reflects the positive principles of traditional African society: humanism, collectivism, and egalitarianism.[5] Each of her major characters – Son, Jadine, Sydney, Ondine, Valerian, Margaret, and Therese – has an opportunity to present his or her particular views on self and others. And while there is an omniscient narrator, this narrator is not given a role superior to that of each of the others but unobtrusively highlights rather than prescribes or defines significant character thoughts and actions. Such a narrative technique offers a more balanced, more objective picture from which to judge the characters.

As class struggle is the dominant theme in *Tar Baby*, it is useful to analyse the novel first by employing a structural framework that examines the two major forces in contention: the ruling class and the subject class (sometimes referred to as the 'people class'). It is also useful to analyse Morrison's attempt to reconcile these forces in bringing together Jadine and Son.

Valerian Street, as well as all who share his aspirations, is a symbol of American capitalism and imperialism. Indeed, he is a typical capitalist who has made his fortune by exploiting the labour of the African masses and by stealing their land. And it is quite significant that his wealth emanates from the production of candy, the main ingredients of which – sugar and cocoa – come from the Caribbean, once the sugar capital of the Western world.[6] This economic fact is made even more poignant after Valerian fires Gideon and Therese for stealing a couple of apples. From Son's, Morrison's, and the reader's perspective, Valerian 'had been able to dismiss with a flutter of the fingers the people whose sugar and cocoa had allowed him to grow old in regal comfort' (p. 174).

Quite aptly, he is named after a plant, the dried roots of which have small clusters of white or pinkish flowers used medicinally as a sedative. And, as his name suggests, Valerian is asleep throughout most of his adult life, unconscious of or unconcerned by the exploitive manner in which he has accumulated his wealth, ignorant of the physical and psychological abuse of his child by his own wife, unsympathetic to the feelings of his servants, and most important for Morrison and her audience, insensitive to the plight of African people.[7] Somnolently, with all of the lush, uncultured, living nature around him, he builds a greenhouse in which to incubate himself from life, but primarily, and in true capitalist fashion, in which to control life. In his words, it is 'a place of controlled ever-flowering life'. So estranged from life is Valerian that he is incapable of love despite the fact that his name suggests this human emotion, for the reader may be tempted to associate Valerian with the name of that day in February on which love is celebrated. Bickering, ridiculing, and name calling constitute the extent of the communication between him and his wife. With his son, Michael, he has no communication. And after thirty years of faithful butlering and cooking, Sydney and Ondine are thought of as mere Uncle Toms (p. 124). Responding to Valerian's inhumanity, Ondine shouts, 'I may be a cook, Mr Street, but I'm a person too' (p. 178). For Valerian, however, one's worth as a human being is measured only by non-human values: wealth and status.

Since his desire is to control life, not live in it, Valerian uses his money to relate to other human beings. He buys Margaret expensive clothes and pays Jadine's college tuition. In fact, it is not until he is confronted with the physical and psychological abuse of his son that he exhibits some genuine emotion, but even this emotional display reeks more of self-pity for his ignorance of the abuse than sorrow for the psychological well-being of his wife and child. For instead of seeking help for Margaret and searching for Michael, Valerian retreats to his greenhouse and to his childhood: 'Valerian wanted his own youth again and a place to spend it' (p. 46).

While it is true that the ruling class in the United States (all of whom are of European descent) consists of those who own and control the means of production, it is also true that there are those (including Africans) who so ardently wish to belong to this class that they exhibit the same behavioural patterns, dress in the same manner, use the same language patterns, and, most unfortunately, share the same ideology as those of their oppressors. Often referred to as the petty bourgeois, this group of people exists between two worlds, denied entry into the ruling class due to their lack of wealth and/or their skin colour and refusing to identify with the African masses to whom they owe allegiance, Jadine, as well as Sydney and Ondine, symbolises the African petty bourgeois.

Called Kingfish and Boulah by Margaret Street, Sydney and Ondine symbolise those unconscious servants who identify more with their employers and their employers' culture than they do with their own people and their own culture. Sydney, in the light of day, proudly refers to himself as 'one of those industrious Philadelphia Negroes – the proudest people in the race' – ignorant of the fact that in the dark of night his 'refreshing' dreams of childhood days in Baltimore are what give him the stamina to cater to Valerian's whims (p. 51) Ondine, painfully reminiscent of Mrs Breedlove in *The Bluest Eye*, calls the Streets' kitchen 'my kitchen' and does not want it violated by the African masses. Living a secondhand life, they accordingly have secondhand furniture, secondhand visitors ('No visitors ever came' for them) and a secondhand daughter. (Because Jadine was a niece, Ondine's relationship with her 'was without the stress of a mother–daughter relationship' [pp. 17, 82]). Perhaps most significant is that they are surnamed Childs, for they are indeed the children of Valerian who do as they are told. Yet, despite the humiliation and degradation of being adults treated as children, they both share the racist, capitalist ideology of their employers. As a consequence, they recognise no bond between themselves and Gideon and Therese, the other African servants who work for the Streets. In fact, Sydney and Ondine are unable to distinguish between them, an unwillingness to recognise 'lower class' Africans as human beings with unique identities: Gideon is referred to as Yardman, and Therese is thought to be several different Marys. On the whole and in true capitalist fashion, these Childses respond to the other Africans as if all African people look alike.

Not only do they embrace the same racist stereotypes as do their exploiters, but the Childses use the same negative jargon to refer to people who look just like them! The poor African masses are niggers who steal; in contrast, the Childses are Negroes, respectable Africans (pp. 32, 87). It is a respectability that prevents them from seeing themselves as a part of the African masses. For instance, in seeking to disassociate himself from Son, Sydney proudly reveals his ignorance of African culture:

> I am a Phil-a-delphia Negro mentioned in the book of the very same name. My people owned drugstores and taught school while yours

were still cutting their faces open so as to be able to tell one of you
from the other.

(p. 140)

Indeed, it is only by understanding Sydney's petty bourgeois men-
tality that we can account for his reaction to Son's humane and
friendly greeting of 'Hi', a greeting that at once establishes a bond
and an equality between the two men. Seemingly, Son's 'Hi' strips
Sydney of his status as head African, and not until Son begins
calling Sydney 'Sir' and 'Mr Childs' does the older man begin to
communicate with the younger.

Morrison's most intricate exploration of the African petty
bourgeois is reserved for Jadine, not Sydney and Ondine.
Significantly called Copper Venus, Jadine is a brown white woman,
a Europeanised African, an art history graduate of the Sorbonne, an
expert on cloisonné, and a cover model for *Elle*. She is one of the
tar babies of the novel, a creation of capitalist America.[8] Her behavioural patterns, dress, language, associations, and ideology are
all those of the ruling class and, as such, demonstrate her hatred of
Africa and all that is associated with it. 'To roam around Europe ...
following soccer games' is her goal in life; her fiancé is a wealthy
European Parisienne who will bring her wealth and unquestioned
status (p. 77). Not surprisingly, her allegiance is more to the Streets,
whom she regards 'like family, almost', than to Ondine and Sydney,
who slave for her (p. 77). In fact, except for her aunt and uncle,
whom she visits only in troubled times, her acquaintances are all
Europeans or Europhiliacs like her. Ideologically, she thinks like the
European, and like her aunt and uncle, she embraces the stereotypes
of the African, calling Son a raggedy nigger and thinking he is
about to rape her. Significantly, Son responds: 'Rape: Why you little
white girls always think somebody's trying to rape you?' (p. 103).

Not only does Jadine think like a European, but also she thinks
she is a European. When Son's presence at L'Arbe de la Croix is
discovered, she questions his reason for stealing as if she too owned
the house: 'It depends on what you want from us.' Surprised by her
irrational, indeed suicidal, association with the Streets, Son replies:
'Us? You call yourself "us"?' (p. 101). Once this association is
made clear, it does not surprise us that Jadine often assumes the
position of adoring daughter to the Streets. At dinnertime, she
'poured [Valerian's] wine, offered him a helping of this, a dab of
that and smiled when she did not have to' (p. 175). And thinking
that Valerian's and Margaret's way of life is normal ('Naturally

they bickered and taunted one another. Naturally. Normal, even' [p. 57]). Indeed the best there is, she belittles African art and she ridicules Michael's attempt to politicise her as to her Africanness: 'Actually we didn't talk; we quarreled. About why I was studying art history at that snotty school instead of – I don't know what. Organizing or something. He said I was abandoning my history. My people' (pp. 61–2).

It is this attempt to be other than herself that causes Jadine's insecurity throughout the novel. As a Europhiliac, she feels threatened by African women who are unashamed of their identity and culture and beautiful not simply because they are, but also because they possess pride and dignity in themselves. The African woman in yellow is an example of one such woman. When Jadine meets her, it is quite significant that Jadine is experiencing one of the happiest times of her life because, as Morrison implies, such happiness can never equal the true happiness felt when one celebrates self. Just chosen for the cover of one of France's most fashionable magazines, courted by 'three gorgeous and raucous men', and told that she had passed her orals, Jadine was at her zenith. Yet this, the most important day of her life, is not sufficient to erase the insecurity that lies behind the facade of any one who abandons self – in the African's case, all things associated with Africa. It is for this reason that the woman in yellow – beautiful, self-confident, proud, and dignified – is such a disturbing and haunting image for Jadine. [...]

Unlike Valerian and Jadine, Son has a sincere love for living things in general, African people in particular, and the African poor especially. He feels at home in natural environments and, as a consequence, is attuned to nature, plucking Valerian's plant to make it bloom and telling Ondine to place banana leaves in her shoes to soothe her sore feet (p. 135). For the African masses, he has a special love, despite his feelings of 'disappointment nudging contempt for the outrage Jade and Sydney and Ondine exhibited in defending property and personnel that did not belong to them from a black man who was one of their own' (p. 124). Unlike Jadine, Sydney, and Ondine, who harbour no love for the struggling African masses, who, in fact, see them as nebulous entities struggling and suffering while they themselves receive only the leftovers of capitalism, Son looks at Gideon and compares this yardman with himself:

[Yardman] was kneeling, chopping at the trunk of a small tree – while he himself was so spanking clean, clean from the roots of his hair to the crevices between his toes, ... now he was as near to crying as he'd been since he'd fled from home ... 'Thanks', whispered Son.

(p. 120)

So conscious is Son of the plight of the African masses that on two occasions the overwhelming oppressiveness of their existence brings him close to fainting. The first occasion occurs when he hears the story of the slaves struck blind when they saw Dominique:[9] the second occurs when he realises the magnitude of the African's self-hatred caused by race and class oppression, a hatred that compels Alma Estee to wear a wig the colour of dried blood: 'He grew dizzy as soon as he saw her.'... "Oh, baby baby baby baby", he said, and went to her to take off the wig' (p. 46). And when he observes an African sister stripped of all dignity and pride, 'word whipping a man on down the street', he is 'made miserable by the eyes inside her eyes, and goes to her, arms wide open and says "Come here"' (p. 258). Such examples of Son's sincere love for African people are present throughout the novel, revealing his sensitivity to his people's oppression and establishing his position as an African revolutionary in the mould of Garvey, Malcolm, and Nkrumah.[10]

Not only is Son race conscious, but also class conscious. He sees himself as a member of the exploited class, although he himself is not directly exploited: 'He saw the things he imagined to be his, including his own reflection, mocked. Appropriated, marketed and trivialized into decor. He could not give up the last thing left to him – fraternity' (p. 144). Clearly, he understands that if African people in general are exploited, then he too is exploited, that if African people are not free, then he is not free. Nowhere is his consciousness of himself as a part of the masses more revealing than in the moment he returns to the United States: African women are crying; African children are mere short people without the vulnerability or laughter associated with them; African men are either avoiding African women, blinding themselves to the woman's pain, or becoming African women, having 'snipped off their testicles and pasted them to their chests' (p. 186). If the psychosis of Africans in America is not manifested in either of these ways, notices Son, it is manifested in a type of Jadism – an abandonment of self, brother, and sister to join forces with the oppressor, becoming 'black people in whiteface playing black people in blackface' (pp. 185–6).

With his unobscured race and class consciousness, Son understands that the primary enemy of African people – that is,

the primary cause of the African's plight – is capitalism/
imperialism:

> Son's mouth went dry as he watched Valerian chewing a piece of
> ham, his head-of-a-coin profile content, approving even the flavor in
> his mouth although he had been able to dismiss with a flutter of his
> fingers the people whose sugar and cocoa had allowed him to grow
> old in regal comfort: ... he turned it into candy, ... and sold it to
> other children and made a fortune ... and buil[t] a palace with more
> of their labor and then hire[d] them to do more of the work he was
> not capable of and pay them again according to some scale of value
> that would outrage Satan himself.
>
> (p. 174)

This passage substantiates Son's class-sightedness. He knows that it
is the African's land and labour, not his skin colour, that primarily
results in his exploitation. It is the African's skin colour that facilitates, not causes, his exploitation. Too, he understands that the
United States is the capitalist capital of the world and, therefore, the
African's worst enemy: 'When he thought of America, he thought
of the tongue that Mexican drew in Uncle Sam's mouth: a map of
the U.S. as an ill-shaped tongue ringed by teeth and crammed with
the corpses of children' (p. 143). [...]

In fact, from the novel's beginning, there are clues that Son, not
Jadine, will be the one to commit class suicide. First, it is Jadine
who is surrounded by ideological reinforcements; she is surrounded
by the lifestyle, the values, the food, the clothes, and the language
and behavioural patterns of the Streets. Son, a loner, struggles to
take Jadine to a higher level, a new state of awareness in regard to
African people while in the midst of capitalist surroundings.
Second, and consequently, it is Son who changes his dress habits to
those of his oppressor. Jadine, sometimes wearing a seal-skin coat,
skin-tight jeans, or a Cheech and Chong T-shirt, never once clothes
herself in the geleelike garb of the African masses. Third, and most
important, Son is not equipped to change Jadine's consciousness,
for, despite his good intentions, his solution, his new and better
society, his alternative to the capitalist way of life, is a return to
African traditionalism as represented by Eloe.[11] Not until Jadine
leaves him, opting for cloisonné rather than Son, does he begin to
realise the utopian nature of his solution:

> Out came the photos [Jadine] had taken in the middle of the road in
> Eloe. Beatrice, pretty Beatrice, Soldier's daughter. She looked stupid.

> Ellen, sweet cookie-faced Ellen, the one he always thought so pretty. She looked stupid. They all looked stupid, backwoodsy, dumb, dead.
> (pp. 234–5)

Eloe is a backwoodsy community, largely illiterate and certainly economically underdeveloped. After experiencing the exploitive systems of slavery, colonialism, neocolonialism, and domestic colonialism, and after being exposed to the ideologies associated with the teachings of Islam and Christianity, neither Son, Jadine, nor African people in general can return to this past, highly romanticised way of life. In the words of Aimé Césaire, 'If the African ... were merely to copy his past, failure would be the inevitable result'.[12] Instead of a return to woebegone days, Son and Jadine in particular and all African people in general must extract the positive from traditional Africa and modern capitalism with Africa as the centre in order to forge a new society.[13] Eloe, with all of its positive elements – humanism, collectivism, and egalitarianism – has its negative characteristics: it is a poor, underdeveloped, uneducated community. Unfortunately, when Son does realise the inadequacy of his solution, he does not try to replace it with a more realistic one. Instead, he willingly forsakes his role as revolutionary and chases Jadine to share hers as reactionary. In this respect, he resembles the blind horsemen who, so devastated by their transition from freedom to slavery, gave up on life by blinding themselves to their oppressive environment. Son's association with these blind men is made from our first introduction to him. Gideon and Therese have always referred to him as the rider or the horseman.[14] Moreover, Therese 'had seen him in a dream smiling at her as he rode away wet and naked on a stallion' (p. 90).

Once again, Toni Morrison creates an unsatisfactory ending, despite her new awareness that the primary cause of the plight of African people is capitalism and despite her knowledge that a return to a past way of life is impractical. Once again, her protagonist escapes reality, this time by blinding himself to the role he must play in liberating African people: 'Looking neither to the left nor to the right. Lickety-split. Lickety-split. Lickety-lickety-lickety-split' (p. 89).

From Doreatha Drummond Mbalia, *Toni Morrison's Developing Class Consciousness* (Selinsgrove, London and Toronto, 1991), pp. 67–82.

NOTES

[Whereas Otten (essay 2) interprets *Tar Baby* largely in terms of the myth of the Fall, Doreatha Mbalia's Marxist reading highlights the myth suggested by the novel's title. The tar baby myth originated in Africa as part of a cycle of trickster tales associated with the spider, Anaanu. It reappeared in nineteenth-century America, initially as an African-American response to slavery, but was then included by Joel Chandler Harris in his Uncle Remus plantation tales. Despite these different versions, the plot elements changed very little. In the Uncle Remus version, Brer Fox sets up the tar baby to catch Brer Rabbit while he watches from the bushes. The tar baby is accosted by the rabbit and when he does not reply is accused of being 'stuck up'. Brer Rabbit tries to teach the tar baby a lesson and ends up becoming stuck in the tar. When the farmers come along, it is Brer Rabbit's wit and ingenuity that gets him out of trouble, persuading them to throw him into the brier patch from which he can escape their clutches.

In *Tar Baby*, the various layers of meaning within the original African myth, which was developed before European contact with the African continent, are reclaimed and adapted to America, especially black America, in the late twentieth century. Mbalia thinks of Jadine as a Europeanised African, as the tar baby intended to lure Africans to European values. Whilst initially we might think of Jadine as the tar baby of the title, the novel is more complex than this and the label seems applicable to different characters at different points in the narrative. Brer Rabbit clearly enters the novel as Son, the trickster figure who turns everything upside down. However, even though the last paragraph of the novel makes this association explicit, Son is never quite reducible to Brer Rabbit. At other points in the novel, he appears to be more tar baby than Brer Rabbit, whilst Jadine trapped in the swamp seems to be a version of Brer Rabbit. The novel reclaims the enigmatic qualities and the open-endedness of the original fable in which the outcome is left to our imagination. We are left with Jadine in mid-air and Son running into the rainforest, presumably to join the mythic, blind horsemen. The novel, which eschews simple binarisms throughout, does not come to a satisfactory solution, probably because there are no easy solutions to the dilemmas which it raises (see note 14).

Even though Son is criticised for not providing an alternative to the capitalist way of life which he condemns, Mbalia is very critical of Jadine for having turned her back on her African ancestry. However, the novel is less sympathetic to Son and more ambivalent about Jadine than Mbalia suggests. From a feminist perspective, for example, Jadine's experiences in Eloe are less one-sided than Mbalia proposes. Admittedly, Mbalia is critical of Eloe and describes it 'as a backwoodsy community, lazily illiterate and certainly economically underdeveloped'. But the emphasis is upon how this exposes the inadequacy of Son's solution. From Jadine's point of view, which is not really given consideration by Mbalia, the overt sexism which she experiences there – Soldier describes her as 'the best pussy in Florida' – is appalling. No wonder she believes that the best place for a black woman is New York. Mbalia accepts, too, Son's view of Jadine's anxiety that he is going to rape her as evidence of her 'white thinking'. She protests at being called white, but interestingly Son balks at her assertiveness as much as at what she actually says. Jadine's denial of her black womanhood which Mbalia, like many other critics, takes as the point behind the visit of the 'night-women', is complicated by the fact that Jadine wants for herself roles other than those which black women have traditionally held. Mbalia sees Jadine's refusal to acknowledge what black women have achieved even in their traditional roles as an arrogant failure on her part. Of course, there is truth in this view of her, but her reaction to the women occurs within the context of her experience of Eloe.

In *Tar Baby*, Jadine's characterisation, as Dubey says of *Sula* (essay 4), is different from earlier representations of black women in fiction. Like Sula, she cannot be easily translated into a familiar format. In rejecting the reproductive function traditionally assigned to black women, the character of Jadine, like Sula, opens up to question the conventional definition of black women. Jadine's desire to achieve different roles for herself is reinforced by her recognition that Eloe offers few challenges or opportunities for fulfilment, intellectual or sexual, for black women. Her frustrations over the place jar with Son's enthusiasm for it. It is these problems and contradictions that Mbalia's essay helps to bring into focus while discussing the novel's politics. Ed.]

1. In discussing the ending of *Tar Baby* with Judith Wilson, Morrison states: 'The problem has been put in the wrong place, as though it's a sexual battle, not a cultural one. Racism hurts in a very personal way. Because of it, people do all sorts of things in their personal lives and love relationships based on differences in values and class and education and their conception of what it means to be Black in this society' (Judith Wilson, 'A Conversation with Toni Morrison', *Essence*, 12 [July 1981], 133). This statement suggests that Morrison, after writing *Tar Baby*, understands the triple plight of African people. It also suggests that she is still unclear about the dominant role of class, although such a clarity is quite evident in the work itself. Perhaps the author had not yet fully digested the information presented in the novel.

2. Kwame Nkrumah, *Class Struggle in Africa* (New York, 1970), p. 87.

3. Toni Morrison, *Tar Baby* (New York, 1981), p. 132. Hereafter, page references in parentheses are to this edition.

4. It is another example of Morrison's heightened consciousness that she chooses two protagonists for this novel – one male and the other female.

5. For additional information on the terms *people capitalism, enlightened capitalism, class peace* and *class harmony*, see Nkrumah, *Class Struggle in Africa*, p. 87.

6. Eric Williams, in Chapter 1 of *Capitalism and Slavery* (New York, 1944), his economic study on the role of African slavery and the slave trade in providing the capital that financed the Industrial Revolution, writes: 'Negro slavery, thus, had nothing to do with climate. Its origin can be expressed in three words: in the Caribbean, sugar; on the mainland, tobacco and cotton' (p. 23).

7. On numerous occasions, Morrison has stated that she writes for an African audience. For example, in an interview with Claudia Tate, she remarked: 'When I view the world, perceive it and write about it, it's the world of Black people' (Claudia Tate [ed.], *Black Women Writers at Work* [New York, 1983], p. 118). On another occasion, she stated: 'I use myself as the Black audience' (Jane Bakerman, '"The Seams Can't Show": An Interview with Toni Morrison', *Black American Literature Forum*, 12: 2 [Summer, 1978], 59). [Although Mbalia cites these examples in support of the argument that Morrison writes for Africans, it has to be noted that in both of them Morrison uses the word 'Black' as opposed to 'African' or 'African-American'. Ed.]

8. According to Morrison, 'In the original story, the tar baby is made by a white man – that has to be the case with Jadine. She has to have been almost "constructed" by the western thing, and grateful to see it'. See Wilson, 'A Conversation with Toni Morrison', 130.

9. Son's dizzy, faint feeling after hearing the story of the race of African blind people may also result from the recognition of his relationship to it. Son's association with this race on the Isles des Chevaliers is made from the beginning. Refer to pages 86, 90, 91, and 130 of *Tar Baby* for relevant passages.

10. Dreams have always played a significant role in Morrison's canon, particularly in reflecting the protagonists' level of consciousness in regard to African people. In *Song of Solomon*, Milkman – during his unconscious stage – dreams of his mother's asphyxiation by plants as he idly stands by and watches. In *Tar Baby*, Son dreams of 'yellow houses with white doors which women opened and shouted Come on in, you honey you! and the fat black ladies in white dresses minding the pie table in the basement of the church and the white wet sheets flapping on a line, and the sound of a six-string guitar plucked after supper while children scooped walnuts up off the ground' (p. 102). That Son has these dreams reveals his sensitivity to and love for African people and the African way of life. However, that he tries to insert these dreams into Jadine as a way of politically educating her reveals his idealism, his fairy-tale belief that real conditions can change by simply wishing that they change.

11. See James Coleman's 'The Quest for Wholeness in Toni Morrison's *Tar Baby*', *Black American Literature Forum*, 20, 1: 2 (Spring–Summer,

1986), 71 for his comment on the idealism of Son's solution: 'Son does not seem able to adapt his folk ways to the modern world.' See also Peter B. Erickson's perceptive remark that 'Morrison juxtaposes Son's romanticised dream-like version of Eloe with the more close-up, qualified view we are given when Son brings Jadine home to visit'. Erickson, 'Images of Nurturance in Toni Morrison's *Tar Baby*', *CLA Journal*, 28: 1 (September 1984), 11–32.

12. Césaire's comment was quoted in Chinweizu's *The West and the Rest of Us: White Predators, Black Slaves and the African Elite* (New York, 1975). More than likely, as editor of *The West*, Morrison was aware of this quotation.

13. Chinweizu makes this point throughout *The West*. See page 303 on the arts as an example. This idea of using our African culture as the foundation and then extracting the positive from our traditional, Euro-Christian and Islamic experiences was best voiced by Dr Kwame Nkrumah in 1964: 'The philosophy referred to as philosophical consciencism; consciencism is the map in intellectual terms of the disposition of forces which will enable African society to digest the Western and the Islamic and the Euro-Christian elements in Africa, and develop them in such a way that they fit into the African personality. The African personality is itself defined by the cluster of humanist principles which underlie the traditional African society' (Kwame Nkrumah, *Consciencism: Philosophy and Ideology for De-Colonization* [New York, 1964]).

14. Various critics have offered their analysis of the ending of *Tar Baby* as well as previous Morrison endings. Most agree that they are unsatisfactory. Perhaps the most insightful of these theories is that of Barbara Lounsberry and Grace Ann Hovet ('Principles of Perception in Toni Morrison's *Sula*', *Black American Literature Forum*, 13: 4 [Winter, 1979], 126–9) and Keith Byerman (*Fingering the Jagged Grain: Tradition and Form in Recent Black Fiction* [Athens, GA, 1985]). Referring to the ending of *Sula*, Lounsberry and Hovet point out that Morrison 'carefully refrains from offering a synthesis of her dialectic between the new and the old. She settles for a clear presentation of the limitations of both' (p. 129). Referring to *Tar Baby*, Byerman writes that both Jadine and Son 'in effect denies [sic] history: Son by believing in the possibility of returning to a previous black purity and Jadine by assuming that blackness was merely an aberration from the truth of Eurocentric Progress' (p. 215).

6

Knowing Our Place: Psychoanalysis and *Sula*

HOUSTON A. BAKER, JR

[...] nowhere is *Sula's* situation as lyrical and symbolic narrative better observed than in the chapter entitled '1922', which begins with the statement 'It was too cool for ice cream'.

It is 'too cool for ice cream' because Nel and Sula, as twelve-year-old black girls 'wishbone thin and easy-assed' (p. 52), are not yet mature enough to participate physically in the sensual, sexual mysteries signified by ice cream. The location of Edna Finch's Mellow House (the ice-cream parlour) in the community is at the end of a gauntlet of young and old black men who stare with 'panther eyes' at the young girls. All of the men are thinking of images summoned by the phrase 'pig meat', but one twenty-one-year-old black 'pool haunt of sinister beauty' named Ajax actually utters the phrase, stirring the budding sexuality of the two girls like confectionary ice on warm and eager tongues.

The opening scene of '1922' is, thus, rife with sexuality. And while the surname 'Finch' carries connotations of a delicate flight and extends the bird imagery of *Sula* (we recall Eva's 'heron' or 'eagle'), 'mellow' indicates 'ripe', or 'mature'. The oxymoron marked by 'sinister beauty' for Ajax is complemented by the innocent lust of adolescent girls and the almost blues' innuendo of Morrison's handling of 'ice cream'. Surely, Edna's mellow confections appear more like the male equivalent of the blues' 'jelly roll' than Baskin–Robbins's multiple flavours. Vanilla and lemon come together as follows:

> The cream-colored trousers marking with a mere seam the place where the mystery curled. Those smooth vanilla crotches invited them; those lemon-yellow gabardines beckoned to them. They moved toward the ice-cream parlor like tightrope walkers, as thrilled by the possibility of a slip as by the maintenance of tension and balance. The least sideways glance, the merest toe stub, could pitch them into those creamy haunches spread wide with welcome. Somewhere beneath all of that daintiness, chambered in all that neatness, lay the thing that clotted their dreams.
>
> (p. 51)

This mutual dream of Sula and Nel is scarcely one of real 'ice cream'. What brings the two girls together, in a word, is the Phallus, the Law of the Fathers, whose 'mystery' makes it a creamy veil for their adolescent dreams.[1] The PHALLUS is, of course, to be distinguished from the penis. The PHALLUS is not a material object but a signifier of the Father, or, better, of the Father's LAW.

In the writing of Freud, infantile drives institute a tripartite pattern of lack-absence-differentiation. Originally 'at one' with the breast of the Mother, the child experiences hunger (lack) as an absence of the breast. Eventually, he or she discovers in the Mother's absence his or her *difference* or differentiation from the Mother. A twofold relationship results. The child makes demands; the Mother has desires. The child wishes to become the desired of the Mother. (A simple instance is alimentary – the child demands food; the mother desires toilet training.) In order for CULTURE to occur, this dyad of desire must be interrupted by a third term. That term is the Father as PHALLUS, as the LAW.

Here we come to the Oedipal stage in which those children possessed of a penis want to be the absent PHALLUS *for* the Mother but find the Father always already there. Hence, they tremble before the thought of death (castration/lack) and subjugate themselves to the master, the LAW of the PHALLUS. They know they will accede to Fatherhood in due course.

Children without a penis substitute a baby – as a sign of presence and satisfaction, and a possible fulfilment of desire – for the absent PHALLUS. What Jacques Lacan makes of the traditional corpus of Freud is a signifying drama in which the PHALLUS represents the condition of possibility of socio-sexual differentiation and cultural production by *standing for* the third term, or Father. It is the marker, as it were, of male power and familiarly patriarchal discourse. It is both precultural and culture-founding.

The PHALLUS, in a word, is the signifier that institutes male-dominant cultural discourse and mandates a division of physiologically differentiated children into two, unequal sexes. To create a habitable space beyond the LAW of the PHALLUS, symbolic manipulation – an unveiling – is *necessary*.

In fact, what causes the discourse of '1922' to coalesce (or clot) is the triple repetition of Sula's and Nel's exorcising ritual of the Phallus. It is important to say at the outset, however, that Sula and Nel, for all their apparent bonding, do not share a single perspective. While the Phallus may be an object common to their dreams, how very different are their dreams! Nel lapses easily into a 'picture of herself lying on a flowered bed, tangled in her own hair, waiting for some fiery prince. He approached but never quite arrived' (p. 51). Sula, by contrast, 'spent hours in the attic behind a roll of linoleum galloping through her own mind on a gray-and-white horse tasting sugar and smelling roses' (p. 52). Different fantasies, to be sure. Sula is a rider and a taster of confections; Nel awaits a fire that never quite kindles. The visions of both girls, however, include not only an implied relationship to the Phallus, but also the presence of some further person, a dream companion of the same gender.

This third party signals a triangulation described by Nancy Chodorow in *The Reproduction of Mothering*:

> Girls cannot and do not 'reject' their mother and women in favour of their father and men, but remain in a bisexual triangle throughout childhood and into puberty. They usually make a sexual resolution in favour of men and their father, but retain an internal emotional triangle.[2]

Discussing the work of the psychologist Hélène Deutsch, Chodorow explains that when women are involved in heterosexual erotic relationships with men, relational triangles represent a reproduction of the type of mother–daughter bonding described in the foregoing quotation. There can be little doubt about both Nel's and Sula's erotic attraction to 'the thing that clotted their dreams'. Similarly, there can be little doubt about the 'nontraditional' character of that signifier in their lives. For both girls are 'daughters of distant mothers and incomprehensible fathers (Sula's because he was dead; Nel's because he wasn't)' (p. 52). In a sense – and as a consequence, at least in part, of a 'nigger joke' – Nel and Sula are *not* members of a traditional 'family', and, hence, cannot play out the usual family romance.

For example, Sula cannot maintain any affectional pre-Oedipal bonding with a mother who, pressed by the exigencies of her need for touching, admits to not liking her daughter, to seeing Sula (quite justifiably in the male-bereft economies of the Bottom) as a burden and a cross to bear. Hence, a rejected Sula watches her mother burn to death without so much as stirring a muscle. Similarly, Nel, as the diminished product of a mother bent on eradicating sexuality along with her daughter's distinguishing physical identity, is incapable of finding a maternal perch for her affections. The two girls, therefore, come to stand to each other as more MOTHER than their actual mothers. They enact their supportive displacement as a function of the incumbencies of a black 'village' existence.

Similarly, Sula and Nel are required to construct the role of the FATHER from that assembly that marks the male gauntlet from the Time-and-a-Half Pool Hall to Edna Finch's Mellow House. This further displacement mystifies the Phallus even further in their mutual imaginings. And it is, ultimately, the displacements occasioned by the 'nigger joke' that necessitate a threefold enactment of Phallic rites in '1922'.

First, there is a ludic enactment in which 'the beautiful, beautiful boys ... [whose] footsteps left a smell of smoke behind' (p. 56) are metaphorically appropriated as 'thick' twigs peeled 'to a smooth, creamy innocence', like ice cream (p. 58). Sula's first act is an artist's response; she 'traced intricate patterns ... with her twig' (p. 58). But soon both Nel and Sula are hollowing out holes in earth. Their separate holes join, and Nel's twig snaps. Both girls, then, throw their twigs into the hole and collect all the debris from the clearing around them and bury it, with the twigs, in the earth. The first rite is completed. The Phallus has been metaphorically exposed and exorcised; its mystery has been appropriated by the absorptive (earth) womb, which seems capable of serving as the whole (as opposed to the broken or fragmented twig) ground of bonding between the girls. It is as though a 'creamy' pleasure can be shared by a common hole. Demystification and burial (a purgative burial and 'cleaning') are engaged as common ritual acts.

In the second instance of the Phallic rites, however, the girls' responses dramatically differentiate them. Chicken Little comes into the clearing, and while Nel badgers him about his polluting behaviour (i.e., picking his nose), Sula accepts him as he is. In an adolescent figuration of her mother's relationship to male lovers, Sula suggests that Chicken 'didn't need fixing' (p. 43). And it is Sula alone who climbs the tree with the little boy, showing him a world beyond the river. Nel remains on the ground and, hence, is not party to a Freudian reading of tree climbing.

In the section of the *Interpretation of Dreams* entitled 'Representation by Symbols', Freud observes, 'I added [in explanation of one of his patient's dreams] from my own knowledge derived elsewhere that climbing down, like climbing up in other cases, described sexual intercourse in the vagina.' Nel is further excluded from the scene when she takes no active part in burial. Sula alone responds in mocking revelry to Chicken's infantile boast of (sexual) achievement: 'I'm a tell my brovver' (p. 60).

> She picked ... [Chicken Little] up by his hands and swung him outward then around and around. His knickers ballooned and his shrieks of frightened joy startled the birds and the fat grasshoppers. When he slipped from her hands and sailed away out over the water they could still hear his bubbly laughter. The water darkened and closed quickly over the place where Chicken Little sank.
>
> (pp. 60–1)

Morrison's own mocking designation of the Phallus, in all of its mystery, as a false harbinger of apocalypse – 'Chicken Little' – begins the demystification that is completed in the little boy's burial by water. Immediately after he sinks below the surface, Sula rushes across the footbridge to Shadrack's shack. Overwhelmed by the neatness of its interior, she forgets to ask the mad ritualist if he has seen her throw Chicken Little in the river. He, thinking she seeks reassurance about the permanence of human life, speaks the single word 'Always'.

Sula has just discovered the absence of benevolent design and the limits of conscious control in the universe. Hence, Shadrack's reassurance is absurdly comic. And in the absurdity of what is (given Shadrack's fiery history) a common knowledge of disorder, the two characters are bonded. Sula becomes one in the party of Shadrackian antinomianism.

The final enactment of Phallic rites in '1922' expands the cate-gorisation of 'the mystery' from false herald of apocalypse to Christian sign of the Transcendental Signifier – the Law itself. In its burial rites for Chicken Little, the community of the Bottom summons Jesus Christ as the metonym for the son – the son, who, as Eva tells Hannah in reference to Plum, is 'hard to bear'. 'You wouldn't know that', she explains to her daughter, 'but they is' (p. 71).

The women of Greater Saint Matthews take Jesus 'as both son and lover', and in his 'downy face they could see the sugar-and-butter sandwiches and feel the oldest and most devastating pain there is: not the pain of childhood, but the remembrance of it' (p. 65). Phallic mystery, even in its most transcendental form as the Law, has its woman's redaction: loss, pain, absence. The actual fathers are disappeared by a 'nigger joke' in *Sula* that emasculates them and denies them any legitimate means of production. They desert children, who, thus, become reminders of dismemberment, dispossession. The joke's consequences demand a compensating ritual, and in *Sula*, it is a funereal exertion of religious frenzy: 'They [the women of Greater Saint Matthews] danced and screamed, not to protest God's will but to acknowledge it and confirm once more their conviction that the only way to avoid the Hand of God is to get in it' (p. 66).

And so 'in the colored part of the cemetery, they sank Chicken Little in between his grandfather and aunt' (p. 66). Butterflies mark the scene of this third burial – butterflies that signify graceful flight and sexual delight and unite, once more, at a higher level of ab-straction and joke-compensation, the dreams of Sula and Nel: 'Two young girlfriends trotting up the road on a summer day wondering what happened to butterflies in the winter' (p. 66).

The butterflies return as 'lemon yellow' delight when Ajax releases a jar of them in Sula's bedroom on one occasion when they make passionate love. And how, with his lemon yellow as sign, could we mistake Ajax as other than one of the party of New Orleans, Sundown House conjurations? Rochelle Sabat, in an early instance of *Sula's* bird imagery, appears as 'the woman in the canary-yellow dress' wafting an odour of gardenias (p. 25).

From Houston A. Baker, Jr, *Working of the Spirit: The Poetics of Afro-American Women's Writing* (Chicago and London, 1991), pp. 145–50.

NOTES

[As for Jennifer FitzGerald in the next essay, also a psychoanalytic reading of Morrison's work, Houston Baker's starting point is that the characters about whom he is writing are not members of a traditional 'family' and, therefore, cannot play out the usual family romance. Consequently, a psychoanalytic reading of the text requires a more hybrid theoretical approach than is normally allowed in traditional psychoanalysis. As mentioned in the Introduction, this essay is from Baker's book-length study of current critical approaches to black women's writing from his own perspective of the theoretical state of African-American intellectual history. He argues that theoretical models are 'always partial and shifting, tentative and reflexive, always hybrid instalments on understanding' (p. 1). This conviction is evident here in his own approach to *Sula* which draws on Sigmund Freud but also on Jacques Lacan who was himself influenced by Freud. Lacan placed more emphasis than Freud on the role of language in gender identity formation. While Freud attributes importance to the biological penis, Lacan highlights the importance which is given to its cultural construction, the phallus. For Lacan entering a language is entering a symbolic order within which the male is privileged over the female. Baker's reading of *Sula* is concerned with the necessity of 'unveiling' in order to create 'a habitable space' beyond the phallus, and 'male-dominated discourse'. Baker finds in *Sula* the triple repetition of the ritual by which Sula and Nel exorcise the phallus to which they both have a different relationship.

In addition to Freud and Lacan, Baker suggests that Nancy Chodorow's work is pertinent to a psychoanalytic reading of this aspect of the novel, particularly her concept that women do not reject their mothers but stand in a bisexual triangle throughout childhood and into puberty. However, Morrison's novel challenges Chodorow's concept because neither Sula nor Nel is able to maintain an affectional pre-Oedipal bonding with her mother. Thus, the two girls stand to each other as more MOTHER than their actual mothers. In her essay, FitzGerald also identifies importance being attached to what Melanie Klein calls 'the internal mother'. Beloved's vehement attachment to a woman on land and on the ship playing the role of the primary caregiver, FitzGerald argues, acts as a double for Klein's 'internal mother'. In this respect she takes further Baker's emphasis on the ways in which psychoanalytic models and relationships echo broader political tensions and difficulties within African-American life. Ed.]

1. For valuable accounts of the phallus in the work of Freud and Lacan, see Juliet Mitchell and Jacqueline Rose (eds), *Feminine Sexuality: Jacques Lacan and the école freudienne* (New York, 1982); Juliet Mitchell, *Psychoanalysis and Feminism: Freud, Reich, Laing and Women* (New York, 1975); Jane Gallop, *The Daughter's Seduction: Feminism and Psychoanalysis* (Ithaca, NY, 1982).

2. Nancy Chodorow, *The Reproduction of Mothering: Psychoanalysis and the Sociology of Gender* (Berkeley, CA, 1978), p. 140.

7

Selfhood and Community: Psychoanalysis and Discourse in *Beloved*

JENNIFER FITZGERALD

I

When Paul D urges Sethe to 'Go as far inside as you need to, I'll hold your ankles. Make sure you get back out' (p. 46), he is inviting her to 'work through' past traumas with himself as psychotherapist.[1] The novel's intertwined narratives can be viewed as a form of 'talking cure': consequently, several critics have taken a psycho-analytic approach to *Beloved*.[2] But many theorists, especially black and feminist, have grave reservations about psychoanalysis.[3] Although Freud demonstrated the specific cultural construction of the psychic processes he analysed, both he and his successors have tended to generalise from limited data unproblematically, positing a model which is both normative and universalised. As a result, psychoanalysis isolates psychic experience from the diversities of ethnicity and class; furthermore, it focuses intensively on the interaction of infant and mother as if this existed as a freestanding relation, independent of the economic, political or social conditions which affect the circumstances of parenting. In doing so, it defines mother-hood according to a very specific, restricted norm, and places a huge burden of responsibility, not to say blame, on mothers.[4] It patholo-gises non-normative families, privileging the healthy development of individual autonomy, highly valued by white Western capitalism.

How appropriate is such a model to African-Americans, whose family history – as *Beloved* shows – has been (forcibly) shaped along non-hegemonic lines?[5] At the same time, how not to draw on psychoanalysis in discussing a novel which explores the aftermath of appalling hurts, the psychic as well as material damage inflicted by slavery?

Among psychoanalytic schools of thought, one may prove useful. Object relations theory proposes that the psyche is constructed within a wide system of relationships, offering a model of how social, cultural and political forces become internalised.[6] As Elizabeth Abel points out, it is at least potentially capable of recognising the range of relationships which influence the psyche, although in practice it has confined itself to the Western nuclear family.[7] This essay, therefore, draws on the vocabulary and insights of object relations psychoanalysis in suggesting a reading of *Beloved*. But first, an explanation of my methodology.

Literary criticism examines texts, not people; it analyses discourse, not psyches. Psychoanalysis is only one of the discourses circulating through the novel, one of the range of positions and meanings available to *Beloved*'s characters under, and after, slavery. It is therefore not offered as a truth to which the characters, *qua* patients, must be led. It is nevertheless worth noting the resemblances between the discourses of psychoanalysis and slavery. The discourse of slavery privileges humanity, autonomy, and participation in a family – by denying these values to slaves. It is not a coincidence that the major focus of psychoanalysis is on precisely these practices: the socialisation of the newborn 'animal', the human baby, and its acquisition of autonomous identity within the context of the nuclear family. Both discourses obviously derive from the same ideology, individualistic Western capitalism.

Such similarities are to be expected, since 'the systematic character of a discourse includes its systematic articulation within other discourses'.[8] But they remind us of the wider context which a purely psychoanalytic focus might obscure. Although each of the characters in *Beloved* has been damaged by slavery, they are not only victims – they are also agents. Discourse analysis draws attention to the variety of subject positions of which they avail themselves. Paul D, for example, moves from the position of object in the discourse of slavery to the position of subject in the discourse of masculinity; the discourse of the good mother offers Sethe a similar shift. This essay therefore reads the novel through various discourses, including the repressed pre-Oedipal discourse triggered as each character confronts a psychic trauma.[9] As these past hurts surface, Denver, Sethe and Paul D work through them in ways which offer an alternative to classic psychoanalytic therapy. The discourses circulating in *Beloved* include:

(1) The dominant discourse of slavery, which produces meanings of humanity, autonomy and familial relationship in order to deny them to slaves – 'trespassers among the human race' (*Beloved*, p. 125). This is how schoolteacher is able 'to show ... that definitions belonged to the definer – not the defined' (p. 190) and why Paul D doubts his own humanity: 'Garner called and announced them men ... Was he naming what he saw or creating what he did not?' (p. 220). Paul D is fascinated by large black families – 'he made them identify over and over who each was ... who, in fact, belonged to who' (p. 219) – as a contradiction to slavery's definition of 'belonging' as property: 'Anybody Baby Suggs knew, let alone loved, who hadn't run off or been hanged, got rented out, loaned out, bought up, brought back, stored up, mortgaged, won, stolen or seized' (p. 23).

(2) The discourse of the good mother. This discourse has been theorised in twentieth-century psychoanalysis but it has deep roots. It conceives of the (usually biological) mother as so instrumental to the child's well-being as to allow her no separate interests. Thus Sethe's concern is not for her own life but 'for the life of her children's mother' (p. 30). It nevertheless offers her status and a position as subject against the discourse of slavery. She internalises this value system by priding herself on the fact that she 'had milk enough for all' (p. 198), by taking and putting her babies 'where they'd be safe' (p. 164). A more generalised maternal discourse is also invoked, undercutting the discourse of slavery – 'No notebook for my babies and no measuring string neither' (p. 198) – and undercut by it: 'What [Baby Suggs] called the nastiness of life was the shock she received upon learning that nobody stopped playing checkers just because the pieces included her children' (p. 23).

(3) The discourse of masculinity: 'Because he was a man and a man could do what he would' (p. 126). When Paul D's subject position in this discourse is threatened (by Beloved's undermining of his will), he reasserts it by the desire to 'document his manhood' (p. 128), to make Sethe pregnant.

(4) The discourse of black solidarity: slaves and ex-slaves depend on, and risk themselves for, each other. While the previous discourses articulate the values of the dominant culture, this discourse prevails among the marginalised African-American community. One material practice of this discourse is the Underground Railroad. Another is Baby Suggs' mission of love. In conscious contradiction to slavery's material practices of torture and mutilation, the ex-slaves are exhorted to value and cherish themselves: 'Yonder they do not love your flesh. They despise it ... *You* got to love it, *you*!' (p. 88).

(5) The pre-Oedipal discourse of object relations psychoanalysis was first articulated by Melanie Klein (whose name provides a useful shorthand for the practices she described). Briefly, Kleinian theory argues that a pre-Oedipal infant's identity is constructed through a complex process during which it experiences very powerful, conflictual emotions, which in an adult would be diagnosed as paranoia, neurosis, even psychosis. The baby projects these emotions onto external 'objects', people with whom it comes into contact (in the first place, the primary caregiver, usually the mother), transforming these persons into fantasy objects, 'imagos'. These fantasy objects are then introjected back into the infant's own psyche. The process is only completed when the child has forged a sense of its own identity out of its experience and fantasies, and has also recognised the autonomy of others, no longer as imagos but as individuals living their own separate lives. Thus selfhood is socially constructed through interaction with others, aspects of whom have been internalised by the child as part of itself.

The discourse of slavery inscribes *Beloved*'s protagonists as objects: they therefore have an investment in inscribing themselves in other discourses in which they act as subjects. But their unconscious also has an investment in Kleinian discourse, in which pre-Oedipal fantasies are inscribed. Since Kleinian discourse articulates the psychic struggle prior to the achievement of subjectivity, it cannot offer a subject position, but neither does it enforce object status. Instead, it speaks the return of the repressed: as each protagonist confronts a crisis which evokes psychic trauma, he or she articulates infantile reactions in the practices of this discourse, projecting emotions onto others as external objects and introjecting the resultant imagos as part of themselves. This process is most evident in the character of Beloved, who is inscribed almost exclusively in terms of projection and introjection.

II

Beloved's obsession with Sethe can be characterised psychoanalytically as pre-Oedipal. She also functions as a figure onto whom others can project their fears and desires. She can thus be read in two ways, as Morrison herself suggests:[10] both as a psychically damaged real-life slavegirl and as a ghost (fantasy object for the emotions of others). Beloved narrates her story in the fragmented monologue which appears to describe her abduction from Africa and transportation in a slave ship. It expresses her vehement attachment to a woman on land and on the ship who, in psychoanalytic terms, plays the part of the mother or primary caregiver (whether she is her mother or not). This woman fits Melanie Klein's notion of the 'internal mother', who is a 'double' of the external person playing the caregiving role.[11] The double is psychologically created by the infant's ambivalent emotions – of both love (and dependence) and hate (and fear of dependence) – for the person who looks after it. She is both idealised and demonised, both all loving and all abandoning.

Beloved repeats this pattern of dependence in her relationship with Sethe, hovering '[l]ike a familiar', waiting for her after work, 'as though every afternoon she doubted anew the older woman's return' (p. 57). Later, she regales Sethe with accusations 'of leaving her behind. Of not being nice to her, not smiling at her' (p. 241). She projects onto Sethe the imago of her internal mother, the woman who was about to smile at her and who then left her behind.

Beloved's excessive dependence corresponds to the symbiosis of mother and infant Klein describes, a state in which the child does not yet recognise its separateness from the world, and in particular from the primary caregiver; she says of the woman on the ship: 'I am not separate from her' (p. 210). She expresses an exaggerated anxiety to help this woman in an attempt to guarantee against abandonment. Her insistence that the woman has her face also makes sense in psychoanalytic discourse, which suggests that babies see themselves reflected back in their mothers' faces, in the loving gaze which assures them of acceptance.[12] Hence Beloved's anguished desire that the woman should smile at her. But, like Winnicott's inadequate mother, the woman is otherwise preoccupied: 'she empties out her eyes' (p. 211). This is the first step in the process of abandonment. The woman 'who was going to smile at me' (p. 213) chooses instead to join the dead man in the sea.

Psychically still a pre-Oedipal infant, with no autonomous sense of self, Beloved experiences this loss as an existential crisis.

Like the baby in Kleinian discourse, she is prey to ambivalent feelings. Although she yearns for the 'join', she fears it involves annihilation by incorporation. She externalises it as chewing and swallowing and then reinternalises it:

> in the night I hear chewing and swallowing and laughter it belongs to me she is the laugh I am the laugher I see her face which is mine ... my face is coming I have to have it I am looking for the join I am loving my face so much my dark face is close to me I want to join she whispers to me she whispers I reach for her chewing and swallowing she touches me she knows I want to join she chews and swallows me I am gone now I am her face my own face has left me I see me swim away.
>
> (pp. 212–13)

At the end of the monologue, Beloved transfers the role of 'internal mother' onto Sethe, now the 'double' of the woman on the ship: 'the sun closes my eyes when I open them I see the face I lost Sethe's is the face that left me Sethe sees me see her and I see the smile her smiling face is the place for me' (p. 213). Sethe's face acts as a mirror to her own: she wants Sethe to gaze into the water with her, 'touch[ing] the rocking faces with her own' (p. 241). She has projected ambivalent emotions onto each 'mother', split into 'good' feelings, such as love (when each woman is idealised) and 'bad' feelings (when she believes each has abandoned her).

Psychoanalytically, such split projections breed insecurity: according to Klein, they result 'in the feeling that the ego is in bits'.[13] This conflates with Beloved's experience, confirming her fears:

> Beloved, inserting a thumb in her mouth along with the forefinger, pulled out a back tooth. ... Beloved looked at the tooth and thought, This is it. Next would be her arm, her hand, a toe. Pieces of her would drop maybe one at a time, maybe all at once. ... Among the things she could not remember was when she first knew that she could wake up any day and find herself in pieces. She had two dreams: exploding, and being swallowed. When her tooth came out – an odd fragment, last in the row – she thought it was starting.
>
> (p. 133)

But the insecurity also intensifies aggression, the paradigmatic 'attack on the mother' Kleinian discourse highlights the anger of the infant who cannot yet conceive of its mother's autonomy. Like this infant, Beloved sees other people only as a function of her own needs. She therefore refuses to accept – or more accurately, is incapable of accepting – Sethe's explanations for leaving her behind. Just as her dependence has been projected into fantasies of feeding – 'Sethe was licked, tasted, eaten by Beloved's eyes' (p. 57) – so her aggression is characterised through the fantasy of cannibalism: 'The bigger Beloved got, the smaller Sethe became. ... She sat in the chair licking her lips like a chastised child while Beloved ate up her life, took it, swelled up with it, grew taller on it' (p. 250).

The apparently twenty-year-old Beloved (p. 55) occasionally 'behave[s] like a two-year-old' (p. 98). This is the age not only at which the crawling already? baby was killed, but at which, according to classic psychoanalysis, children begin to undergo the Oedipal crisis which should instigate their development into separate selfhood. Beloved confronts the typically Oedipal primal scene when she witnesses Sethe and Paul D in the bath tub. However, she avoids negotiating the conflict and coming to terms with her exclusion from this sexual dyad by 'moving' Paul D into sexual relations with herself. Sex does not initiate her into adult relations but allows her to prolong infantile dependence: by breaking Sethe's sexual tie with Paul D, she has found a means of keeping Sethe to herself.

The Oedipal crisis is supposed to encourage the child to repress its immediate desires, in order to accommodate the norms of its surrounding family, society and culture. The caregiver usually begins this process of socialisation by denying the child its importunate demands, making it consider the needs of others. Sethe fails to perform the role of 'the unquestioned mother whose word was law and who knew what was best' (p. 242), humbly abdicating her 'maternal' authority over Beloved: '[N]obody said, Get on out of here, girl, and come back when you get some sense. Nobody said, You raise your hand to me and I will knock you into the middle of next week. ... I will wrap you round that doorknob, don't nobody work for you and God don't love ugly ways' (p. 242). When eventually Sethe 'leav[es] Beloved behind. Again' (p. 262) to attack Bodwin, Beloved's fears – and her psychosis – are confirmed. Isolated and inconsolable, she 'erupts into her separate parts, to make it easy for the chewing laughter to swallow her all away' (p. 274).

Beloved is almost exclusively inscribed in the pre-Oedipal practices of Kleinian discourse. Sethe and Paul D initially repress this discourse, due to their investment in taking up a valued position in other discourses, but as we shall see, the surface is broken through the practices of splitting, projection and introjection. [...]

At first glance, we have no doubt that Sethe has been capable of adult responsibilities, but closer scrutiny calls into question the discourse in which she inscribes herself. Because slavery denies parental claims, Sethe insists upon her role as mother. She thus refutes her position as object in the discourse of slavery by asserting her position as subject in the discourse of the good mother. But the version of motherhood she articulates offers an exaggerated, idealised view of exclusive maternal responsibility. As she tries to maintain control of this discourse, another set of significations slips through, of Sethe as daughter. Practices which signify motherly devotion activate memories of her own babyhood. [...]

This daughterly discourse articulates a psychic trauma of infantile abandonment. Slavery severed Sethe's bond with her mother before she had developed a separate identity; consequently, her sense of self and of the boundaries to that self is dangerously weak. Like a pre-Oedipal infant, she 'didn't know where the world stopped and she began' (p. 164). She replaces her individual identity with her maternal role, but the discourse of the good mother draws on the same lack of boundaries which the pre-Oedipal infant experiences: 'I wouldn't draw breath without my children' (p. 203). Sethe projects 'all the parts of her that were precious and fine and beautiful' (p. 163) onto external objects, her children. The discourses become hopelessly entangled; her excessive investment in mothering is an impossible attempt to make up for her own loss as a daughter:

> My plan was to take us all to the other side where my own ma'am is. They stopped me from getting us there, but they didn't stop you from getting here. Ha Ha. You came right on back like a good girl, like a daughter which is what I wanted to be and would have been if my ma'am had been able to get out of the rice long enough before they hanged her and let me be one ... I wonder what they was doing when they was caught. Running, you think? No. Not that. Because she was my ma'am and nobody's ma'am would run off and leave her daughter, would she? Would she, now?
>
> (p. 203)

Like Beloved, she cannot accept that her mother was a person with separate interests, who could decide to escape even when it involved leaving her daughter behind. This psychic investment in a dogged belief that mother and child are inseparably one, with identical selfhood and interests, is then articulated in the murder of her two-year-old daughter.

Object relations theory suggests that just as the infant refuses to see the mother as a separate individual, so the mother may be tempted to treat her child as a part of herself: '[J]ust as the mother is to the child, so is the child to the mother – an object of gratification. And just as the child does not recognise the separate identity of the mother, so the mother looks upon her child as a part of herself whose interests are identical with her own.'[14] Such a mother may well believe that she killed her child for its own good. The fusion of good mother and pre-Oedipal discourses provides the logic that makes sense of such an action. Sethe says to Paul D: 'Grown don't mean nothing to a mother. A child is a child. They get bigger, older, but grown? What's that supposed to mean? In my heart it don't mean a thing' (p. 45). To which psychoanalysis offers a gloss: 'For the mother the child is never grown up, for when grown up he [*sic*] is no longer her child.'[15] One can keep a critical distance from the universalising implications of this statement while recognising its specific relevance to the practices of slavery, in which 'it wasn't worth the trouble to try to learn [your child's] features [which] you would never see change into adulthood anyway' (*Beloved*, p. 139).

Ultimately, then, the responsibility for Sethe's confusion lies in slavery, which positioned her as object and denied her the experience of bonding with her own mother through which she could arrive at a separate subjectivity, and which precipitated her entry into good motherhood, whose practices equally denied a sense of individual self. Not recognising the separateness of her children, Sethe makes life-and-death decisions for them. She only begins to reassemble her several parts (no longer projected onto external objects) when Paul D washes her in sections, taking up where Baby Suggs left off. This functions as an alternative version of mothering, articulated in ways quite opposed to the discourse of the good mother, dispensing with both the exclusivity of biology (only biological parents have responsibility) and of gender (only women can be mothers). Paul D gives her back her self: 'You your best thing, Sethe. You are.' ... 'Me? Me?' (p. 273).

Just as Sethe refuses her negative inscription in the discourse of slavery by taking a positively valued position as good mother, so Paul D plumbs for the discourse of masculinity and its signifying practices of free will and self-control:

Because he was a man and a man could do what he would: be still
for six hours in a dry well while night dropped; fight raccoon with
his hands and win; watch another man, whom he loved better than
his brothers, roast without a fear just so the roasters would know
what a man was like.

(p. 126)

He encourages other people's emotions but he cannot acknowledge
his own vulnerability: instead he projects (his own) goodness and
beauty onto external objects such as trees. He has a psychic investment in repressing unspeakable tortures into a tobacco tin lodged in
his chest, because the masculine discourse of unified self-control
positions him as a subject, contradicting his dehumanising position
as object in the discourse of slavery. But Beloved undermines his
rigid discipline, 'moving' him from room to room and then to sex
against his will. [...] Through the fissures of the masculine, the
Kleinian discourse emerges. When she asks him to call her by her
name, he says 'Red heart' instead of 'Beloved', indicating that she
functions as a projection of Paul D's own 'red, red heart' (p. 235).
And he says, 'She reminds me of something. Something, look like,
I'm supposed to remember' (p. 234). He has projected the vulnera-
ble, emotional part of himself onto Beloved, whom he now intro-
jects (witness his impression that she is invading him).

The self-doubt he has externalised in Beloved's control over him
undermines not only his masculine self-image but, crucially, his
human identity, reinscribing him in the discourse of slavery. Hence
his agonising uncertainty with regard to his status as a human
being. Just as the discourse of slavery projects white fears of their
own animality – 'the jungle they had made' (p. 199) – onto people
of colour, so Paul D projects the suspicion he harbours about
himself onto Sethe, replaying schoolteacher's taxonomy of 'animal
characteristics': 'You got two feet, Sethe, not four', ... 'How fast he
had moved from his shame to hers' (p. 165).

Sethe, therefore, also functions as a projection for the aspects of
himself that he cannot bear to acknowledge. As his self-controlled
unified subjectivity fragments, he feels himself falling apart: 'His
tobacco tin, blown open, spilled contents that floated freely and
made him their play and prey' (p. 218). In Kleinian discourse the
splitting of the self is part of the ongoing process of achieving
human identity in relationship. Paul D has a model in Sixo, who
was able to project multiple selves (represented by his name) onto

an external object, the Thirty Mile Woman, and then introject them again: 'The pieces I am, she gather them and give them back to me in all the right order' (pp. 272–3). As he acknowledges the validity of Sixo's sense of self, Paul D can give up his unified position within masculinity, learning to introject the pieces of himself which constitute his relation to and dependence on others. He remembers that on the day of his capture at Sweet Home, Sethe had reflected back the same integration Sixo gained from the Thirty Mile Woman. In delicate recognition of his humanity and without invoking masculine repression, she overlooked his slave condition – 'collared like a beast' – and 'left him his manhood' (p. 273). In reciprocity, as we have seen, Paul D helps her to identify the value that lies in her own self.

III

Thus, each of the protagonists has experienced not only the material horrors of slavery but a psychic trauma which undermines their sense of self. As Paul D learns, the unified self proposed in the discourse of masculinity is an illusion, but some grasp on one's position as a subject is required for negotiation with the world.

Kleinian psychoanalysis argues that selfhood is gained in relation to others: first to the mother, and gradually to all those who form the individual's environment. In this novel, Baby Suggs facilitates the community in forging its members' identities: the community thus performs the function of an extended 'mother'. She, too, is a mother-deprived daughter: 'If my mother knew me would she like me?' Her sense of self is also weak: 'the sadness was at her center, the desolated center where the self that was no self made its home' (p. 140). But when she attains freedom, that is, when the discourse of slavery has lost its power, she discovers what it means to identify one's *own* hands, heartbeat, person. Her response is to foster the selfhood which racism has denied to each of the exslaves. Her mother love extends beyond the bounds of the nuclear family, which Eurocentric psychoanalysis has universalised as *the* psychic environment. She insists on a collective act of self-appreciation, in which all those damaged by dehumanisation and hate can learn to love – or 'mother' – themselves, in a manner that fosters tenderness for their joint humanity:

> 'Here', she said, 'in this here place, we flesh; flesh that weeps, laughs; flesh that dances on bare feet in grass. Love it. Love it hard. Yonder

they do not love your flesh. They despise it. ... *You* got to love it, *you*! ... This is flesh I'm talking about here. Flesh that needs to be loved.'

(p. 88)

Thus, while encouraging the therapeutic practice of 'lay[ing] it all down' (p. 86), Baby Suggs radically revises classic psychoanalytic discourse, involving 'a wide range of changing social relations'[16] in the construction of identity. She envisages the adult healing the traumas of childhood, with the help not of professional therapists, but of those who have shared the pain. The practices of this revised psychoanalysis can be juxtaposed to those generated by slavery.

Suggs' discourse of communal self-love challenges the significations of other discourses: the discourse of masculinity is replaced by that of the family of colour when she asserts: 'A man ain't nothing but a man. ... But a son? Well now, that's *somebody*' (p. 23). It opposes the Eurocentric privileging of separateness and autonomy supported by masculinity[17] and which Sethe has internalised in her good mother position. It is not her valuing of motherhood which draws the community against Sethe, but her arrogance and self-sufficiency, 'trying to do it all alone with her nose in the air' (p. 254). As a good mother Sethe insists: 'I did it. I got us all out. ... had help, of course, lots of that, but still it was me doing it; me saying, *Go on*, and *Now*' (p. 162). But as Baby Suggs knows, 'Nobody could make it alone. ... You could be lost forever, if there wasn't nobody to show you the way' (p. 135). Sethe does not explicitly deny the help she was granted, but in the expectation – articulated through the killing of her children – that she has a right to an idealised family life, she is resisting a communal identification with the deprivation all the ex-slaves have experienced. Sethe not only had 'the amazing luck of six whole years of marriage' but also took this 'blessing ... for granted' (p. 23); when it was threatened, she performed a 'miracle' – the escape of all her children, plus herself, delivering her last child on the run. Her good mother discourse makes pretensions to an overweening responsibility, which includes overreaching rights. Paul D recognises that 'more important than what Sethe had done was what she claimed' (p. 164).

Motivating communal resentment of Sethe's extraordinary good fortune is not merely envy but what is seen as indifference to, or denial of, others' pain. The counterreaction to Baby Suggs' feast stems from the same source – the community sees her as unfairly privileged. [...] In a process akin to that described by psychoanalyst Alice Miller, those who have suffered feel very uncomfortable in the presence of those who (apparently) have not; the freedom of the latter reminds the former of the pain which they have been able to survive solely by repression; the only means to externalise this pain is to inflict it on the fortunate and as-yet pain-free Sethe.

As a result, the community fails to warn her of the approach of schoolteacher and the slavecatchers, and later, after the murder and arrest, deprives her of the communal 'mothering' which it would otherwise have offered:

> Otherwise the singing would have begun at once, the moment she appeared in the doorway of the house on Bluestone Road. Some cape of sound would have quickly been wrapped around her, like arms to hold and steady her on the way. As it was, they waited till the cart turned about, headed west to town. And then no words. Humming. No words at all.
>
> (p. 152)

This song is a version of Baby Suggs' song and dance in the Clearing, and is repeated nineteen years later in a reverse action, when the community joins to 'save' Sethe from Beloved. [...] This is the maternal semiotic – 'In the beginning there were no words. In the beginning was the sound, and they all knew what the sound sounded like' (p. 259) – which challenges the privileged and impossible discourse of the good mother.[18] In place of Sethe's outrageous claims to *exclusive* responsibility, the African-American community offers an extended social network of care and support. Crucially, it encourages *self*-love, by means of which the individual can receive the 'mothering' of which politics or circumstance may have deprived him- or herself.

Beloved's exposition of communal mothering offers an alternative to the individualism and autonomy privileged by classical psychoanalysis. According to this revised version, identity is constructed not within the narrow confines of the hegemonic nuclear family but in relation to the whole community. As Joan Riviere, an object relations theorist, puts it:

> There is no such thing as a single human being, pure and simple, unmixed with other human beings. Each personality is a world in himself [*sic*], a company of many. That self, that life of one's own ... is a composite structure which has been and is being formed and

built up since the day of our birth out of countless never-ending influences and exchanges between ourselves and others.[19]

Communal solidarity was nevertheless withheld from Sethe for nineteen years. The novel draws attention to the fine line that has to be drawn between support and indulgence in two significant instances. At one stage it appears that Sethe, Denver and Beloved offer each other a version of reciprocal mothering. The monologues of part two are finally intertwined into a polyphonic threnody, in which the three voices, initially distinct, merge into a single unified cry:

> I waited for you
> You are mine
> You are mine
> You are mine
>   (p. 217)

But while the mothering of community takes place in the social sphere of everyday life (exemplified in the care Denver receives when she looks for help), pre-Oedipal symbiosis between mother and grown-up infant is anti-social and destructive. Stamp Paid hears:

> a conflagration of hasty voices – loud, urgent, all speaking at once so he could not make out what they were talking about or to whom. The speech wasn't nonsensical, exactly, nor was it tongues. But something was wrong with the order of the words and he couldn't describe or cipher it to save his life. All he could make out was the word *mine*. The rest of it stayed outside his mind's reach.
>   (p. 172)

This is narcissism, not reciprocity. Secondly, Baby Suggs disapproves of 'extra': "'Everything depends on knowing how much,'" she said, and "Good is knowing when to stop"' (p. 87). She nevertheless ignores her own lesson in the celebration which so angers her neighbours, 'because she had overstepped, given too much, offended them by excess' (p. 138). Both incidents demonstrate a disregard for boundaries.

Once again the discourse of slavery circulates the same meanings as psychoanalysis. Pre-Oedipal dependence refuses to acknowledge the separate selfhood of the other; the brutal possessiveness of slavery, by defining one group of people as the property of another,

refuses to recognise their separate humanity. Slavery's greediness –
like the pre-Oedipal child's – is all-consuming. Sethe's inability to
recognise 'where the world stopped and she began' (p. 164) repli-
cates what Baby Suggs had 'learned from her sixty years a slave and
ten years free', that '[white people] ... don't know when to stop'
(p. 104). White functions as a metaphor for this indiscriminate
merging: Baby's final years are spent craving colour, a black
signifier, in opposition to '[t]hose white things [who] have taken all
I had or dreamed ... and broke my heartstrings too' (p. 89).
Whiteness, as an 'identity without boundaries, without definition,
without question',[20] swallows up difference, as the infant incorporates the mother, and then projects its own brutality onto the
signifiers of the other. [...] What has been projected is thus introjected, reproducing the savagery of white racism.

By juxtaposing a psychoanalytic discourse with its practices of
projection and introjection to the dominant discourses of slavery,
masculinity and the good mother, this essay has highlighted their
shared significations. Despite its individualistic pathologising, classical psychoanalysis, vigorously modified by object relations theory,
can be explored as one of the set of meanings which can be read
into, or onto, *Beloved*. The marginalised discourse of the black
community conveys solidarity and support not only through material practices of helping and sharing, but also through the social relations which nurture the individual's sense of self. Deprived of
pre-Oedipal bonding with mothers or caregivers, African-Americans
can learn to mother themselves through reciprocal self-love. At the
novel's close, Denver, Sethe and Paul D have all proceeded from re-
pressive isolation to a developed sense of self, reflected back from
the love they see in the eyes of others. No one, however, is looking
for (or at) Beloved, who is forgotten 'like a bad dream' (p. 274).
Thus a psychoanalytic reading of the novel allows us to explore not
only the psychic damage of slavery but its therapeutic alternative,
the cooperative self-healing of a community of survivors, forging a
'livable' (p. 198) life for themselves.

From *Modern Fiction Studies*, 38: 3–4 (Fall/Winter, 1993), 669–87.

NOTES

[As suggested in the Introduction, Jennifer FitzGerald is one of the critics
who see themselves as addressing not only Morrison's fiction but also

larger debates in black literary criticism. FitzGerald is concerned with the way in which psychoanalysis has isolated psychic experience from the diversities of ethnicity and class. For this reason, she suggests that psycho-analysis may not be a wholly appropriate methodology with which to approach African-American literature. FitzGerald's argument is that among psychoanalytic schools of thought, object relations theory (explained briefly in the Introduction) may be the most appropriate because it proposes that the psyche is constructed within a wide system of relationships. Her paper, like Cynthia Davis's essay (1), addresses how external social, cultural and political forces become internalised within the psyche. The publication of these two papers in the same volume affords an opportunity to compare psychoanalytic and Marxist-sociological approaches to the same subject, albeit in relation to different texts. While Davis appropriates Fredric Jameson's notion of the 'Third' and the institutionalisation of the 'Look', FitzGerald focuses on the processes of 'projection' and 'intro-jection' (described by Melanie Klein: see Introduction, p. 15) which she sees as characterising most relationships in the novel. This process is evident in each character who confronts psychic trauma. Kleinian discourse is concerned with the psychic struggle prior to subjectivity. *Beloved* is con-cerned with characters trying to acquire the subject position of which slavery has robbed them. Like many critics of Morrison's work, FitzGerald has found that discussion of the wider relationships in which African-American psyches are constructed demands a complex theoretical base. In order to analyse the different subject positions to which Morrison's characters avail themselves in response to traumatic experiences, she draws both on object relations theory and on discourse analysis. This dual approach, together with the widened perspective of object relations compared with classical psychoanalysis, enables FitzGerald to explore not only the psychic damage of slavery but its therapeutic alternative, the supportive community.

Critics, such as Rigney (essay 3), employing other methodologies have, like FitzGerald, arrived at the importance of community in Morrison's work. Some critics such as Dubey (essay 4) in the extract reprinted from her book, *Black Women Novelists and the Nationalist Aesthetic*, have argued that the representation of community in Morrison's fiction is often ambivalent. The original aspects of FitzGerald's essay are her argument that the existence of the wider black community confounds classic psycho-analytic approaches to African-American writings and her use of Kleinian psychoanalysis to rationalise the relationships between characters in *Beloved*, especially that between Beloved and Sethe. Thus Beloved as a character can be read as a psychically damaged child – locked within the pre-Oedipal state – and as a fantasy object for the emotions of others. Beloved's obsession with Sethe is characterised by FitzGerald as pre-Oedipal. Like the baby in Kleinian psychoanalysis, she displays excessive dependence and is prey to ambivalent feelings – the resultant insecurity of which intensifies her aggression. In a part of the essay which for reasons of space we have not been able to reproduce, FitzGerald argues that Denver, too, transfers her dependence from Sethe on to Beloved and thus experiences a similar psychic disintegration. But she eventually negotiates her way into selfhood and society. Ed.]

1. An excerpt from this essay was presented at the Colloquium 'African-American Literature Today: Critical Approaches' in May 1993 at the Institut Charles V, Université de Paris VII. I should like to thank Maria Stuart, and especially Maureen McNeil and Peter Stoneley, whose suggestions and feedback on previous versions have been invaluable.

2. These critics include Marianne Hirsch, *The Mother–Daughter Plot: Narrative, Psychoanalysis, Feminism* (Bloomington, IN, 1989); Rebecca Ferguson, 'History, Memory and Language in Toni Morrison's *Beloved*', in Susan Sellers (ed.), *Feminist Criticism: Theory and Practice* (Hemel Hempstead, 1991), pp. 109–27; Barbara Offutt Mathieson, 'Memory and Mother Love in Morrison's *Beloved*', *American Imago*, 47:1 (1990), 1–21; Mae G. Henderson, 'Toni Morrison's *Beloved*: Re-Membering the Body as Historical Text', in Hortense Spillers (ed.), *Comparative American Identities* (London and New York, 1991), pp. 62–86; Barbara Schapiro, 'The Bonds of Love and the Boundaries of Self in Toni Morrison's *Beloved*', *Contemporary Literature*, 23 (1991), 194–210; Stephanie A. Demetrakopoulos, 'Maternal Bonds as Devourers of Women's Individuation in Toni Morrison's *Beloved*', *African American Review*, 26 (1992), 51–9; and Jean Wyatt, 'Giving Body to the Word: The Maternal Symbolic in Toni Morrison's *Beloved*', *PMLA*, 108 (1993), 474–88.

3. See Elizabeth Abel, 'Race, Class, and Psychoanalysis? Opening Questions', in Marianne Hirsch and Evelyn Fox (eds), *Conflicts in Feminism* (London and New York, 1990), pp. 184–204; Elizabeth V. Spelman, *Inessential Woman: Problems of Exclusion in Feminist Thought* (1988; rpt London, 1990).

4. See Denise Riley, *War in the Nursery: Theories of the Child and Mother* (London, 1983); Valerie Walkerdine and Helen Lucey, *Democracy in the Kitchen: Regulating Mothers and Socialising Daughters* (London, 1989); Valerie Nice, *Mothers and Daughters: The Distortion of a Relationship* (London, 1992).

5. See Andrew Billingsley, *Climbing Jacob's Ladder: the Enduring Legacy of African-American Families* (New York, 1992); Herbert G. Gutman, *The Black Family in Slavery and Freedom: 1750–1925* (New York, 1976); bell hooks, 'Homeplace: A State of Resistance', *Yearning: Race, Gender and Cultural Politics* (London, 1991), pp. 41–9; Deborah Gray White, 'Ain't I a Woman?', *Female Slaves in the Plantation South* (New York, 1985).

6. The object relations school is based on and developed out of the work of Melanie Klein. See Juliet Mitchell (ed.), *The Selected Melanie Klein*

(1986; rpt London, 1991); Alice Balint, 'Love for the Mother and Mother Love' (1939), in Michael Balint, *Primary Love and Psycho-Analytical Technique* (New York, 1986), pp. 109–27; D. W. Winnicott, *Playing and Reality* (London, 1971); Nancy Chodorow, *Feminism and Psycho-Analytic Theory* (New Haven, CT, 1989); Jessica Benjamin, *The Bonds of Love: Psychoanalysis, Feminism, and the Problem of Domination* (1988; rpt London, 1990).

7. Elizabeth Abel, 'Race, Class, and Psychoanalysis? Opening Questions', p. 186.

8. Julian Henriques et al., *Changing the Subject: Psychology, Social Regulation and Subjectivity* (London, 1984), pp. 105–6.

9. For other integrations of psychoanalysis and discourse theory, see Wendy Holloway, 'Gender Difference and the Production of Subjectivity', in Henriques et al., pp. 227–63.

10. Marsha Jean Darling, 'In the Realms of Responsibility: A Conversation with Toni Morrison', *Women's Review of Books* (March, 1988), 5–6.

11. Juliet Mitchell (ed.), *The Selected Melanie Klein*, pp. 148–9.

12. D. W. Winnicott, *Playing and Reality* (London, 1971), pp. 111–18.

13. Juliet Mitchell (ed.), *The Selected Melanie Klein*, p. 120.

14. Michael Balint (ed.), *Primary Love and Psycho-Analytic Technique*, p. 120.

15. Ibid., pp. 119–20.

16. Elizabeth Abel, 'Race, Class, and Psychoanalysis? Opening Questions', p. 185.

17. Deborah Ayer Sitter, 'The Making of a Man: Dialogic meaning in *Beloved*', *African American Review*, 26 (1992), 24.

18. Kristeva's account of the semiotic quotes another revision of the scriptual phraselogy from Celine: 'In the beginning was emotion. The Word came next to replace emotion as the trot replaces the gallop.' See Julia Kristeva, *Desire in Language: A Semiotic Approach to Literature and Art*, ed. Leon S. Roudiez, trans. Thomas Gora, Alice Jardine and Leon S. Roudiez (Oxford, 1980), p. 144.

19. Quoted by Nancy Chodorow, *Feminism and Psychoanalytic Theory*, p. 158.

20. Claire Pajaczkowska and Lola Young, 'Racism, Representation, Psychoanalysis', in James Donald and Ali Rattansi (eds), *Culture and Difference* (London, 1992), pp. 198–219.

8

Knitting and Knotting the Narrative Thread – *Beloved* as Postmodern Novel

RAFAEL PÉREZ-TORRES

Beloved weaves a story on a singular frame: interpretation represents an integral part of black cultural and social identity. In Toni Morrison's book, the fictional characters and communities – as objects of exploitation in both slave and free-market societies – transform an essential absence into a powerful presence. A sense of self emerges from experiences of exploitation, marginalisation and denial. Analogously, Morrison's narrative, confronting a facelessness the dominant culture in America threatens to impose on black expression, forges out of cultural and social absence a voice and identity. *Beloved* creates an aesthetic identity by playing against and through the cultural field of postmodernism.

At a very basic level, this engagement with postmodernism manifests itself in the aesthetic play of the novel. Throughout, *Beloved* demonstrates its concern with linguistic expression: the evocation of both oral and written discourses, the shifting from third person narration to omniscient narration to interior monologue, the iteration and reiteration of words and phrases and passages. While this linguistic and narrative variation is evocative of an oral literature that shapes and retraces various tellings of the same story, it also demonstrates a concern (characteristic of experimental twentieth-century literary discourses) with the production and meaning of language. The text thus spins a story woven of myth that creates a

128

pattern of sophisticated linguistic play. There is a crossing of genres and styles and narrative perspectives in *Beloved* that suggests it filters the absent or marginalised oral discourse of a pre-capitalist black community through the self-conscious discourse of the contemporary novel. The narrative emerges, then, at the point at which premodern and postmodern forms of literary expression cross.

The action in *Beloved* turns on processes of reinscription and reinterpretation. It intertwines the mythic, folkloric and poetic threads of an oral literature with the rhetorical and discursive trajectories of a postmodern literary landscape. The novel stands amid a cultural context in which play, allusion, quotation serve as privileged aesthetic techniques. *Beloved* and other novels that emerge from multicultural histories diverge from classically postmodern texts – Pynchon's *V*, Barth's *Giles Goat-Boy*, Barthelme's *The Dead Father* – in their relation to socio-historical realities. Henry Louis Gates has, for example, discussed the theoretical basis of black literature. His work has placed in a new light a tired issue: what distinguishes black literary production in the Americas from other literary works? He positions the question thusly: 'the problem, for us, can perhaps be usefully stated in the irony implicit in the attempt to posit a "black self" in the very Western languages in which blackness itself is a figure of absence, a negation. Ethnocentrism and "logocentrism" are profoundly interrelated in Western discourse as old as the *Phaedrus* of Plato, in which one finds one of the earliest figures of blackness as absence, a figure of negation.'[1] The question from this view becomes not how African-American literary production distinguishes itself from other forms, but rather how – given socio-historical conditions compelling it towards silence – the literature manages to speak at all. Gates's work looks at the ways linguistic structures at once mask and reveal the social and political structures from which they arise and which they create. How can black writers, Gates questions, use a language in which blackness signifies absence to write about their own 'blackness' as a source of identity? Gates will finally come to argue that black writers have had to digest both Western and non-Western forms of literary production. Out of this process they forge a literary discourse that transforms notions of blackness.

The 'blackness' of black literary texts, historically read to signify a lack in Western discourse, becomes in Morrison's hands an important thread tying together the sometimes (especially in a North American context) all too disparate realms of politics and aesthetics. The 'not' signified by blackness becomes for Morrison a means by which to weave her tale. A process of interpretation and reinterpretation in *Beloved* serves to form an 'is' out of the 'nots', helps untie the tangled threads by which Morrison knits together her novel. *Beloved* challenges us to rethink the relationship between the postmodern and the marginal, to bind together seemingly separate cultural realms. The novel forces us to retrace the distinct threads of the historically marginal that colour the weave of postmodern culture.

Absence informs several levels of the narration and is made tangible from the first page of *Beloved*. The several historical and geographical facts we are given (the action is set near Cincinnati, Ohio; the year is 1873; the address of the house is 124 Bluestone Road) do nothing to obviate the sense of loss that pervades the narrative's opening. We are told that the grandmother, Baby Suggs, is dead and the sons, Howard and Buglar, have run away. Only the escaped slave Sethe, married to Baby Suggs's son Halle, and her daughter Denver remain. Though free, they are scorned by their community and are the victims of a ghostly presence, a 'spite' that fills the house at 124 Bluestone Road. The concrete historic and geographic specificity that opens the narrative stands opposed to the equally concrete absences evident in the story: the missing ancestor and the missing descendants. Readers are placed generationally in a space that floats somewhere between an absent past and an absent future. Into this static fictional present a ghostly past perpetually attempts to insert itself.

Absence is also present through to the last page of the novel. The reader is told numerous times that Beloved's story 'is not a story to pass on' (p. 275). 'Pass on' signifies both rejection and acceptance. Beloved's story cannot be repeated, the narrative warns, cannot be allowed to occur again in the world. The repeated warning also means that this is a story that cannot be forgotten, that cannot be rejected or 'passed' on. Thus the close of the novel evokes again the motif of absence and presence by ambiguously suggesting that Beloved's story should neither be forgotten nor repeated.

The interplay between presence and absence, accepting and rejecting, appearing and disappearing, repeats and resurfaces throughout the course of *Beloved*. The demarcation in the text between life and death (the ultimate distinction in the modern world between existence and extinction) blurs and is erased. Obviously this is the case as Beloved, Sethe's murdered child, returns incarnate. It is a motif, however, evident from the very first scene of the book. Though dead, Baby Suggs is from beginning to end a felt and seen presence in the narrative. We are given her image: an old crippled woman, lying in bed, hovering between the memories of an uneasy life and the certainty of a restless death. Too demoralised to care that her grandsons have run off, she is concerned only with the small satisfaction of meditating upon scraps of coloured cloth: 'suspended between the emptiness of life and the meanness of the dead, she couldn't get interested in leaving life or living it, let alone the fright of two creeping-off boys. Her past had been like her present – intolerable – and since she knew death was anything but forgetfulness, she used the little energy left her for pondering color' (p. 6). We come to learn of Baby Suggs's slave past that had 'busted her legs, back, head, eyes, hands, kidneys, womb and tongue' (p. 87). Her son Halle, who had at the old plantation Sweet Home hired himself out every Sunday for five years in order to buy her freedom, has not managed to make it north to be with his mother, wife and daughter. Baby Suggs has had to become accustomed to absences. And in this she is not alone.

The story of slavery invoked by *Beloved* and endured by Baby Suggs is premised on the absence of power, the absence of self-determination, the absence of a homeland, the absence of a language. The action of the novel incorporates these historical conditions and draws attention to their many results. The absence of Mr Garner, who had been a temperate force of oppression at Sweet Home, leads to the slaves' flight. The absence of her children who had escaped earlier and gone ahead of their parents drives Sethe to continue her arduous journey north to Ohio. The absence of Halle leads her to wait for his return and is one of the causes for Baby Suggs's withdrawal into her small world of coloured cloth. Sethe learns the lessons of absence and refuses to turn her children over to the slave catchers who have come to take her family back to Sweet Home, eluding capture only by murdering her child. The presence of her baby's ghost as well as its eventual reincarnation serve as a constant reminder of the absence and longing that have led Sethe and Denver to take refuge in their isolated world at 124 Bluestone.

Absence thus comprises the past and the present of the characters' lives in *Beloved*. Before a presence can be forged from all these absences, the logic that equates black with blank needs to be examined. Consistently, the main absences the characters endure lie in the insulting and violating practice of commodification Baby Suggs and all her people have had to learn to survive:

> in all of Baby's life, as well as Sethe's own, men and women were moved around like checkers. Anybody Baby Suggs knew, let alone loved, who hadn't run off or been hanged, got rented out, loaned out, bought up, brought back, stored up, mortgaged, won, stolen or seized. So Baby's eight children had six fathers. What she called the nastiness of life was the shock she received upon learning that nobody stopped playing checkers just because the pieces included her children.
>
> (p. 23)

Commodity and exchange serve as the only form of interaction between blacks and whites in *Beloved*. This exchange on its most basic level involves the marketing of human beings, but exchange also occurs in a more subtle though no less invidious manner. The abolitionists who use Sethe's plight to further their cause turn her story into currency. Their concern is not with her as an individual, but with her as a case. Her story disappears in their rush to turn her case into abolitionist propaganda. This causes Sethe to shy away from repeating her narrative and leads her to put her story away so it can neither be misused nor misunderstood. Only later, with Beloved's re-emergence, does the story of a mother driven to desperation and murder too re-emerge. The relation of Sethe's story opens between her, Beloved and Denver channels of exchange (aesthetic, social, personal) similar to the channels of charitable exchange evident among the black community in the novel. The novel thus posits forms of exchange that provide alternatives to modern forms of market exchange.

Morrison's narrative sketches a relation between the black community and material goods that is governed by the use value of those commodities. Her aesthetic creation is spun out of a historical period in which the industrial has not yet infused the lives of the characters. This aspect in some measure explains how many of Morrison's works explicitly or implicitly focus on elements of rural, pre-industrial life. By presenting monetary exchange only through the buying or selling of slaves, the narrative suggests a nostalgia for the premodern that implicitly focuses criticism on contemporary social organisation.

The evocation of exchange within the text does not suggest that absences are tied solely to economic exploitation. The reason Baby

Suggs's children are used as pieces in the slave traders' game is, of course, because of their colour. Thus one begins to grasp a vague pun woven into the text: Baby Suggs's fascination with colour comes as the result of her suffering a life of deprivation, a life, like her room, that is absent of colour ('except for two orange squares in a quilt that made the absence shout' [p. 38]). Colour becomes a metonym for the richness of life. Yet Baby Suggs's suffering is due precisely to the colour of her skin. The punning on Baby Suggs's fixation with 'color' is an appropriate verbal device for a narrative concerning and arising from a black culture. The word 'color' in this context is a sign for the literal concept of hue and visual perception. The concept undergoes a literary transformation whereby colour serves as a metonym for luxuriousness, comfort, pleasure. Simultaneously it serves to signal not just a racial group called 'black', but also the recent transformation in our language system in which the term 'colour' and 'coloured' were replaced by the terms 'African-American' and 'black'. The pun helps trace literal as well as historical, political and social patterns within the weave of the narrative. The language of the text, the effect of pun and play, constructs and dissolves structures that are at once linguistic and ideological.

So while Morrison's text shares narrative affinities with classically postmodern texts, it also suggests a connection between its narrative strategies and the socio-historical realities of Africans in the Americas. Gates argues that the Signifyin(g) of black narratives – the linguistic playing, punning, coding, decoding and recoding found in African-American texts – emerges from the pressing necessity for political, social, and economic survival:

> Black people have always been masters of the figurative: saying one thing to mean something quite other has been basic to black survival in oppressive Western cultures. Misreading signs could be, and indeed often was, fatal. 'Reading', in this sense, was not play; it was an essential aspect of the 'literacy' training of a child. This sort of metaphorical literacy, the learning to decipher codes, is just about the blackest aspect of the black tradition.[2]

The term 'play' suggests freedom, innocence, rebellion. The linguistic 'play' evident in *Beloved* results from the crossing of several discourses that have deadly serious political, social, and cultural implications. There is in *Beloved* no innocence, no aesthetic word play that does not simultaneously trace and erase various structures of political and cultural meaning. In this respect, *Beloved* and other multicultural novels distinguish themselves from the full-blown fancy found in texts often associated with the postmodern.

The allusions and processes of symbolic exchange evident in *Beloved* work over and over to re-entrench the narrative in a painful social and historical reality. Late in the novel, for example, Denver goes among the community in search of food and work in order to support her mother who has been incapacitated by the demanding return of her murdered daughter, Beloved. Seeking to enter the service of the Bodwins, the abolitionist family that helped settle Baby Suggs and Sethe on their arrival in Ohio, Denver notices a small figure of a black boy on the shelf:

> His head was thrown back farther than a head could go, his hands were shoved in his pockets. Bulging like moons, two eyes were all the face he had above the gaping red mouth. His hair was a cluster of raised, widely spaced dots made of nail heads. And he was on his knees. His mouth wide as a cup, held the coins needed to pay for a delivery or some other small service, but could just as well have held buttons, pins, or crab-apple jelly. Painted across the pedestal he knelt on were the words 'At Yo Service'.
>
> (p. 255)

The caricature here is cruel. Its image at once suggests commercial exchange (the coins held for delivery or small service), servitude (the kneeling figure), and the grotesquely twisted neck of a lynching victim. With this brief image the text exhibits a comprehensive critique of the commercial, racist and potentially violent nature of the dominant social order. The passage also evokes a series of puns: the 'service' of blacks equated with the 'service' of the small cup full of change, the taking of money from out of the black boy's mouth suggestive of the drawing upon the services performed by blacks, the presence of the grotesque boy 'At Yo Service' evident just as Denver is going to enter the service of the Bodwins. One meaning slides into the next.

The image of the black figurine suggests an instability of symbolic exchange at work in the novel. The significances of such words as 'color' and 'exchange' and 'service' configured by the image of the subservient change cup move towards a critique of social realities. The 'slipperiness' of language is foregrounded in the novel as words glide from one frame of reference to another, just as characters glide from one defining identity to another, and the form of the narrative from one genre to another. This shifting is due to the inadequacy of – the absences left by – previous literary, discursive, and social forms. As multiplicity and transformation come to form the privileged components of *Beloved*, the inadequacies of other avant-garde forms of literary expression are made present. In large part, the reason classically postmodern texts move away from connection with socio-historical reality is their commitment to the hermetic isolation of the aesthetic object. By comparison, multicultural texts place in the foreground the relation between language and power. In order to understand alterity and decentralisation as historically grounded phenomena rather than reified fetish, a critical postmodernism needs to take into account the profound relationship between language and power that multicultural texts address. [...]

The past mercilessly consumes Sethe. She has not found a language to effectively counteract the intolerance and violation traced by other discourses. Despite her best efforts to respond to a hopeless situation, despite her attempts to assert agency by becoming a speaking subject, Sethe finds herself subject to the tyranny of history.

Over and over, Sethe finds this tyranny associated with signs and language. She becomes a text upon which her white masters inscribe a discourse of slavery. She also becomes a text upon which patriarchy seeks to write. Sethe ponders why Paul D would want her, suddenly, to bear him a child. She suspects that he wants to use her body as a marker for establishing a legacy for himself: he will use her to have a child and thus leave a sign that he had passed that way. [...]

It is this tyranny to which Paul D refers when he tells Sethe, 'me and you, we got more yesterday than anybody. We need some kind of tomorrow' (p. 273). Paul D tries to move Sethe away from the destructive past towards a new beginning. Suggesting a movement beyond the structures of patriarchy and the violence of slavery, Paul D realises the need to rename and re-identify what their past was and, as a result, what their future may be. He wants to put his story next to hers, to rewrite and so reroute the course of their narrative.

After all, Beloved's story 'is not a story to pass on' (p. 275). Beloved passes away without a trace so that her memory, like a dream, can be forgotten. Her story needs to be closed off in order for new stories to be created. The world imaged in the narrative is shut off from further scrutiny. The last word of the text merges with the title of the novel. Together they form an inscription that creates a sense of finality even a tombstone could not provide: Beloved.

The drawing together of stories signals the primary strategy of Morrison's text. The novel works to weave together into one narrative stories seemingly as dissimilar as those Sethe and Paul D possess. Throughout, the text highlights the various processes by which stories, both traditional and contemporary, oral and written, are told. The tale of Sethe's escape and Denver's birth, the infanticide and the aftermath, are all told by or remembered through the consciousness of various characters – Denver, Sethe, Stamp Paid, Beloved – as well as through the voice of the modern narrator who frames the entire narrative. From the first page of the novel, this twentieth-century voice creates a tension between the fictional past and the moment of narration. The narrator explains that the site of the novel, 124 Bluestone Road, 'didn't have a number then, because Cincinnati didn't stretch that far. In fact, Ohio had been calling itself a state only seventy years ...' (p. 36). The narrative brings to the fore the temporal disjuncture between the narrative present and the fictional past characteristic of the novelistic form. *Beloved* also focuses on how stories are told by one person to another as a means of articulating the accumulated wisdom of communal thought and of hearing the dead through the voices of the living. The novel thus evokes numerous forms of narrative as it melds together ancient and contemporary literary forms in a critical postmodern pastiche.

Pastiche has become a loaded term within a contemporary discussion of postmodernism. On one hand the debate, as articulated by such critics as Hal Foster, views artists engaging in pastiche as 'foot-loose in time, culture, and metaphor'.[3] Fredric Jameson argues that pastiche is a neutral practice of parody 'without any of parody's ulterior motives, amputated of the satiric impulse, devoid of laughter. ... Pastiche is thus blank parody'.[4] In another camp, David Antin, discussing postmodern poetry, argues that the 'weaker' logical relations between the assembled objects of pastiche allow 'a greater degree of uncertainty of interpretation or, more specifically, more degrees of freedom in the reading of the sign-objects and their ensemble relations'.[5] Contra Jameson, in *Beloved* the use of pastiche is not a 'blank' parody, but rather a liberating technique which frees the signifier from a fixed frame of reference. In *Beloved*, the pastiche suggests that each narrative form evoked by the novel – novelistic, modernistic, oral, preliterate, journalistic – becomes a metanarrative at play in the field of the novel. Each form therefore loses its authoritative status. The levelling this implies – the seeming 'blankness' that so concerns Jameson – does not undercut the critique implicit in the novel. By evoking a historically decentred narrative – the communal voice articulating African-American experiences, for example – and placing it within the same discursive space as a powerful narrative – an aesthetically decentred but culturally privileged modernism – *Beloved* takes quite literally the decentring impulse that is supposed to inform postmodern culture.

From *Modern Fiction Studies*, 39:3–4 (Fall/Winter, 1993), 689–707.

NOTES

[Rafael Pérez-Torres' essay has similar starting points to some of the other essays included in this volume. Like other contributors, particularly Cynthia Davis and Jennifer FitzGerald, Pérez-Torres is concerned with how a sense of self in Toni Morrison's fiction emerges from experiences of exploitation, marginalisation and denial. As we saw earlier, Davis (essay 1) approaches the subject from a Marxist perspective derived largely from the work of Fredric Jameson. She focuses on how the institutionalisation of the white 'Look' reduces blacks to objects and then makes them feel inferior as objects. FitzGerald (essay 7), on the other hand, approaches the subject from an object relations psychoanalytic perspective emphasising the representation of psychic struggle prior to subjectivity. Pérez-Torres focuses on how absence is turned into a powerful presence in Morrison's fiction. The creation of a black identity out of exploitation and oppression is seen as analogous to Morrison's creation of an aesthetic identity in *Beloved* which counters the marginalisation and invisibility of black expression.

Like Rigney (essay 3), Pérez-Torres reminds us of a conundrum to which Henry Louis Gates, Jr, has drawn attention: how African-Americans have managed to write at all given the socio-historic forces determined to silence them. Whereas Rigney's solution is to turn to what she characterises as the radical nature of Morrison's prose, evidenced (as mentioned in the Introduction) in its use of songs, music and silence, Pérez-Torres is concerned with the ways in which the novel intertwines threads of myth and folklore from an oral culture with the sophisticated linguistic strategies of postmodern literature such as pastiche and metanarrative. Although they approach the novel from very different perspectives, both FitzGerald and

Pérez-Torres identify twin processes at work in *Beloved*. For FitzGerald, employing a Kleinian psychoanalytic perspective, the novel turns on a process of projection and introjection, while for Pérez-Torres, employing a postmodern perspective, it turns on a process of reinscription and reinterpretation. The texts which those in power inscribe with meaning are reinscribed by those who recode themselves as the subjects rather than the objects of that discourse.

Like many other critics of Morrison's work, including Rigney, Pérez-Torres highlights the importance of the power of naming and renaming. This is discussed as part of the interplay throughout the novel between presence and absence. The key absences upon which *Beloved* is premised are identified as the absences of power, of self-determination, of homeland, and of language. Like Rigney and FitzGerald, Pérez-Torres is concerned with the necessity of adapting European models to black literature. He argues that the postmodern features of *Beloved* coexist with African-American literary characteristics. These African-American features include punning, linguistic playfulness, coding, decoding and recoding and are what Henry Louis Gates, Jr, has labelled the 'Signifyin(g) practices' of black literature to which I referred in the Introduction. In *The Signifyin(g) Monkey: A Theory of African-American Literary Criticism* (New York and Oxford, 1988), Gates, Jr, finds that Signifyin(g) is an important trope in African-American literature originating in the vernacular traditions to be found in African, Latin-American and Caribbean culture, especially the tales of the Signifyin(g) Monkey. By Signifyin(g), he means the way one text Signifies upon another, by tropological revision or repetition and difference. So black people as the objects of racial parody are able to distance themselves from it by Signifyin(g) upon it.

Pérez-Torres argues that the specific historical reality with which *Beloved* is concerned is the major difference between African-American and Euro-American texts (Pérez-Torres labels the latter 'classically postmodern'). Rebecca Ferguson in 'History, Memory and Language in Toni Morrison's *Beloved*' (Susan Sellers and Linda Hutcheon [eds], *Feminist Criticism: Theory and Practice*, Toronto, 1991) argues that for African-American writers abandoning the constraints of realism and naturalism does not mean abandoning the traditional narratives of myth and legend or neglecting history. Pérez-Torres takes the argument further than Ferguson, suggesting that the African-American postmodern text highlights the relationship between language and power. He also argues that whereas *Beloved* is re-entrenched in a specific history where commodification and exchange serve as the only form of interaction between blacks and whites, the novel, like all Morrison's fiction, relies upon a communal, historically decentred narrative. Ed.]

1.   Henry Louis Gates, Jr (ed.), *Black Literature and Literary Theory* (London and New York, 1984), p. 7.

2.   Ibid., p. 6.

3.   Hal Foster, 'Against Pluralism', in Hal Foster (ed.), *Recordings: Art, Spectacle, Cultural Politics* (Port Townsend, 1985), pp. 13–32.

4.   Fredric Jameson, 'Postmodernism, or the Cultural Logic of Late Capitalism', *New Left Review*, 146 (1984), 53–92.

5.   David Antin, 'Modernism and Postmodernism: Approaching the Present in American Poetry', *boundary 2*, 1.1 (1972), 98–133.

9

Daughters Signifyin(g) History: The Example of Toni Morrison's *Beloved*

ASHRAF H. A. RUSHDY

Despite the dangers of remembering the past, African-American artists have insistently based a large part of their aesthetic ideal on precisely that activity. John Edgar Wideman prefaces his novel *Sent For You Yesterday* with this testament: 'Past lives in us, through us. Each of us harbours the spirits of people who walked the earth before we did, and those spirits depend on us for continuing existence, just as we depend on their presence to live our lives to the fullest.' This insistence on the interdependence of past and present is, moreover, a political act, for it advocates a revisioning of the past as it is filtered through the present. Wideman elsewhere has asked, 'What is history except people's imaginary recreation?' Racial memories, he suggests, 'exist in the imagination'. They are in fact a record of 'certain collective experiences' that 'have been repeated generation after generation'.[1]

As Toni Morrison has said, 'if we don't keep in touch with the ancestor ... we are, in fact, lost'. Keeping in touch with the ancestor, she adds, is the work of a reconstructive memory: 'Memory (the deliberate act of remembering) is a form of willed creation. It is not an effort to find out the way it really was – that is research. The point is to dwell on the way it appeared and why it appeared in that particular way.' This concern with the appearance, with the ideology of transmission, is though, only part of the overall trajectory of her revisionary project. Eventually her work, she states, must 'bear witness and identify that which is useful from the past and that which ought to be discarded'.[2] It must, that is, signify on the past and make it palatable for a present politic – eschewing that part of the past which has been constructed out of a denigrative ideology and reconstructing that part which will serve the present.

Morrison is both participant and theorist of this black aesthetic of remembering, and she has recently set out some of the mandates for establishing a form of literary theory that will truly accommodate African-American literature – a theory based on an inherited culture, an inherited 'history', and the understanding of the ways that any given artistic work negotiates between those cultural/historical worlds it inhabits. Moreover, not only does Morrison, following the line of Pauline Hopkins, delineate the 'dormant inmost feelings in that history'; she takes up, delicately yet resolutely, the task of reviving the very figures of that history.[3]

By taking a historical personage – a daughter of a faintly famous African-American victim of racist ideology – and constructing her as a hopeful presence in a contemporary setting, Morrison offers an introjection into the fields of revisionist historiography and fiction. She makes articulate a victim of a patriarchal order in order to criticise that order. Yet she portrays an unrelenting hopefulness in that critique. She does not inherit, as Deborah McDowell maintains some writers do, 'the orthodoxy of victimage', nor does she reduce her narrative to anything resembling what Henry Louis Gates Jr has called a 'master plot of victim and victimiser'.[4] She, like Ralph Ellison, returns to history not to find claims for reparation or reasons for despair, but to find 'something subjective, wilful, and complexly and compellingly human' – to find, that is, something for her art. She does so, moreover, by doing what Hortense Spillers claims Ishmael Reed does with the discursive field of slavery in his *Flight to Canada*: 'construct[ing] and reconstruct[ing] repertoires of usage out of the most painful human/historical experience.'[5] In articulating a reconstructive – critical and hopeful – feminist voice within the fields of revisionist historiography and contemporary fiction, what Morrison does is create daughters Signifyin(g) history.

RAISING *BELOVED*: A REQUIEM THAT IS A RESURRECTION

Morrison thought that her most recent book would be the least read of her novels because it would be perceived to be a work dealing with slavery, an institution that is willingly placed under erasure by what she calls a 'national amnesia': 'I thought this has got to be the least read of all the books I'd written because it is about something the characters don't want to remember, I don't want to remember, black people don't want to remember, white people don't want to remember.' But *Beloved* is not about slavery as an institution; it is 'about those *anonymous* people called slaves'.[6]

Morrison's sense of ambivalence, of wishing to forget and remember at the same time, is enacted in her attitude to the story and its characters. Speaking about the writing of *Beloved*, she declares her wish to invoke all those people who are 'unburied, or at least unceremoniously buried', and go about 'properly, artistically, burying them'. However, this burial's purpose, it would appear, is to bring them back into 'living life'. This tension between needing to bury the past as well as needing to revive it, between a necessary remembering and an equally necessary forgetting, exists in both the author and her narrative. We might better understand that tension by attending to the author's construction of the scenes of inspiration leading her to write this novel.

Morrison has said that the idea of *Beloved* was inspired by 'two or three little fragments of stories' that she had 'heard from different places'.[7] The first was the story of Margaret Garner, a slave who in January 1856 escaped from her owner Archibald K. Gaines of Kentucky, crossed the Ohio River, and attempted to find refuge in Cincinnati. She was pursued by Gaines and a posse of officers. They surrounded the house where she, her husband Robert, and their four children were harboured. When the posse battered down the door and rushed in, Robert shot at them and wounded one of the officers before being overpowered. According to Levi Coffin, 'at this moment, Margaret Garner, seeing that their hopes of freedom were vain, seized a butcher knife that lay on the table, and with one stroke cut the throat of her little daughter, whom she probably loved the best. She then attempted to take the life of the other children and to kill herself, but she was overpowered and hampered before she could complete her desperate work.'[8] Margaret Garner chose death for both herself and her most beloved rather than accept being forced to return to slavery and have her children suffer an institutionalised dehumanisation. The story of Margaret Garner was eventually to become the historical analogue of the plot of *Beloved*.[9]

Morrison said that what this story made her realise was that 'the best thing that is in us is also the thing that makes us sabotage ourselves' ('Conversation', 585). The story of Margaret Garner stayed with Morrison, representing, albeit unclearly, something about feminine selflessness. It took another story to clarify more precisely what Margaret Garner and her story meant.

Morrison found that story in Camille Billops's *The Harlem Book of the Dead* – an album featuring James Van der Zee's photographs of Harlem funerals. These were photographs, Morrison has said, that had a 'narrative quality'. One photograph and its attendant story in particular caught her attention:

> In one picture, there was a young girl lying in a coffin and he [Van der Zee] says that she was eighteen years old and she had gone to a party and that she was dancing and suddenly she slumped and they noticed there was blood on her and they said, 'What happened to you?' And she said, 'I'll tell you tomorrow. I'll tell you tomorrow.' That's all she would say. And apparently her ex-boyfriend or somebody who was jealous had come into the party with a gun and a silencer and shot her. And she kept saying, 'I'll tell you tomorrow' because she wanted him to get away. And he did, I guess; anyway, she died.
>
> ('Conversation', 584)

After reading the narrative of Margaret Garner, Toni Morrison had thought she glimpsed an opaque truth that she had always known, somehow: 'But that moment, that decision was a piece, a tail of something that was always around, and it didn't get clear for me until I was thinking of another story.'

When Van der Zee provided that next story, Morrison saw clearly what she'd glimpsed through a darker glass: 'Now what made those stories connect, I can't explain, but I do know that, in both instances, something seemed clear to me. A woman loved something other than herself so much. She had placed all of the value of her life in something outside herself. That the woman who killed her children loved her children so much; they were the best part of her and she would not see them sullied' ('Conversation',

584). In 1978, nine years before the publication of *Beloved*, Morrison started attempting to formulate the terms of that tension between remembering and forgetting, burying and reviving. In the Foreword to *The Harlem Book of the Dead* she writes: 'The narrative quality, the intimacy, the humanity of his photographs are stunning, and the proof, if any is needed, is in this collection of photographs devoted exclusively to the dead about which one can only say, "How living are his portraits of the dead". So living, so "undead", that the prestigious writer, Owen Dodson, is stirred to poetry in which life trembles in every metaphor.'[10] One of Owen Dodson's 'living' poems is on the page facing the picture of the young girl as she lies in her coffin:

> They lean over me and say:
> 'Who deathed you who,
> who, who, who, who ...
> I whisper: 'Tell you presently ...
> Shortly ... this evening ...
> Tomorrow ...'
> Tomorrow is here
> And you out there safe.
> I'm safe in here, Tootsie.
>   (pp. 52–3)

If Van der Zee's photographs give renewed life to the dead, so does Dodson's poetry give renewed voice. Across from a picture of a girl in a coffin resides her living voice, her expression of the safety of death. As early as 1973, Morrison had been concerned with making the dead articulate. When Sula dies, she feels her face smiling: '"Well, I'll be damned", she thought, "it didn't even hurt. Wait'll I tell Nell".'[11]

In 1987, with *Beloved*, Morrison goes further in giving the dead voice, in remembering the forgotten. *Beloved* is, in effect, a requiem that is a resurrection. The most obvious example of this commemoration is Beloved herself, the ghost of Margaret Garner's unnamed child: 'So I just imagined the life of a dead girl which was the girl that Margaret Garner killed, the baby girl that she killed. ... And I call her Beloved so that I can filter all these confrontations and questions that she has in that situation' ('Conversation', 585). Beloved is more than just a character in the novel, though. She is the embodiment of the past that must be remembered in order to be forgotten; she symbolises what must be reincarnated in order to be buried, properly: 'Everybody knew what she was called, but nobody anywhere knew her name. Disremembered and unaccounted for, she cannot be lost because no one is looking for her.'[12]

In the end, though, Beloved is not the most important character in Morrison's revisionist strategy. That character is Denver, the other daughter. Morrison's original intent in the novel, she said in 1985, was to develop the narrative of Beloved into the narrative of Denver. First she would imagine the life of the murdered child, 'to extend her life, you know, her search, her quest, all the way through as long as I care to go, into the twenties where it switches to this other girl'. This 'other girl', Denver, is the site of hope in Morrison's novel. She is the daughter of history. Nonetheless, as Morrison emphasises, even when Denver becomes the focus of the narrative's attention, 'Beloved will be there also' ('Conversation', 585). Before turning to the novel, and determining how Morrison inscribes hope into a critical revision of history, let us return briefly to the narrative of Margaret Garner in order to see the history that she revises.

TOWARDS *BELOVED*: MARGARET GARNER

It was sometime in January 1856 that Margaret Garner attempted her escape and killed her daughter. The story and the ensuing court case were reported in the Cincinnati newspapers and reported again in *The Liberator* in March 1856. Another detailed narrative appeared in the *Annual Report of the American Anti-Slavery Society* in 1856.[13] The newspaper coverage may have been motivated by a variety of reasons, some of them, one intuits, having to do with the exoticism of the story. In much the same way, Jim Trueblood of Ralph Ellison's *Invisible Man* becomes the focus of white attention after he commits incest with his daughter:

> The white folks took up for me. And the white folks took to coming out here to see us and talk with us. Some of 'em was big white folks, too, from the big school way across the State. Asked me lots 'bout what I thought 'bout things, and 'bout my folks and the kids, and wrote it all down in a book ... That's what I don't understand. I done the worse thing a man could ever do in his family and instead of chasin' me out of the country, they gimme more help than they ever give any other colored man, no matter how good a nigguh he was.[14]

In *Beloved* Morrison has Paul D respond to the media attention Sethe gets for infanticide in much the same way as the 'invisible man' responds to Trueblood's story:

> Because there was no way in hell a black face could appear in a newspaper if the story was about something anybody wanted to hear. A whip of fear broke through the heart chambers as soon as you saw a Negro's face in a paper, since the face was not there because the person had a healthy baby, or outran a street mob. Nor was it there because the person had been killed, or maimed or caught or burned or jailed or whipped or evicted or stomped or raped or cheated, since that could hardly qualify as news in a newspaper. It would have to be something out of the ordinary – something white-people would find interesting, truly different, worth a few minutes of teeth sucking if not gasps. And it must have been hard to find news about Negroes worth the breath catch of a white citizen of Cincinnati.[15]
>
> (pp. 155–6)

As Levi Coffin noted, the Margaret Garner case 'attracted more attention and aroused deeper interest and sympathy' than any other he'd known (I'll return to the importance of this critique of print media later).

The case became a forum for 'that noble anti-slavery lawyer' John Jolliffe, counsel for the defence, to argue that the 1850 Fugitive Slave Law was unconstitutional. Lucy Stone, who visited Garner in jail, spoke to the crowd outside her trial, describing Garner as a quintessentially American hero: 'I thought the spirit she manifested was the same with that of our ancestors to whom we had erected a monument at Bunker Hill – the spirit that would rather let us all go back to God than back to slavery.' A year and a half after her trial, Garner had become a symbol for what Frederick Douglass called his 'philosophy of reform'. Addressing an assembly celebrating the twenty-third anniversary of West Indian Emancipation, Douglass proclaimed:

> The whole history of the progress of human liberty shows that all concessions yet made to her august claims, have been born of earnest struggle. The conflict has been exciting, agitating, all-absorbing, and for the time being, putting all other tumults to silence. It must do this or it does nothing. If there is no struggle there is no progress. ... This struggle may be a moral one, or it may be a physical one, but it must be a struggle. Power concedes nothing without a demand. It never did and it never will. Find out what any people will quietly

submit to and you have found out the exact measure of injustice and wrong which will be imposed upon them. ... The limits of tyrants are prescribed by the endurance of those whom they oppress. ... If we ever get free from the oppressions and wrongs heaped upon us, we must pay for their removal. We must do this by labor, by suffering, by sacrifice, and if needs be, by our lives and the lives of others.

 Hence, my friends, every mother who, like Margaret Garner, plunges a knife into the bosom of her infant to save it from the hell of our Christian Slavery, should be held and honored as a benefactress.[16]

As late as 1892, the story of Margaret Garner could be used to signify the extreme measures a person would take to escape what the lawyer Jolliffe called the 'seething hell of American slavery' and Douglass the 'hell of our Christian Slavery'.

In Frances E. W. Harper's *Iola Leroy*, Margaret Garner's case symbolised in the heroine's life what the author calls 'school-girl notions'. Iola is the daughter of the slaveowner Eugene Leroy and his wife Marie, who has 'negro blood in her veins'; Iola, when she attends school in the North, does not yet know her maternal racial background. In discussion with her fellow school-girls in the Northern school, Iola defends the institution of slavery, claiming that their slaves are 'content'. One of her schoolfriends disagrees: '"I don't know," was the response of her friend, "but I do not think that that slave mother who took her four children, crossed the Ohio River on the ice, killed one of the children and attempted the lives of the other two, was a contented slave".'[17] Significantly, when Iola does discover her racial heritage she begins a mission of education, the biggest part of which is the paper she reads to the Council Meeting at Mr Stillman's house, a paper entitled 'Education of Mothers'. Nameless now, Margaret Garner had become a political symbol for discontent. By 1948, Herbert Aptheker would cite the Margaret Garner case to argue why 'the Negro woman so often urged haste in slave plottings'. By 1981, Angela Y. Davis would echo him in arguing that the Margaret Garner case demonstrated not only the willingness of slave women to organise insurrections but also the unique desperation of the slave mother.[18]

 By 1987, Margaret Garner's story would inspire a Pulitzer prize-winning novel. Morrison has said that she does not know what eventually happened to Margaret Garner.[19] There are conflicting reports. According to Coffin and *The Liberator*, while Garner was being shipped back to Kentucky she jumped overboard with her baby; she was saved but her baby drowned. According to a report in the Cincinnati *Chronicle* and the Philadelphia *Press*, Margaret and her husband Robert worked in New Orleans and then on Judge Bonham's plantation in Mississippi until Margaret died of typhoid fever in 1858.[20] Whatever her fate, at Morrison's hands she has been buried in order to be resurrected into a new life, and she has been remembered in order that the institution she suffered may be forgotten.

SIGNIFYIN(G) ON HISTORY

Beloved, according to Stanley Crouch, one of its harshest reviewers, 'means to prove that Afro-Americans are the result of a cruel determinism'.[21] This criticism is a good place to start our discussion of the novel, not because Crouch has hit upon some truth regarding *Beloved* or Morrison (he has not) but because he demonstrates the sort of conclusion a reader may reach if unburdened by knowledge of the historical place of *Beloved's* writing, its historical analogue, and its critical position in the African-American aesthetic and politics of remembering history.

Beloved is the product of and a contribution to a historical moment in which African-American historiography is in a state of fervid revision. The debate currently ranges between those who argue that slavery led to the 'infantilisation' of adult Africans because the most significant relationship in any slave's life was that between the slave and the master, and those who argue that slaves formed viable internal communities, family structures, and protective personae that allowed them to live rich, coherent lives within their own system of values.[22] One premise underlying this debate is the question of whether slaves were acquiescent or resistant to the institution, whether they conformed to the 'Sambo' or 'Mammy' stereotypes who accepted their stations or whether they were in perpetual opposition to them – both in daily resistance and in sensational insurrections.[23] It is within this revisionary fray that *Beloved* may profitably be examined. The novel both remembers the victimisation of the ex-slaves who are its protagonists and asserts the healing and wholeness that those protagonists carry with them in their communal lives. Crouch, unfortunately, reads the novel as if it were a rendition only of victimisation, only of determinism; in other words, he misreads it.

Morrison has on more than one occasion asserted that she writes from a double perspective of accusation and hope, of criticising the past and caring for the future. She claims that this double perspective is the perspective of a 'Black woman writer' that is, 'one who look[s] at things in an unforgiving/loving way ..., writing to repossess, re-name, re-own'. In *Beloved*, this perspective is described as 'the glare of an outside thing that embraces while it accuses' (p. 271). It is on precisely this issue of a dual-vision that she marks the distinction between black men's writing and black women's: 'what I found so lacking in most black writing by men that seems to be present in a lot of black women's writing is a sense of joy, in addition to oppression and being women or black or whatever.'[24]

Morrison writes out of a dual perspective in order to re-possess, as I've suggested earlier, by remembering the ancestor, not only an aesthetic act but an act of historical recovery: 'roots are less a matter of geography than sense of shared history; less to do with place, than with inner space.'[25] Each act of writing a novel is for her an act of discovering deep within herself some relationship to a 'collective memory'. Memory itself, write Mary Frances Berry and John Blassingame, is for African-Americans 'an instrument of survival'. It is an instrument, writes Morrison, that can be traced back to an African heritage: 'it's true what Africans say: "The Ancestor lives as long as there are those who remember".'[26]

In the novel this truth is expressed by Sethe's mother-in-law. Baby Suggs knows that 'death was anything but forgetfulness' (p. 4). That remembering is both a resurrection and a pain is testified to by Amy Denver, who assisted in the birthing of Sethe's daughter: 'Anything dead coming back to life hurts.' The daughter Amy delivered testifies to that: 'A truth for all times, thought Denver' (p. 35). [...] In the novel [...] all the double perspectives of this black woman writer are expressed – remembering and forgetting, accusing and embracing, burying and reviving, joy and oppression.

From *American Literature*, 64: 3 (September, 1992), 566–97.

NOTES

[Ashraf Rushdy's essay is the opening argument of a paper which is unfortunately too long to reproduce in full here and which illustrates in substantial detail how Morrison Signifies history in *Beloved*. Rebecca Ferguson in 'History, Memory and Language in Toni Morrison's *Beloved*' (see head note to essay 8) argues that black writers such as Morrison have a complex perspective on black history. They see that it is a history of oppression which many African-Americans may rather forget – Morrison initially thought that *Beloved* would be the least read of her books because it dealt with slavery – but they also believe that it must be remembered and accounted for. Morrison's view that black history has been 'disremembered and unaccounted for' is considered in detail in Rushdy's paper from a new historicist perspective. Like Pérez-Torres (essay 8), Rushdy draws on the concept of Signifyin(g) which Henry Louis Gates, Jr, identified as a key trope in African-American literature. Rushdy reads *Beloved* as Signifyin(g) on the story of Margaret Garner, a slave who escaped from her owner and made the decision to kill her daughters and herself rather than return to slavery. Here Rushdy is using a definition of the concept of Signifyin(g) which is removed from its vernacular origins. Morrison's most important introjection into the Garner story is seen as establishing a context for what Sethe has done. In other words, Rushdy recognises that an important moment in the novel is Sethe's realisation, brought about with the help of Baby Suggs, that the responsibility for what she has done must lie with the system of slavery and the white slaveowners.

Rushdy's essay explores the nature of Morrison's own historicist perspective within the Signifyin(g) framework of the novel. Central to its thesis is Morrison's assertion that black women writers have a double perspective on the past, one which 'embraces while it accuses'. For Morrison, it is not for the black writer to discover what the past was really like, but to consider why it was like it was. Rushdy's new historicist approach has two areas of focus – the ideology of transmission and eschewing those aspects of the past which have been constructed out of a denigrative ideology. Rushdy sees the representation of Beloved, one of history's anonymous victims, as the most important revisionist strategy in the novel. As the incarnated memory of Sethe's guilt, Beloved is a symbol of unrelenting criticism. But while for Rushdy, Beloved is the unforgiving view of the past, Denver, who is in effect one of the children who survived the Garner story, is seen as embracing the past. Ed.]

1. John Edgar Wideman, *Sent For You Yesterday* (1983; rpt New York, 1988), prefatory page; John O'Brien (ed.), *Interviews With Black Writers* (New York 1973), pp. 220–1.

2. Toni Morrison, 'Rootedness: The Ancestor as Foundation', in Mari Evans (ed.), *Black Women Writers (1950–1980): A Critical Evaluation* (New York, 1984), pp. 339–45, especially p. 344; Morrison, 'Memory, Creation and Writing', *Thought: A Review of Culture and Idea*, 59 (December, 1984), 385–90, especially 385, 389. Cf. Morrison, 'City Limits, Village Values: Concepts of the Neighbourhood in Black Fiction', in Michael C. Jaye and Ann

Chalmers Watt (eds), *Literature and the Urban Experience: Essays on the City and Literature* (New Brunswick, 1980), pp. 35–43.

3. Toni Morrison, 'Unspeakable Things Unspoken: The Afro-American Presence in American Literature', *Michigan Quarterly Review*, 28 (Winter, 1989), 1–34, especially 11; cf. 25, where she describes how in the writing of *Tar Baby* she had to deal with 'the nostalgia for the history; the violence done to it and the consequences of that violence'. See Pauline Hopkins, *Contending Forces: A Romance Illustrative of Negro Life North and South* (Boston, 1900), pp. 13–14.

4. Deborah E. McDowell, 'Boundaries: Our Distant Relations and Close Kin', in Houston A. Baker, Jr and Patricia Redmond (eds), *Afro-American Literary Study in the 1990s* (Chicago, 1989), pp. 51–70, especially p. 70. Henry Louis Gates, Jr, 'Introduction', in Gates, Jr (ed.), *Reading Black, Reading Feminist: A Critical Anthology* (New York, 1990), pp. 1–17, especially p. 16.

5. Hortense J. Spillers, 'Changing the Letter: The Yokes, the Jokes of Discourse, or Mrs Stowe, Mr Reed', in Deborah McDowell and Arnold Rampersad (eds), *Slavery and the Literary Imagination* (Baltimore, MD, 1989), pp. 25–61, especially 52. See also Ralph Ellison, 'A Very Stern Discipline', in *Going to the Territory* (New York, 1986), pp. 275–307, especially pp. 276, 287–8. The term theory and typographical notation of 'Signifyin(g)' are all derived from the work of Henry Louis Gates, Jr, from his two formative essays, 'Literary Theory and the Black Tradition' and 'The "Blackness of Blackness": A Critique of the Sign and the Signifying Monkey', both in *Figures in Black: Words, Signs, and the 'Racial' Self* (New York, 1987), pp. 3–58, 235–76, and especially from his consummate book, *The Signifying Monkey: A Theory of African-American Literary Criticism* (New York, 1988).

6. Bonnie Angelo, 'The Pain of Being Black' [An Interview with Toni Morrison], *Time* (22 May 1989), 68–70, especially, 68. Morrison also expressed the difficulty of her chosen subject matter in *Beloved* to Sandi Russell, 'It's OK to Say OK', *Women's Review*, 5 (March 1986), 22–4; rpt in Nellie Y. McKay (ed.), *Critical Essays on Toni Morrison* (Boston, 1988), 43–54.

7. Gloria Naylor and Toni Morrison, 'A Conversation', *Southern Review*, 21 (1985), 567–93. [Cited as 'Conversation' in further text references.]

8. Levi Coffin, *Reminiscences of Levi Coffin* (Cincinnati, 1876), pp. 557–67.

9. The story of Margaret Garner's escape will seem familiar to some readers as a historical event replicating (four years after) the literary

event of Eliza's escape in Harriet Beecher Stowe's *Uncle Tom's Cabin*, chs 7 and 8. Eliza, too, crosses the semi-frozen Ohio River from Kentucky to escape Shelby. For the sources for the Eliza episode, see Stowe, *The Key to Uncle Tom's Cabin* (1853; rpt Port Washington, NY, 1968), pp. 21–3.

10. Toni Morrison, Foreword, Camille Billops, *The Harlem Book of the Dead* (New York, 1978).

11. Toni Morrison, *Sula* (New York, 1987), p. 149.

12. Toni Morrison, *Beloved* (New York, 1987), p. 274.

13. The story was reported in *The Liberator*, 26 (21 March 1856), 47, reprinted from the Cincinnati *Commercial*. [...] it was also reported in the Philadelphia Press (14 March, 1870). For the *Annual Report of the American Anti-Slavery Society* (New York, 1856), 44–7, see Philip S. Foner (ed.), *The Life and Writings of Frederick Douglass* [5 vols] (New York, 1950–75), 2, 568 n. 30.

14. Ralph Ellison, *Invisible Man* (New York, 1952), pp. 53, 67.

15. While hearing Trueblood relate this story to him and the white Mr Norton, the 'invisible man' thinks to himself 'How can he tell this to white men ... when he knows they'll say that all Negroes do such things?' (p. 57).

16. For Levi Coffin, John Jolliffe and Lucy Stone, see Coffin, *Reminiscences*, pp. 557, 548, 561, 562, 564–5. *Frederick Douglass*, 'West India Emancipation', *The Life and Writings*, 2, 426–39, especially 437.

17. Frances E. W. Harper, *Iola Leroy, or Shadows Uplifted* (1982; rpt Boston 1987), pp. 65, 98.

18. Herbert Aptheker, 'The Negro Woman', *Masses and Mainstream*, 11 (February 1948), 10–17; Angela Davis, *Woman, Race and Class* (New York, 1981), pp. 21, 29, 205.

19. Naylor and Morrison, 'A Conversation', 584.

20. Coffin, *Reminiscences*, p. 567.

21. Stanley Crouch, 'Aunt Medea', *New Republic* (19 October 1987), 38–43; especially 42.

22. See, for instance, Stanley M. Elkins, *Slavery: A Problem in American Institutional and Intellectual Life*, 3rd rev. edn (1959: Chicago, 1976), esp. pp. 223–310. [Rushdy provides a comprehensive list – too long to reprint here – of responses to Elkins. The reader should see George P. Rawick, *From Sundown to Sumup: The Making of the Black Community* (Westport, CT 1972). Ed.]

23. See Herbert Aptheker, *American Negro Slave Revolts* (1943; New York, 1987) and Rawick, *From Sundown to Sunup*, pp. 53–75.

24. Robert Stepto, '"Intimate Things in Place": A Conversation with Toni Morrison', in Michael S. Harper and Robert B. Stepto (eds), *Chant of Saints: A Gathering of Afro-American Literature, Art and Scholarship* (Urbana, IL, 1979), pp. 213–29, especially p. 225.

25. Russell, 'It's OK to Say OK', 43–7.

26. Claudia Tate, 'Toni Morrison [An Interview]' in Claudia Tate (ed.), *Black Women Writers at Work* (New York, 1983), pp. 118–31. Berry and Blasingame, 'Long Memory' and Morrison 'Foreword', *The Harlem Book of the Dead*.

10

Experiencing *Jazz*

EUSEBIO L. RODRIGUES

I

We may as well enter the novel by way of the one word title, *Jazz*, a stop consonant and a flatted monosyllable that extends into a voiced double sibilant. Like the muted soundsplash of a brush against a snare drum. 'Sth, I know that woman', a woman's voice cautions in a whisper, then it suddenly drops us, without warning, into a confusing world.

The confusion arises from the speed of the telling. Fragments of information rush along unconnectedly. A woman and a flock of birds; a man both sad and happy; he has shot an eighteen-year-old girl; Violet (the voice drops briefly, between commas, to touch on the woman's name) cuts up the girl's dead face at a funeral, then hurries back to her apartment where she sets the flock free 'to freeze or fly' (an unusual yoking of verbs and choices); one is a parrot that says, 'I love you'.

The voice, a written voice, hurtles along offering no explanations, dropping more bits of information that stubbornly refuse to come together and make sense: that the man, Joe Trace, is Violet's husband, that Violet is fifty and skinny, that the dead girl had a creamy face, that the girl has an aunt, that there's an upstairs neighbour, Malvonne. We read on impatiently, wanting to interrupt and ask questions, but this voice is in a reckless hurry to tell everything at once without stopping. It throws in additional information, about spring, about another girl, another threesome. It slows down at last, a little out of breath, hinting at some kind of mystery at the end: 'What turned out different was who shot whom' (p. 6). We read on, on, bewildered but intrigued, looking at the words, listening to their rhythm, their rhythms, seeking desperately to discover the meanings of the text. Halfway through the novel we pause to take stock, to put things together, to get our bearings.

A visual examination of the layout of *Jazz* reveals that it has no numbered chapters and no chapter titles to act as guides. The text has been cut into unnumbered unequal sections, ten of them, divided by blank pages that compel even the fast page turner to slow down. Each section is further cut into a number of unequal subsections: the first (pp. 1–21) has three subsections separated by two-line gaps; the last (pp. 219–29), seven.

Here is a musical score that has to be made to spring into audial life, into sound and rhythm and beat. The inner ear listens to what one reads, and the words begin to take wing, to leap into sound:

> Blues man, Black and bluesman. Blacktherefore blue man.
> Everybody knows your name.
> Where-did-she-go-and-why man. So-lonesome-I-could-die man.
> Everybody knows your name.
>
> (p. 119)

[...]

Jazz is made up of a number of such rhythmic paragraphs, subsections and sections that together compose a musical score. The novel has a loose fluid non-Aristotelian experimental form. Not the tight, climactic, Freytag-pyramid structure of conventional fiction, but the form of a jazz piece.[1] Toni Morrison oralises print. She also uses her language instrument to try out some daring modes and techniques of play and to create the informal, improvisatory patterning of jazz.

The visual layout – the lack of rigid chapter divisions, the unnumbered sections with blank pages in between, the unequal subsections separated by two-line gaps – appears to dissolve as word sounds begin to move. Toni Morrison produces a textual continuum by using transitional slurs and glides across sections. 'In a *hat* in the morning' ends one section; 'the *hat* pushed back on her forehead ...' the next section begins (pp. 87, 89; italics mine). 'Pain' opens another section, picking up the last wordsound, 'pain', of the previous section (pp. 216, 219). Two words 'spring' and 'city' act as a *glissando* causing two sections to slide together (pp. 114, 117).

'But where is *she*?', at the end of a section, is a dramatic question about Wild, the mother whom Joe hunts for in Vienna for the last time in 1906; the answer, two blank pages later, 'there she is', opens the next section and refers, strangely, not to Wild but to Dorcas in 1926 in the City (pp. 184, 187).

Such carry-overs make for rhythmic flow. Unlike the clearly demarcated movements of a symphony, the sections of *Jazz* never come to a complete stop. Like nonstop sequences during a jam session, they keep moving restlessly on and on giving the text a jazz feel. For Morrison tries to approximate not only the sounds of jazz but also the patterning. The first few pages, like a twelve-bar jazz 'tune' or set melody, tell in summary the whole story of Violet and Joe and Dorcas, a story repeated and modulated at the end by that of Violet and Joe and Felice, Dorcas' friend, 'another true-as-life Dorcas' (p. 197), as the narrator informs us. In between the beginning and the end are amplifications, with improvisations, variations and solo statements, a virtuoso display of jazz play. Morrison wants her fiction 'to recreate play and arbitrariness in the way narrative events unfold' ('Memory', p. 388). *Jazz* is a shimmering network of characters and of strands of action.

The characters are cross-connected in strange ways. Joe's Dorcas (whose biblical name means 'gazelle') is a city version and a repeat of the deer-eyed Wild, the mother who orphaned her newly born baby, never looked at it, or held it in her arms (p. 170). Young Joe hunted for a mother he never could find, and then discovers there-she-is Dorcas in the City in 1926. His Violet helped Joe escape the emptiness within himself in 1893, when he fell out of a walnut tree into her life. By marrying Violet, Joe rescued her from the dark memory of her mother, Rose Dear, who had flung herself into a well in 1892.

These story strands do not assume a plot pattern. Nor do they build to a climax or climb steadily to a crescendo. The narrative sets its own pace and meanders along through place and time, shifting between the City and the country, presenting freeflowing associated events in the lives of Joe and Violet and Dorcas, wandering off at times to relate the experiences of their friends and relations. And so we get to know a whole cast of tangential characters and events seemingly unconnected. We are told what happened to Joe and Violet before the move to the City in 1906. Orphan Joe's story is connected with that of Hunters Hunter, who was present when Wild gave birth to Joe and, as a father figure, taught him hunting skills and shaped his sensibility, especially his protective regard for women.

We also come to know in some detail the story of Hunters Hunter who, as a boy, was briefly involved with a rich landowner's daughter, Vera Louise Gray. The strange by-product of their sexual escapades would have been just a 'mortification' to be disposed of (p. 178), had the baby not had radiantly golden skin and, later, gray eyes. Golden Gray was raised and spoiled by his mother in Baltimore, helped by her servant, True Belle, Violet's grandmother, who also adored the little boy with his golden curls.

At eighteen, told by his mother that his father was 'a black-skinned nigger' (p. 145), in despair perhaps at the paradox of being a white black, then told what he has to do by True Belle, Golden Gray journeys to Vienna to discover and, perhaps, to kill his father. On the way he encounters Wild and, fascinated by her, she 'of luminous eyes and lips to break your heart' (p. 155), forgets his mission of vengeance and disappears with her into the woods, after assisting at the birth of Joe. The strange story of Joe, the strange attendants at his strange birth and his unsuccessful quest for his mother, reads like a primitive folk tale with mythic overtones.

More down to earth is the interconnected story of Violet and her family, a tragic story of poverty and dispossession, with an absent father (involved in some way with the Virginia Readjusters, but of no real help to his own family) and a mother who commits suicide. It is the grandmother, True Belle, a former slave, who rescues the family from despair and teaches them the lessons of laughter and survival. She is what Morrison has termed the 'advising, benevolent, protective, wise Black ancestor' ('City Limits', p. 39), the tribal mother in whom rests the wisdom of the race, the saviour figure who propels Violet to Palestine where she meets Joe and acquires inner strength and confidence.

These intertwined strands of stories seem to lead nowhere and appear to lack coherence and pattern. Of all the characters, only Joe and Violet migrate to the City where they are involved with Malvonne, the Traces's upstairs neighbour from whom Joe rents a room for his meetings with Dorcas, and with Alice Manfred, Dorcas' aunt, who brought the eight-year-old orphan from riot-torn East St. Louis to live with her in Harlem. The other stories are incomplete. Some characters disappear. We never know what happens to Hunters Hunter – neither does Joe. Nor is the mystery of Wild and of Golden Gray ever solved. We never see them again.

What we are left with is what Joe sees in 1906: a cave, sunlit and set in a rock formation above a flowing river named Treason by white folks, and unmistakable signs of domesticity and peace within (p. 184). But where is *she*, Joe's question, triggers other questions never answered: what? who? why?

Why? we too ask. Why the strange patterning, the crazy chronology, why not focus on the story of Joe and Violet and Dorcas? Answers suggest themselves. More than just a story of three individuals, the novel, a continuation of *Beloved*, jazzifies the history of a people. Morrison extends the range of her fictional world by giving us rapid and vivid glimpses of their life in the rural South after emancipation.

The stories of Joe and Violet are set against the bleak conditions in the South at the time: segregation, the exploitation of labour by white landowners, the miserable wages paid, brutal eviction from lands and houses, the injustices and deceptions practised on people deliberately kept illiterate. This sociopolitical context is not just background detail presented in the detached language of sociology. It is brought to dynamic life by breaking up chronology (so that time-fragments can be moved and can be kept moving) and by using light irony and wry humour to undercut the pain.

Morrison appropriates the blues mode to distance and so to intensify and refine the suffering in order to strip it of sentimentality. Four years after the dispossession, in 1892, the narrator twice tells us, Rose Dear jumped in the well and missed all the fun (pp. 99, 102). In 1901 Joe and Violet were evicted from a piece of land they had bought, but Joe does not complain, only stating, 'Like a fool I thought they'd let me keep it. They ran us off with two slips of paper I never saw nor signed' (p. 126). The technique is like that used in a Louis Armstrong jazz piece: 'What did I do', he asks, 'what did I do, to be so black and blue?', playing on words lightly, uncomplainingly, repeating them softly. 'My only sin', he sings, 'is in my skin', the echo-rhyme giving the words an ironic edge. His raspy growl with its tonal spread (on the words 'do' and 'black'), the accompanying groundbeat, both intensify and deepen what he means.

The rhythm changes for the presentation of the race riots of the time, but the technique does not. Facts are set down coldly, matter-of-factly, the voice never raised. Over two hundred dead in East St Louis, the narrator tells us and then adds a deadly aside: 'So many whites killed the papers would not print the number' (p. 57). Dorcas' father is 'pulled off a streetcar and stomped to death', her mother 'burned crispy' (p. 57). Joe does not elaborate on the 1917 summer riots of New York when he was almost burned alive. There were four-day hangings in Rocky Mount, the narrator tells us. But it wasn't messy at all, no, an orderly decorum was maintained: 'the men on Tuesday, the women two days later' (p. 101). A young tenor is tied to a log and castrated. The narrator focuses not on visual horror but on the grandmother, 'refusing to give up his waste-filled trousers, washing them over and over although the stain had disappeared at the third rinse' (p. 101). The obvious is never stated: that the act of repeated washing is the grandmother's way of expressing her helpless inexpressible grief. Distancing intensifies horror.

One of the ways of escape from the horror and the suffering in the South was to go north. The rhythm changes once again to present the theme of migration, of people on the move, on the go. It has a quick beat that accelerates to capture the excitement, the anxieties laced with hope, the joy and the abandon of a million people entering a land where the cities of the North dissolve into one big City, Harlem.[2] Trains carry them there, and Morrison's phrasing enacts both the rhythm of the wheels and the cascading swirl of sensations and feelings just before entry:

> When the train trembled approaching the water surrounding the City, they thought it was like them: nervous at having got there at last, but terrified of what was on the other side. Eager, a little scared, they did not even nap during the fourteen hours of a ride smoother than a rocking cradle. The quick darkness in the carriage cars when they shot through a tunnel made them wonder if maybe there was a wall ahead to crash into or a cliff hanging over nothing. The train shivered with them at the thought but went on and sure enough there was ground up ahead and the trembling became the dancing under their feet. Joe stood up, his fingers clutching the baggage rack above his head. He felt the dancing better that way, and told Violet to do the same.
>
> (p. 30)

[...]

II

This sequence initiates the setting up of the novel's major theme: the impact of their most recent move on the psyche of a people. The earlier 'move', over two hundred years ago, had taken place on black slaveships from a land beyond the sea.[3] This time the journey, from the rural South – which for many of the uprooted had begun to feel like home (p. 111) – to the industrial North, from country to city, was not as traumatic but was profound. It changed them.

In order to record and present this continuing process of change in fictional form, Morrison had to use unusual narrative strategies. A totally objective narrator would have been too distant, too impersonal; an ordinary first-person one too involved, too limited, to understand the tribulations of a people. Morrison makes use of a number of voices and tellers. These voices blend and change, then shift into viewpoints that switch (at times in the same paragraph) and slide, then become voices again. The process of thinking turns into a point of view, then changes into a voice. A mysterious 'I' enters and speaks for a while, turns objective, disappears, and re-enters again and again. We have to be alert at all times, the ear at the ready, to pick up and put together the 'arrangement' of echoes of sound and meaning that these connected voices release. Morrison adapts the oral/musical mode of storytelling that relies on listening and memory.

Section four (pp. 89–114), which revolves around the activities of Violet, illustrates this mode vividly. It is late March 1926, and we enter a drugstore (Duggie's) with Violet. The narrator takes us into a Violet aware of another Violet, '*that* Violet', within her. The angles of the telling keep shifting constantly, shuttling between the Violet that was, in the country, and the Violet that is, the one whose psyche has been deformed by her twenty years in the City, so that people call her 'Violent'. At times Violet recalls the past briefly, she talks with Alice Manfred, at times she uses the first person (p. 97); at other times the strange narrator slips into an 'I', quite unobtrusively (p. 101). We move back and forth in time (between 1888 and 1926) and in place (from Vesper County, Virginia, to the City), coming to know almost the whole story of Violet, bits and pieces of which we had been told in the first three sections.

We come to know details about Dorcas' funeral, about Violet's first meeting with Joe, about Rose Dear's suicide. We are now aware of the reasons behind Violet's 'public craziness' (p. 22), of the forces in her that made her pick up (not steal) the baby with the 'honey-sweet, butter-colored face' (p. 19) so that people thought she was crazy. And of the two hungers in her: the unfulfilled 'mother-hunger' (p. 108) – she and Joe didn't want babies at first; she had three miscarriages; later she sleeps with a doll in her arms –

and the stories True Belle had fed Violet about the golden-skinned baby that made her yearn to be 'White. Light. Young again' (p. 208),[4] as she later confesses to Alice. Amid the whirl of detail a truth hits Violet about Joe and about herself: 'Standing in the cane, he was trying to catch a girl he was yet to see, but his heart knew all about, and me, holding on to him but wishing he was the golden boy I never saw either. Which means from the very beginning I was a substitute and so was he' (p. 97). We easily make the cross-connections: that Joe's heart drew him inevitably, via Wild, to Dorcas, and that for Violet, Joe was a substitute for Golden Gray. Perhaps Violet will be able to solve the 'mystery of love' (p. 5).

We are given more hints about the mystery. Morrison offers three sections that take us into the inner beings of three major characters, Joe, Dorcas and Felice. She does not use the Joycean stream-of-consciousness, perhaps because she wants to do more, penetrate below consciousness into the psyche. She makes use of the first-person talking voice, a voice that talks not to someone else but to one's unpolluted self. Joe talks to himself and, towards the end of his section, to Dorcas, his other self. His section, placed in quotation marks (pp. 121–35), compels us to realise how the city has changed him.

In the country, hunting in vain for Wild, having tracked her down to an isolated rock formation above a river teeming with fish, aware of the music of her unseen presence everywhere around, Joe had first whispered a loud plea to her to say something, to give him a sign, at least to show him a hand. What he got was a nothing (which lodged within him) and a resounding silence. Then desperate when four redwings (a sure sign of Wild's presence) 'shot' up out of the base of a strange white-oak tree (it was entwined in its own roots as though nourishing and protecting itself), Joe had 'shot' at it with an unloaded shotgun, discharging his anger harmlessly. In the City, hunting for Dorcas, who has abandoned him, Joe is driven by his hunter self to shoot her using a silencer: 'But if the trail speaks, no matter what's in the way, you can find yourself in a crowded room aiming a bullet at her heart, never mind it's the heart you can't live without' (p. 130).

Dorcas too is driven by forces the City unleashes in her. Lacking the sustenance provided by nature and by the country, cut off suddenly from her mother's nurturing love, strictly disciplined by her terrified aunt, Dorcas is a rebel, a wild creature of the City who takes in the intoxicating words of that 'knowing' woman: you got to get it bring it and put it right here or else (p. 60). Her talk to her self, just after she is shot, compresses all we need to know: 'They need me to say his name so they can go after him. Take away his sample case with Rochelle and Bernadine and Faye inside. I know his name but Mama won't tell. The world rocked from a stick beneath my hand, Felice. There in that room with the ice sign in the window' (p. 193). A dying girl talking urgently to her inner self, and to Felice, her other self, telling what she now knows about her self. Joe's sample case with its Cleopatra products dissolves into the cigar box with the clothespin dolls she had loved. The room with the ominous iceman's sign in the window becomes not just a place for assignation but one where human love, noble and pure, and almost cosmic ('the world rocked'), and warmly sexual ('a stick beneath my hand') also fleetingly manifests itself. Her love is so generous and self-sacrificial that she allows herself to bleed to death rather than reveal his name for the police to find him.[5] 'Mama won't tell', she says, using a vibrant word that refers beyond herself to the primal source out of which all love springs.

The story of Dorcas reveals the tremendous impact the City makes on the young and the defenceless. It deludes them into believing that they are free to do what they want and get away with it. They do not realise the insidious 'plans' of the well laid-out streets of the City that makes people do what it wants. The intoxicating rhythms of its music with its jazz beat never stop, they urge everyone every day to 'come and do wrong' (p. 67). City life is essentially street life (p. 120). Country images, when used for city life, become charged with irony. Young men are sheiks 'radiant and brutal' (p. 120) or else 'roosters' that never pursue but lie in wait for the 'chicks' to pass by and find them. Country tracks for hunting become city trails as Joe discovers. The City pumps desire (p. 34) and transforms love into a soaring 'love appetite' (p. 67). Only a nameless parrot in a cage can utter an 'I love you' in the City.

Even the older women are affected by the City. Some await the arrival of 'Imminent Demise' (p. 56) or the coming of the God of Wrath. The call-and-response give-and-take of church preaching generates a jazz patterning with words repeated, questions asked, answers given:

> He was not just on His way, coming, coming to right the wrongs done to them, He was here, Already. See? See? What the world had done to them it was now doing to itself. Did the world mess over

them? Yes but look where the mess originated. Were they berated
and cursed? Oh yes but look how the world cursed and berated itself.
Were the women fondled in kitchens and the back of stores? Uh huh.

(pp. 77–8)

Questions trigger staccato responses like 'yes' qualified by a 'but'
and confirmed by an 'uh huh'. Lacking a wise ancestor, some turn
for support to 'leagues, clubs, societies, sisterhoods' (p. 78). Others
turn wild, for there's no helping hand to rely on. They arm themselves with 'folded blades, packets of lye, shards of glass taped to
their hands' (p. 78) in order to attack, and to defend themselves
from attack.

III

Morrison had to create a special narrator who could survey and
present the City's far-ranging impact and also maintain the jazz
pace of the story. Not one who was objective (too cold, human in-
volvement was essential), not one who was omniscient (that kind
wouldn't be dramatic and couldn't produce tempo), not one of the
characters (that kind would limit story range). She made use of an
overarching narrator who could be both detached and involved
and, perhaps, unlike the other voices and tellers, attempt to understand the significance of the story of a people, the meaning of their
history.

Sth', this narrator begins, using a cautionary female whisper. We
read on wanting to discover to whom this first-person voice
belongs. Our first clue is a tantalising proclamation: 'I'm crazy
about this City' (p. 7). Almost immediately the mystery deepens,
for we are offered a series of strange statements:

> I haven't got any muscles, so I can't really be expected to defend
> myself. But I do know how to take precaution. Mostly it's making
> sure no one knows all there is to know about me. Second, I watch
> everything and everyone and try to figure out their plans, their rea-
> sonings, long before they do. You have to understand what it's like,
> taking on a big city: I'm exposed to all sorts of ignorance and
> criminality. Still, this is the only life for me.
>
> (p. 8)

Patiently we play detective, note the clues, make deductions about
this narrator who tries to be self-effacing, never intrusive. No

muscles: a disembodied voice perhaps, the voice of the City. It uses city idiom: its language is simple and colloquial, but not quite clear. What does it mean to take on a city, why is this the only life? I watch everything and everyone, it says. Perhaps this 'I' is an all-seeing eye, all-piercing too, one that can penetrate human motives and plans. We think suddenly of the myths of Plato and of the *Bhagavad Gita*.

And then of the epigraph of *Jazz* which we had bypassed:

> I am the name of the sound
> and the sound of the name.
> I am the sign of the letter
> and the designation of the division.
> ('Thunder, Perfect Mind',
> *The Nag Hammadi*)

'Thunder', a short tractate in the Nag Hammadi collection, is a revelation discourse uttered by a goddess figure whose name is Thunder, which in Greek is feminine. Thunder is the way in which Zeus *tonans* makes his presence known on earth, a heavenly voice. In this tractate, according to Douglas M. Parrott, 'Thunder is allegorised as Perfect Mind, meaning the extension of the divine into the world' (p. 296). That it is the thunder goddess who narrates the story becomes clear at last in the first paragraph of the final section of *Jazz*, where the words 'thunder' and 'storm', the phrase 'I the eye of the storm', and the statement, 'I break lives to prove I can mend them back again', are heard (p. 219).

A strange narrator this, this female immanence of the divine, perplexing, full of contradictions, a narrator that changes as her story moves on. By the time the end draws near, she has lost the city confidence she had in herself and in her telling. At first she claims to be 'curious, inventive and well-informed' (p. 137). But then she accuses herself of being careless, stupid and unreliable (p. 160). She bewails her racially determined mistake about Golden Gray's motive: not out of revenge related to skin colour does he drive to Vienna, but because of his desperate need for a father figure and for authentic being (p. 159). The narrator-deity hastens to mend matters. What she does is unclear: she uses her powers to invoke the spirit of love that rises mysteriously out of a well (surely the one into which Rose Dear flung herself)[6] and enters Golden Gray's being. That's why, perhaps, he and Wild go away together.

Despite all her powers, this female deity cannot really penetrate human hearts and understand what being human means. She is surprised at the way the story of Violet and Joe and Dorcas/Felice ends, for she had overestimated the powerful impact of the City and underestimated the human resilience that enables a whole people to believe they will overcome. She had expected that 'one would kill the other' (p. 220). Instead Violet and Joe come together and heal each other. Felice heals Joe by telling him that Dorcas loved him at the end, that she let herself die for his sake. Unlike Dorcas who allowed the City to shape her, Felice, urged on by the changed Violet, will not allow the world to change her self, but will make up her own world. And will be happy, as her name suggests.

At the end it is spring, a time of awakening. We now know the many implications of the question that had sounded simple at the beginning: 'who shot whom' (p. 6). We know, even though City people think that the threesome on Lenox Avenue is 'scandalizing' (p. 6), that all three have somehow managed to put their lives together.

[...]

Jazz doesn't solve but does celebrate instead the mystery of human love. Of human life, too. It asks questions, not cosmic questions like *unde malum*, but questions about the presence of evil in the city streets. The story of Joe and Dorcas is associated with the Garden of Eden and the apple.[7] Human beings (as Morrison's other novels, especially *Tar Baby*, imply) have to move out of Paradise to enjoy the fruit of knowledge and to experience love and pleasure and pain. After twenty years in the City, fifty-three-year-old Joe has not lost his country innocence and is still a sixteen-year-old 'kid' (p. 121), until he meets Dorcas. Through Felice, Dorcas sends Joe a cryptic message, 'There's only one apple ... Just one' (p. 213). The message confirms Joe's interpretation of the Eden story: 'I told you again that you were the reason Adam ate the apple and its core. That when he left Eden, he left a rich man. Not only did he have Eve, but he had the taste of the first apple in the world in his mouth for the rest of his life' (p. 133).

Violet, at fifty, aware that the place of shade without trees awaits her (p. 110), sighs out her disappointment with life. It is Alice Manfred who tells her what to do: don't just accept life, but 'make it, make it' in this world (p. 113). Through what happened to Dorcas, Alice was taught 'just how small and quick this little bitty life is' (p. 113) and that it doesn't help to live in fear. She turns into the city version of True Belle, who taught Violet and her family how to survive, with the truth that laughter is more serious than tears.

Dorcas' 'Mama?', hurled up into the overarching sky, is a question that has no answer. It is a personal cry of anguish, a cry for help. It is also the cry of a whole people seeking a way out of suffering and injustice and despair. No answers are provided. Help is perhaps possible, suggested by the word 'hand', which people seek, and offer, and sometimes find, and by 'love', which can rise up like a Rose Dear smile out of a dark well, and which never really dies, even in the City. And also by jazz and the blues, music that quickens the sad bird Violet bought for Joe and for their apartment, a music that can render a people's pain and so transmute and transcend it.

What all this leads to is a question not to be asked. Like jazz, *Jazz* hits us below the Cartesian belt and offers us a powerful experience that does not insist on definite meanings. Hunters Hunter stops speculating about his encounters with the mysterious Wild: 'there's no gain fathoming more' (p. 166).[8] *Jazz* does not offer us any solutions, or even a resolution.

Like Louis Armstrong's classic 'West End Blues' (1928), the novel ends with a closing ensemble of interludes and breaks and brief solos. Played in a low register, at a slow blues tempo, the seven subsections (pp. 219–29) use stretched blue notes to restate and to purify earlier experiences of joy and pain. We catch, as in a break, a glimpse of fifty-eight-year-old Alice Manfred, who has gone back to Springfield, where she has 'someone who can provide the necessary things for the night' (p. 222). We see Felice walking with slow confidence on the City streets. A musical interlude gently evokes the memory of Violet, in 1906, in the country, tired and asleep after a day's hard work, laughing and happy as she lies dreaming, with Joe watching over her protectively. Another interlude: Joe and Violet, together again, walk the streets of the City together, or lie in bed together under a satin quilt as memories filter through to them:

> Lying next to her, his head turned toward the window, he sees through the glass darkness taking the shape of a shoulder with a thin line of blood. Slowly, slowly it forms itself into a bird with a blade of red on the wing. Meanwhile Violet rests her hand on his chest as though it were the sunlit rim of a well and down there somebody is gathering gifts (lead pencils, Bull Durham, Jap Rose Soap) to distribute to them all.
>
> (pp. 224–5)

Darkness dissolves as we listen to this slow soft music that, like Joe's two-coloured eyes, like Joe himself, is both sad and happy, a music of sibilants. The bloodred streak on Dorcas' shoulder turns into one of Wild's escort of redwings, while sunlight rims Rose Dear's well for Violet and a phantom father returns bearing small tokens of love (p. 101).

The lead player then begins an improvisatory solo (pp. 226–8) using a moderate tempo. The words and notes and sounds stir our musical memories, for we have heard them all before: click and clicking, tap and snap and snapping fingers, shade and crevices, wells and the world, and golden hair, and hand. We now know better than to try to figure out what the solo means. What we experience is language trying to become music as it tries to capture the flow of human time.

At the very end the narrator-goddess, awakened by the mysterious power of human love, acutely conscious now of the 'division' of the divine she had mentioned in the epigraph, intensely aware of her own aloneness and of her need for a hand and for a healing of division, utters a loud silent plea that is almost human: 'If I were able I'd say it. Say make me, remake me. You are free to do it and I am free to let you because look, look. Look where your hands are. Now' (p. 229).[9]

From *Modern Fiction Studies*, 39: 3–4 (Fall/Winter, 1993), 733–53.

NOTES

[Although jazz is clearly an important influence on the novel, many of *Jazz's* narrative features, such as telling the same story from different perspectives, cross-connecting different story lines and even the call-and-response, are to be found in Morrison's previous novels and may even be traced back to the influence of the English novelist Virginia Woolf, upon whom Morrison wrote her MA thesis. *Jazz* is typical of Morrison's fiction in its concern with place and displacement, the interrelatendness of past and present, and with characters who, as Jan Furman has said, 'are alienated from the places and people who give them identity' (*Toni Morrison's Fiction* [Columbia, 1996], p. 92). Morrison herself felt that the novel was especially indebted to her writing *Beloved* (see her interview with Christopher Bigsby, 'Jazz Queen', *The Independent*, 26 April [1992], 28–32). Both novels are concerned with obsessive love and seem, as Eusebio Rodrigues says of *Jazz*, to penetrate below consciousness into the psyche. Indeed, the central storyline of *Jazz*, like that of *Beloved*, was inspired by Camille Billops's *The Harlem Book of the Dead* in which Morrison read the Margaret Garner story which is reconfigured in *Beloved*. James Van der Zee's photograph, and the story of the young girl lying in her coffin from Billops's book are clearly the source for two of the incidents in *Jazz* including the opening event in which Violet tries to disfigure the face of Dorcas's corpse in the open coffin. That the girl in Van der Zee's photograph was killed at a party with a gun and silencer by someone who was jealous mirrors Dorcas's death. Morrison provides a fuller picture of Dorcas as she did of Sethe (her version of Margaret Garner) in *Beloved*, and in both novels constructs a narrative that links the past with the present; offering the suggestion that Dorcas's jealous lover kills her because he associates her abandoning him for another man with the fact that his mother abandoned him years before. Rodrigues' essay highlights how Morrison, as in *Beloved*, develops what she finds in Billops's book in order to explore problems and tensions within the wider African-American community shaped by a particular historicised context.

One of the effects of the detective work which *Jazz* requires of the reader is to cast a degree of uncertainty and ambivalence over the novel. Thus, for example, it becomes clear, as indeed the narrator herself eventually recognises, that Joe killed Dorcas because he cannot bear to be abandoned a second time, as he was by his mother, who might or might not be Wild of whom Dorcas reminds him. But at the same time such an explanation seems to rob the novel of its complexity. As Jan Furman has pointed out: 'Morrison suggests, as she always does of deranged episodes in otherwise rational lives, that no definitive, easy-to-grasp explanation exists for the exception' (*Toni Morrison's Fiction*, p. 88). Dorcas has tended to be seen either, following the hints in the text, symbolically as Joe's substitute for his mother, Wild, or as exemplifying what the City unleashes in people. Indeed, Dorcas is a complex character (see, for example, Furman, pp. 86–8) and through her behaviour, her attitudes and what is reported of her, Morrison anchors her concerns with the kind of culture which impacted on African-Americans in the Jazz era. Ed.]

1. Walter Ong in *Orality and Literacy* (New York, 1982) refers to the well-known Freytag's pyramid, an upward slope followed by a downward slope. He also writes about oral patterning, stating that 'an oral culture has no experience of a lengthy, epic-size or novel-size climactic linear plot. It cannot organise even shorter narrative in the studious, relentless climactic way that readers of literature for the past 200 years have learned more and more to expect – and, in recent decades, self-consciously to depreciate' (pp. 142–3).

2. There are over 80 references in the novel to Harlem, which is always the City, with a capital C.

3. Morrison smuggles in a reference to the earlier 'move' in *Jazz*. Watching Alice Manfred ironing, Violet is reminded of True Belle, who always used to do the 'yoke' last. At one moment Alice forgets

to lift the iron off the board, and both women see their slave past in the scorch mark: 'the black and smoking ship burned clear through the yoke' (p. 113). The middle passage reverberates in this line.

4.   A faint echo of Pecola's yearning in *The Bluest Eye*.

5.   *The Harlem Book of the Dead* has, next to the photograph of a dead girl, the photographer's version of what happened to her (p. 84). [See Rushdy's essay (9) in this volume and my note on it. Ed.] Own Dodson, the poet, composed a 'Dorcas' poem for the book (p. 52):

> They lean over me and say:
> 'Who deathed you who,
> who, who, who, who ...
> I whisper: 'Tell you presently ...
> Shortly ... this evening ...
> Tomorrow ...'
> Tomorrow is here
> And you out there safe.
> I'm safe in here, Tootsie.

6.   Rose Dear, with her leftover smiles (p. 161), is not just a suicide. She turns into an embodiment of 'some brief benevolent love' (p. 161) that rises out of the darkness of the well to influence others. She does not 'abandon' her children, for she loves them very much. She waits for four long years after the arrival of True Belle, and only after she knows they will be looked after does she surrender to her despair.

7.   References to the biblical story can be found on the following pages: Eve (p. 133), apple (pp. 34, 40, 133, 134, 213), core (pp. 63, 133, 134), Eden (pp. 33, 180), Paradise (p. 63), snake (p. 76).

8.   We cannot violate the mystery that is Wild but can perhaps offer some tentative thoughts: that she is associated with a Kali-like 'mother' nature; that she seeks refuge from modern man and his violence, that she is, according to Joe, everywhere and nowhere, like the memory of Dorcas for Violet (pp. 179, 28).

9.   My deep thanks to my colleagues Patricia O'Connor, Keith Fort, and Ray Reno for ear-reading this piece with great care (in both senses). I also thank Terence McPartland who transferred *Jazz* into the 'word cruncher' set up.

11

Signifyin(g) Abjection: Narrative Strategies in Toni Morrison's *Jazz*

ANGELA BURTON

Toni Morrison's status as a recognised commentator on black America seems to rest uneasily with the centrality she gives to black disempowerment in her fiction. Her major protagonists resort to bizarre types of crisis resolution including murder, incestuous rape, bestiality and self-mutilation, often within the context of parent–child relationships.[1] Tensions arise when one seeks to read these representations as affirmations of black, rather than white, power. The following essay seeks to resolve this tension by arguing that, throughout her fiction, Morrison employs the strategy of Signifyin(g) on abjection, illustrating this in relation to her most recent novel, *Jazz*,[2] and discussing Morrison's representation of the mixed-race figure – Golden Gray – as a trope of abjection. I begin by explaining the term 'Signifyin(g) abjection'.

SIGNIFYIN(G)

Henry Louis Gates, Jr, identifies the black American practice of Signifyin(g) as a significant tradition in relation to black writing.[3] By 'Signifyin(g)' Gates refers to the way in which, in black vernacular discourse, the ambiguities, ambivalences and indeterminacies of language are played upon, to powerful effect: '"Signifyin(g) [is] the language of trickery, that set of words or gestures which arrives at "direction through indirection"'.[4] Clarence Major defines 'Signification' as 'negative talk, using irony', and 'Signifyin(g)', in part, as 'speaking ironically'.[5] Gates notes that virtually antithetical meanings exist between the standard English usage of 'signifying' and black American speakers' usage of 'Signifyin(g)'. He differentiates visually between these discrete meanings by referring to white usage of the term as 'signifying' and its black usage, as 'Signifyin(g)'. One illustration of how a word can 'Signify' as opposed to 'signify' is the title of a Michael Jackson song 'Bad', which uses the African-American vernacular usage of 'Bad', where 'bad' is used to mean 'positive to the extreme' and 'a simple reversal of the white standard, the very best; good'.[6] Gates's exposition, then, offers me the means by which I come to read the figuring of abjection in Morrison's fiction as one which enables us to see 'abjection' as a sign capable of 'signifying' a conventional and 'Signifyin(g)' an oppositional meaning simultaneously.

ABJECTION

My understanding of 'abjection' derives from Julia Kristeva who theorises it in relation to the dynamics of the psyche and the practice of writing.[7] Kristeva analogises psychic construction to bodily construction to explain how the psyche functions. To maintain its healthy constitution, the body engages in a dynamic process, exchanging things it takes in (food, air, water), for things it expels (excrement, menstrual blood, vomit, pus). Things taken in are either assimilated or expelled. When something enters the body which can be neither assimilated nor ejected (for example, a fatal virus), an untenable situation arises and the body collapses irredeemably. This is the condition of physical abjection. This bodily process parallels the psyche's construction of identity. We constitute our sense of a stable healthy identity by constantly taking ideas in and assimilating positive, whilst expelling negative, views of ourselves. If this dynamic exchange mechanism breaks down, and we introject unassimilable yet unejectable concepts – which Kristeva terms 'the abject' – into the psyche (for example, untenable views of ourselves), we experience psychological abjection, and suffer a breakdown of identity.

KRISTEVA'S DEFINITIONAL CRITERIA OF THE ABJECT

Discourses on purity and pollution inform our definitions of the abject in that the binary relation which sets purity in opposition to impurity (or pollutant) informs its conception. Whilst what is deemed abject can vary (for example, cultural and historical attitudes to excrement or menstrual blood vary greatly) and is never universally agreed, the inverse binary (the relation of mutually exclusive opposites) by which pollutants are distinguished from the pure *is* a common factor, and the one which universally informs relations between ourselves and what we deem 'the abject'. This relationship of imagined difference – by which we distinguish those things we perceive of as constituting the 'I' versus those we perceive of as constituting the 'not-I' – describes the way we constitute ourselves physically and psychologically.

Kristeva suggests that whatever is deemed abject has two major qualities: firstly, it is *imagined* as *absolutely* 'Other' to ourselves; secondly, it is (in fact) only *relatively* (or *provisionally*) 'Other' to us. Thus despite our imagining it is 'Other' to us, by reason of its potential *similarity* to us the abject has the capacity to transgress bodily and psychological boundaries and, having penetrated us (physically or psychologically), has the specific potential to take us over, physically becoming our body, or psychologically becoming 'us'. From this we can see that HIV viruses (or cancers) exemplify the abject, since they enter the body, and from within take over, destroying its immune (or cell reproduction) systems to the extent that the body becomes wholly abject, and dies. The corpse, according to Kristeva, is the trope signifying the ultimate in physical abjection, whilst the collapse (or 'death') of identity signifies the ultimate psychological abjection.

KRISTEVA'S DEFINITIONAL CRITERIA OF ABJECTION

When the abject penetrates us (or when that which we perceive of as 'not-I' penetrates that we perceive to be 'I') an untenable situation arises. As a result of this we experience a schism of affective feeling, sometimes registered somatically and sometimes as a schism of identity, wherein we experience ourselves as a 'split subject', that is to say, as both subject and object simultaneously. For example, cancer patients commonly perceive the cancer as something which both is, and isn't, part of their own body (and therefore themselves) simultaneously. Yet the boundary distinguishing the abject tumour from the patient's body is an ambivalent one. Cancer both *is*, and *is not*, the body we perceive of as 'us'. Cancer actually *is* the body, since it is the body's own cells growing at an abnormal rate, but this overgrowth produces expendable tumours in the body, which emotionally we perceive are not 'us', but some outside object or imagined 'Other' within.

Popular mythology equates cancer with 'death' and 'disease'. By reason of this equation we come to perceive of it as life-extinguishing based on an inverse binary which sets the healthy 'I' against the 'not-I' of 'death' and of 'disease'. The one seems to preclude the other. Thus the cancer patient becomes anomalously situated between 'life' and 'death', 'health' and 'disease'. This explains the psychological ambivalence which cancer generates, both in society and in individuals. Yet it is not universally true that everyone who develops cancer will die of it, or that they will not recover with treatment, or that they will not die of something else first. It is the fact that we *imagine* that 'all people who get cancer will die', which generates our horror. Thus we can see that an important mechanism involved in generating abjection involves both the process of imagining and the logic of the equations by which we determine what is abject. For these reasons, things which we perceive to be abject, in penetrating us and 'becoming' us, inspire ambivalence, a confusion of emotional responses causing us to become caught between desire[8] and revulsion and unable to know which way to turn in our responses. This is the condition of psychological abjection.

THE ABJECTION OF THE MIXED-RACE FIGURE IN *JAZZ*

In *Jazz*, Morrison Signifies on the abjection generated by miscegenation in order to reformulate the mixed-race figure in three ways. Firstly, she reconfigures the myth of origins associated with the mixed-race figure. Secondly, she deconstructs and reconfigures the identity politics of the central miscegenated figure, Golden Gray, so that he is no longer a negrophobe who (when confronted by the return of his repressed African genetic trace) despises himself. Thirdly, she reconfigures *our* attitudes (as readers and members of social communities) towards the mixed-race figure, in order to bring this occluded and problematic figure back into the corpus of black America.

ORIGINS

Miscegenation is only brought into conceptual being by racist discourse. It invokes the ambivalent and phobic responses characteristic of abjection because it involves a transgression of the discrete boundaries by which races are differentiated. The desire for absolute physical racial separateness concomitantly involves a fear of 'pollution' of one racial group by another. For these reasons, the mixed-race figure has historically been a trope of cultural anxiety within both black and white American discourses on cultural identity, so that, for example, Barbara Christian draws attention to its appearance as a common trope in literature of the ante-bellum American south. Christian explains this was because of its location at the interstice between at least two (often conflicting and always racial) cultural paradigms. The mixed-race figure (sometimes referred to as the mulatto) was thus an 'in-between', a problematic figure in relation to debates on cultural identity. Christian points out that through pejorative stereotyping, they have commonly been represented as a cultural anomaly or aberration:

> the mulatto is often tragic. Often she is shown as caught between two worlds, and since she is obviously the result of an illicit relationship, she suffers from a melancholy of the blood that inevitably leads to tragedy.[9]

As Frederick Douglass noted in 1845, the increasing genesis of mixed-race children in nineteenth-century America created a new and discrete population:

> *a very different-looking class of people are springing up at the south*, and are now held in slavery, from those originally brought to this country from Africa; and if their increase will do no other good, it will do away the force of the argument, that God cursed Ham, and therefore American slavery is right.[10] [my italics]

Douglass's comments are pertinent in several ways. Firstly, he notes that the new mixed-race generations signified the birth of a new cul-

tural group, markedly different in *appearance* from prior generations of Africans in America. In this, the body of the mixed-race
figure can be seen as a semiotic trope of the new 'very different
looking' community – the African-Americans Douglass describes.
Secondly, he observes that these new looking people were perceived
of as a different *class*. This implies that a sense of internal division
within black communities accompanied the advent of mixed-race
African-Americans (as Douglass elsewhere confirms, giving examples of domestic friction in the households of slaveholders who sustained 'the double relation of master and father' to their mixed-race
offspring).[11] Thirdly, of mixed race himself, Douglass did not share
the dominant cultural anxieties towards this group, seeing their
inception as a force for change which would ultimately end racism
in America.

As neither wholly black nor wholly white, and as (in Douglass's
examples) neither clearly slave nor clearly son, the mixed-race
figure, then, has historically existed as an anomaly in the ideological
system of racist economies. In generating cultural anxieties (in both
black and white communities) such figures have functioned as the
abject, threatening the stability of both sides of the racist binary. In
Jazz, Morrison focuses on the identity politics of such a figure who,
impossibly trapped on the cusp between two mutually exclusive
racial categories, is ambivalently positioned as neither wholly
'white' nor 'black' – hence, he is named 'Gray'. In her figuring of
Golden Gray, Morrison explores abjection in relation to both sides
of the binary: oppressor/oppressed. Simultaneously, Morrison uses
the anomalous, mixed-race figure to deconstruct the authority of
racism itself.

The central significance of the theme of miscegenation (and consequently of Golden Gray) to *Jazz* is highlighted by Morrison's
decision to frame her novel around the themes and structures of
jazz aesthetics. Jazz is a 'mixed race' aesthetic which – despite its
popular association with black culture – is neither a wholly white
nor wholly black tradition. It is *both* in that it has origins in black
Creole *and* in wholly white culture. The first jazz record was made
by a white band and many wholly white bands played it from its
earliest inception. James Lincoln Collier points out that during the
1920s – the temporal setting for Morrison's *Jazz* – jazz was regarded as 'a New Orleans music played in somewhat different styles
by both blacks and whites'.[12] Nelson George further suggests that
'from the 1920s to the 1940s, jazz was seen as white music',[13] and
elsewhere it has been suggested that, during the 1930s, the majority

of Harlem night-clubs (in which we can assume jazz was played) were white-owned.[14] It is precisely for the reason that jazz was influenced, played and appropriated by white musicians, and later adopted by mainstream white culture, that its status within black culture has been ambivalent. This is one possible reason for its occlusion in such histories of black cultural production.[15] Crucially, many 'black' creators of jazz were themselves of mixed race or black Creoles:

> Playing a crucial, and perhaps dominant, role was a group of people of mixed blood called black Creoles, who lived in New Orleans and its environs. The term Creole referred to the original French and Spanish settlers of the city. White Creoles often took mistresses of mixed blood, and their children went on to form a subculture lodged halfway between the white world and the black one. [...] In sum, these black Creoles never took part in what we think of as the typical experience of the early black American – the deadly drudgery of the plantations and the pine camps, the whippings, the children sold down the river, the lynch mobs, and of course the musical forms we associate with that life. The black Creoles were far more European in their habits and attitudes than were even most white Americans.[16]

Certainly, the work of renowned jazz 'greats' indicates the influence of Creole culture. Billie Holiday was of mixed race, Louis Armstrong originally played with King Oliver's Creole Band, whilst Duke Ellington played alongside musicians of mixed cultural origin and in 1931 recorded a seven-minute composition, *Creole Rhapsody*. In both its formal aesthetic structures and its cultural origins, then, jazz developed as a hybrid aesthetic to the extent that, in 1933, it was hailed as the new form of *American* music most capable of representing America's 'melting pot' of ethnic communities.[17]

The appropriateness of Morrison's use of jazz aesthetics to frame a novel dealing with issues of racial hybridity and inter-racial or 'transgressive' love is also supported by the fact that during the 1920s many Harlem night-clubs – where jazz was consumed – were transgressive social spaces. Many broke prohibition laws by serving alcohol, and some transgressed segregation laws by enabling different racial groups and social classes to mix freely and in intimate physical proximity with one another.[18] The fact that hundreds of white (and black) people of all social classes flocked into 1920s Harlem for its nightlife, suggests the attraction this social 'transgression' – among others – held at the time to the consumers of the jazz clubs of Harlem. The inter-racial mixing of the Jazz Age was not confined to the growth of popular culture in Harlem. Houston A. Baker Jr notes that this period also witnessed a fashion for 'inter-racial dinner parties' amongst the American intelligentsia.[19] Morrison's use of jazz aesthetics thus highlights the central significance of the theme of miscegenation and of the mixed-race figure in *Jazz*.

GOLDEN GRAY

In her novel, Morrison invests in the traditional vision of mixed-race figures in her representation of Dorcas (whose fate follows the conventions of stories about mixed-race figures) which counter-points the revisionist representation of Golden Gray. This contrast is initially highlighted by Morrison's decision to signify Gray's skin colour by his name 'Golden', whilst describing Dorcas's complexion by the term 'sugar-flawed' (p. 28). A crucial difference arises in that the former term is less problematically implicated, than the latter, in the complex significations of racial politics. Dorcas's 'sugar-flawed skin' is paler than Violet's 'boot-black' skin, and is part of a series of physical differences listed between the two women who are the objects of Joe's affections. Whilst 'sugar-flawed' ostensibly describes Dorcas's pitted complexion as a result of eating too many sweets, it also Signifies on the history behind skin colouring by alluding to the illicit sexual economy of sugar-plantation culture. In this sense 'flawed' Signifies: white slaveholders' sexual violation of black female slaves (whose sexual purity was 'flawed' by rape); the 'flawed' status of mixed-race skin colouring as perceived within racist semiotics (for example, the assumption that miscegenation has 'flawed' the ethnic purity of African skin); and the ethnic heritage of Africans in America. Sugar is an important trope in Morrison's writing of plantation culture and the discourse of slavery, and elsewhere.[20] In making reference to it in *Jazz*, Morrison strikes a thematic chord linking general female anxieties over appearance with cultural anxieties over mixed-race colouring and the mixed-race figure's position in American society. As representation of the conventions of stories about mixed-race figures – and in the classical sense of tragedy – Dorcas is also, of course, a tragically 'flawed' character. By contrast, through Golden Gray Morrison presents a revisioning of the conventional story about mixed-race figures within the frame of a classical tragedy.

Various cultural traditions intertextually relate to Morrison's texts, notably biblical and classical texts.[21] Black interpretations of these texts have historically informed black American culture,[22] as Constance M. Carroll observes: 'Black women students, much more than white women students, understand and can identify with the situation of Medea.'[23] Clearly Euripides' *Medea*, the story of a mother killing her own children, is the classical tragedy which informs *Beloved*. In *Jazz* Morrison draws on another classical tragedy, that of Oedipus, to inform the story of Golden Gray's quest to meet his father. The myth of Oedipus is well known,[24] and its central protagonist has been described as

> the archetypal tragic hero, whose history embodied the universal human predicament of ignorance – man's lack of understanding of who he is and his blindness in the face of destiny.[25]

The moral of Sophocles' *Oedipus Rex* is that 'however rich, powerful and outwardly fortunate he may appear, no one can be confident of escaping disaster'.[26] Clearly, this myth relates to Golden Gray's quest for identity in *Jazz* in several ways. Golden Gray is geographically distanced from his father at birth and is brought up 'blind' to his origins both literally and culturally. He is not told that his father was a negro slave until he is eighteen, when any potential affiliation to his African lineage has been erased by his white wealthy upbringing and replaced by white negrophobia. Gray's literal ignorance of his paternal origins is an innocent 'blindness', not of his own choosing. However, his adoption of white negrophobic values, apparent as he quests to 'find, then kill [...] his father' (p. 143), is a 'blindness' of his own making, and for this he is culpable. As the narrator points out, his anger at his father is not driven (in the Freudian sense) by sexual rivalry with his father for his mother's attentions, it is driven by his belief that his father has, through the sexual act with his mother, 'polluted' his identity as a 'white' man. His Oedipal angst is driven by the unassimilable negro trace that he has discovered exists in his own 'insulted skin': Golden Gray has 'Come all that way not to insult his father but his race' (p. 143). Gray's Oedipal 'tragedy' then, is that his adopted white racism has rendered him ontologically 'blind' to the humanity of his father, to the extent that he cannot psychologically assimilate or 'see' the idea of his having a negro for a father. It is his racism which prevents him from 'recognising' his own father, and for this he is culpable.

Morrison's attempts to reconfigure the mixed-race figure begin with her revisioning of established myths of origin surrounding the procreation of mixed-race children. A convention of so-called mulatto stories (as typified by Colonel Gray in *Jazz*) is that a white slaveowner overpowers and impregnates his black female slaves, characteristically without the women's consent and in situations more analogous to rape than seduction. Morrison's Lestory, as Black paternal originator of the African-American physical synthesis, reverses these conventions in two ways. Firstly, he *is* sexually desired by the mother of his child, Vera Louise; thus the sex act is one of mutually desired seduction and not rape.[27] Secondly, he is seen as the masculine agent in the cultural fusion he initiates. Thus, it is black, and not white, male desire which brings the mulatto child into being.

In plantation societies mixed-race children were often seen as the legacy of white male abuse and degeneracy, and the products of white control over black bodies. As such, they were commonly aborted but, if allowed to live, were ambivalently received by both black and white communities. By figuring black paternity as a point of agency in the text, and the ensuing child as a product of *black desire*, Morrison problematises established views of the origins of mixed-race children *and* of the passivity (or non-agency) of black males, since, if such children can no longer be seen simply as the products of white degeneracy, the foundations by which people of mixed race have historically been accorded pariah status in black communities are removed.

Allusions encoded in Henry Lestory's name index his status as the seminal and originating figure in all subsequent personal histories told in *Jazz*. Several sources identify the red-light district of New Orleans, a Creole area known as Storyville (named after a local politician, Joseph Story) as the specific area in which jazz music was first developed.[28] It is highly significant, then, that Morrison names her African-American 'ancestral' figure 'Henry Le*story*'. From a black poststructuralist or Euro-American perspective the ambiguity Morrison stages over the name Lestory, 'Henry Lestory or Les Troy or something like that' (p. 148), functions as a postmodernist pun reminding us that the text is a fiction and of the endemic unreliability of any mode of narration, a theme the narrator most frequently highlights in relation to narrating identity:

> What was I thinking of? How could I have imagined him so poorly? [...] I have been careless and stupid and it infuriates me to discover (again) how unreliable I am.
>
> (p. 160)

Rather than reductively consign Lestory's name (or Morrison's fiction) to the undifferentiated heterogeneity of postmodernism, however, we can read it differently, by considering Morrison's technique of Signifyin(g) and her invocation of jazz. The creolised name Lestory Signifies in that it has both black and white connotations. It is a hybridised name which literally means 'the story' in Anglo-French, a linguistic fusion informing the language spoken in Creole cultures such as that of New Orleans. The black trace encoded in Lestory's name, to the 'Story' of 'Storyville', in the central narrative section of *Jazz*, reads as a site of origin. Just as Storyville, in New Orleans, was the originary site of jazz, the musical aesthetic of hybridity, so Henry Lestory is the figuration of a point of origin and of African-American hybridity in the centre of the book. Directly, and indirectly – through his son – traces of Lestory's radical act of procreation (sowing his African seed into a white American Southern Belle) is structured geneaologically and chronologically (in the story as opposed to the narrative) as the point of origin for all subsequent narratives of identity in *Jazz*.

The geographic dissemination of Lestory's descendants to cities in the north mirrors the dissemination of jazz music. In 1917, police closed the red light district of Storyville and the musicians who hallmarked the jazz tradition were forced northwards to find work. Many migrated to Chicago or to Harlem, including Louis Armstrong – himself a native of New Orleans and the musician whose innovative style of jazz (the improvisational solo) Morrison employs in *Jazz*. Just as these musicians took with them and disseminated the distinctive style of New Orleans music which became known as jazz, so Lestory's descendants take with them and disseminate the hallmark of their shared past in stories based on fragments of memory and traces of past events. The figuring of Henry Lestory, then, is a key foundational event within the narrative of *Jazz*. His procreative act of love leaves its traces through his son and consequently links all of the central characters in subsequent generations. By Signifyin(g) on the name of Lestory, Morrison creates a story of a personal black history which is also metonymic of a foundational myth of origin – Lestory originates a communally shared history of hybridity. This clearly begins to revision conventional imaging of the mixed-race figure as a negative stereotype.

The second strategy Morrison employs in her reconfiguring of the mixed-race figure is to focus closely on the identity collapse of Golden Gray, effected by racism and reformulated in abjection. Morrison's strategy is radical. She constructs both oppressor *and* oppressed within the *same* body to interrogate the untenable logic of racism. Gray's identity crisis illustrates the abjection of both racist *and* victim within the exchange mechanism of racism. He is both negrophobe and mixed-race figure and so his identity crisis represents an agonistic struggle between the ideologies of oppressor and oppressed within a single psycho-somatic territory.

Gray's initial crisis is brought about by his negrophobia – evident in his first responses to Wild and Lestory – and figured through the rhetoric of abjection in several ways. Conceptions of the abject are always founded on the binary opposition of purity/pollution. Gray's fears of the 'negro' status of both Wild and Lestory are represented by images of purity and pollution. Gray's negrophobia compels him to notice details of Wild's dirtiness before he notices her humanity. She is a 'filthy woman' (p. 149) 'covered in mud' (p. 144) and '[u]nder the dirt, lacing her coal-black skin, were traces of bad things' (p. 171). Wild's 'blackness' is figured as a disease: 'He leans down, holding his breath against infection or odor or something. Something that might touch or penetrate him' (p. 144). His fears of his own dissembling draw him to notice visceral aspects of the girl, and induce somatic responses in himself. The girl's eyes are 'sealed with blood. A lip of skin hangs from her forehead and the blood from it has covered her eyes' (p. 154). He experiences 'nausea' (p. 144), 'shock' (p. 152), a sharp 'scare' (p. 150) and 'shudders' at the thought of the woman touching him (p. 150).

Lestory invokes his son's greatest abjection since it is *his* negro status which most challenges Gray's 'white' negrophobic identity, confronting him with the fact that what he most despises – the negro trace – exists in himself. Gray's extreme psychic dissemblance at this insight is figured as physical dissembling. He feels his body coming apart as crunching bone, 'sliced flesh', 'tubes of blood cut through' (p. 158). The unassimilable idea of his own racial 'pollution' generates one of 'those violent, dark revolts of being'[29] characterising abjection, and renders Golden Gray a split subject. He is both white and non-white, black and non-black, subject and object (non-subject).

Golden Gray's 'white' identity rests upon his inverse relation to what is 'black', and in order to sustain his myth of difference he must construct a fantasy 'negro' which is 'Other' to him. This occurs when in his revulsion towards Wild he denies her human status, ranking her as less valuable than (yet somehow equivalent to) the horse, seeing her as a subhuman 'thing' (p. 149). In 'avoiding her' (p. 152), he tries 'not to look at the hair on her head either, or at her face, turned away into blades of grass' (p. 152), '[h]e wants nothing to do with what he has seen' (p. 144) and hopes that 'her lean will not shift' (p. 145). Despite his desire to 'avoid' Wild, in abjection Gray experiences ambivalence – the vortex of feelings oscillating between revulsion and desire – and is thus simultaneously and compulsively drawn towards her, driven to notice exact details of her proximity (signifying her symbolic 'nearness') to him – 'Her head is leaning away from him and her feet are touching one of his splendid but muddy boots' (p. 145).

Gray is also compelled to notice details of Wild's sexuality. Despite 'avoiding her', he remains attentive to her as 'a naked berry-black woman' with her 'mouth and legs open' (p. 144), and despite averting his gaze, he is unable to resist thinking of 'her private parts' (p. 152). Despite, too, trying to validate his horror of negroes (by denying Wild's humanity and foregrounding her 'Otherness' to him), he becomes 'uneasy with this picture of himself' (p. 145). The girl invokes his abjection not just because she is black, but because she is also *pregnant*. The womb is the site where the transgressive act of miscegenation physiologically occurs and Wild's pregnancy forces Gray to confront what he seeks to deny, the facts of his own birth.

Wild's figuring as the source of Gray's abjection is imaged by his perceptions of her transgressing boundaries between life and death. She appears both dead – 'She looks dead' (p. 144) – and alive: 'he notices a rippling movement in her stomach. Something inside her is moving' (p. 145). Thus, Golden Gray ambivalently wants to walk away from her, yet is uneasy to picture himself doing this. Wild's pregnancy enhances the novel's theme of myths of origin. '[T]here is something about where he has come from and why, where he is going and why' (p. 145) which prevents him from abandoning her. He is split, partly revulsed by her (because her condition forces him to confront what he wants to repress – the events of his own origin), yet partly compelled to help her (because, simultaneously, he is searching for his origins).

Golden Gray experiences varying intensities of love and hate in his attitudes to different negroes in different contexts. Whilst he despises Wild and Lestory, True Belle, his childhood nurse, 'had been his first and major love' (p. 150). What he truly seeks to avert his gaze from (or repress) when he encounters Wild, is the 'shock of knowing' (p. 152) their *nearness*. Whatever repulses him about this female 'negro' now applies to himself. The trace of the negro is in both of them. They are *equals*, the *same*:

> ...the nigger. But so was he. He had always thought there was only one kind – True Belle's kind. Black and nothing. Like Henry Les Troy. Like the filthy woman snoring in the cot. But there was another kind – like himself.
>
> (p. 149)

This very insight becomes strangely empowering to him. Their 'sameness' allows for an inversion of the false (or imaginary) binary by which he has differentiated himself from negroes. If he and negroes are both alike then they, like he, must be human subjects and not subhuman non-subjects. By means of inverting the logic of the binary opposition of racial difference, Gray achieves the insight which redeems his prior 'blindness', enabling him to 'see' – or realise – the resolution to his abjection. Beginning to 'see' his father as 'like himself' (a man) exposes the false syllogisms inherent in white ideology (exemplified in the following hierarchical binary equation: white = 'human' subject/black = non-'human' subject), the ideology by which he had previously constructed his 'white' identity. By deconstructing these falsehoods through a series of reversals he comes to recognise Lestory primarily as a *man* (and 'human' subject) and only incidentally as a man who is *black*. Following his 'recognition' of Lestory as a *man*, Gray is then able to 'see' him as a significant part of himself which has been missing – a father:

> What do I care what the colour of his skin is, or his contact with my mother? When I see him, or what is left of him, I will tell him all about the missing part of me and listen for his crying shame. I will exchange then; let him have mine and take his as my own and we will both be free, arm-tangled and whole.
>
> (p. 159)

Thus, through her representation of Gray's identity collapse Morrison allows us to 'see' how abjection functions as a deconstructive space in which the false hierarchical binaries of racial difference collapse. In this she Signifies on abjection by showing it as a space of disenfranchisement (Gray's identity collapses with the collapse of white ideology) but *also* as a potential space of empowerment (the collapse of white ideology offers Gray the chance to 'see' beyond it and 'realise' his new identity as a black man's son). In this way, the ambivalence of abjection allows Gray to glimpse beyond his racial prejudices – 'which is maybe why two gallops beyond that hair, that skin, their absence was unthinkable' (p. 150) – and 'see' the way out of his abjection, first with Wild – 'And if he shuddered at the possibility of her leaning on him ... it is also true that he overcame the shudder' (p. 150) – and then with his father:

> Only now, he thought, now that I know I have a father, do I feel his absence: the place where he should have been and was not. Before I thought everyone was one-armed like me.
>
> (p. 158)

In abjection, the collapse of Gray's racist 'blindness' enables him to 'see' that living without a father has been like an amputation, and that this loss – the denial of his father – is what it has cost him to live in white ideology. The trope of disfigurement and amputation is a metaphor Morrison uses to illustrate the idea that the price of white ideology is inversely related to the loss of the (black *or* white) self, psychically or physically. In her fiction it becomes a measure of the cost black Americans pay to live in societies governed by white ideology. Thus, in *Sula* Eva Peace pays the price of an amputated leg in order to remain solvent as a single black parent in white society, whilst her daughter, Sula, pays the price of an amputated fingertip to survive an encounter with white boys. Morrison explains the semantic field of this metaphor in her analysis of Melville's *Moby Dick*, when she interprets the significance of the white whale in Melville's text:

> Melville's 'truth' was his recognition of the moment in America when whiteness became ideology. And if the white whale is the ideology of race, what Ahab has lost to it is personal dismemberment and family and society and his own place as a human in the world. The trauma of racism is, for the racist and the victim, the severe fragmentation of the self, and has always seemed to me a cause (not a symptom) of psychosis.[30]

Clearly, Morrison's use of the body as an allegory for the psyche works by analogy in a similar way to Kristeva's model of abjection. It also comes close to Frantz Fanon's thinking on race. Perhaps we can begin to speculate that the liminal models of identity formation, charted by these three writers, are *so* similar and *so* analogous to one another, that what Kristeva calls abjection the other two call racism. Fanon himself described the psychic trauma of racism in metaphors of somatic injury and amputation:

> On that day, completely dislocated, unable to be abroad with the white man, who unmercifully imprisoned me, I took myself far off from my own presence, far indeed, and made myself an object. What else could it be for me but an amputation, an excision, a hemorrhage that spattered my whole body with black blood?[31]

In *Jazz*, Gray's losses to white ideology are similarly figured by an amputation, indexed by his clothes – the symbolic mask of Gray's 'white' identity – which 'lying on the bed, looked like an empty man with one arm folded' (p. 158). Given the parallels between the writings of Morrison, Kristeva and Fanon on the causes and effects of racism it seems that from their different perspectives and different cultural positionings in time, space and place, the thinking of these three writers converges in a single insight, that the concept of racial difference itself constitutes a universal abject. This certainly seems to be a philosophical touchstone in the fiction of Toni Morrison and leads me to the third way in which Morrison reconfigures the mixed-race figure.

THE READER

Throughout the flashback section of *Jazz* Morrison positions her readers as 'witnesses' to Gray's identity crisis. The effect of this is that we – the readers – are called upon to 'see' our own complicity in generating the abjection of the figure of mixed-race origins. Morrison's narrator is deeply concerned to implicate us in this story by making sure we 'see' (or understand) what she is showing us. This is achieved in two ways. Firstly, through the perspective of a wandering viewpoint, established by the narrator's own improvisational and revisionary 'readings' of Golden Gray's actions during the flashback sequence. Morrison borrows the style of the improvisational solo from jazz aesthetics to structure the sequence of interpretations the narrator makes of Gray. This structure, of sequential interpretation infused with both dissonance and affirmation, mimics jazz improvisation. Importantly, it also functions to mimic our own reading perspective as readers and interpreters of the text. This alignment – of narratorial and reading perspectives – during the narrator's 'reading' of Gray's crisis establishes that we and the narrator are equally positioned in this analysis. The narrator appears to 'see' only what *we* see. Our own implication in Gray's refiguring is confirmed by a second strategy as we are directly implicated in a process of realisation when, in the middle of describing Gray's approach, Morrison's narrator suddenly addresses a direct question to us, seeking confirmation that *we* 'see' what *she* sees:

> Can you see the fields beyond, crackling and drying in the wind? The blade of blackbirds rising out of nowhere, brandishing and then gone?
>
> (p. 153)

Houston A. Baker contends that the Harlem Renaissance was central to the development of black 'modern' identity and to black modernism.[32] The setting of *Jazz* is located temporally and spatially in this period, and Morrison's technique at this point bears analogy to a famous precedent for the modernist attempt to transcend the restrictions of literary communication, that of Joseph Conrad's narrator in *Heart of Darkness* when trying to envision Colonel Kurtz (a personification of the human evil involved in the exploitative racism of nineteenth-century Europe's 'scramble for Africa') to his listeners:

> at the time I did not see – you understand. He was just a word for me. I did not see the man in the name any more than you do. Do you see him? Do you see the story? Do you see anything?[33]

Just as Conrad's text seeks to implicate the reader in the construction of Kurtz, so Morrison's text employs a similar strategy. Through this intertextual reference Morrison invokes the modernist crisis of representation and the modernist idea that the *process* of art was as important as its product, to *Jazz*. In part, this invocation functions to indicate her engagement with a parallel but contemporary crisis of representation to that of the modernist era, namely, the representation of contemporary African-American ethnic identity in an increasingly hybridised society. In part, it implicates her readers in her artistic process of engaging with this issue. Implicating communities of readers in reconfiguring the mixed-race figure is important because, just as 'All of Europe contributed to the making of Kurtz' (*Heart of Darkness* p. 86), so we might deduce all of Euro-America contributed to 'making' the mixed-race figure a cultural anomaly and pariah. The problem of remaking, or reconfiguring, Golden Gray thus involves us, the readers. What *Jazz* demands we 'see' is our own complicity in constructing the abjection of pariah figures of our own societies, intimating that their ultimate 'realisation' as a reconstructed trope lies with us as living 'readers' of the semiotics of cultural ethnicity. Their reconstruction rests upon our own deconstruction as investors in racial difference in the real world of living communities. In this way, not only does Morrison reconfigure Gray's identity through abjection, by exposing his complicitous introjection of white ideology, she simultaneously reconfigures *us*, her readers, making us 'see' our own complicity in the ongoing abjection of racism. The narrative of *Jazz* compels us to 'remake' ourselves as a community of 'readers' in which the mixed-race subject has a 'right to be'.

Morrison rarely foregrounds white experience, more typically representing white presence as 'the ghost in the machine' of black experience, inverting her own observations about the nineteenth-century American literary canon's suppression of the Afro–American presence.[34] This explains why Morrison does not interrogate white racism through white figures. By contrast, what her texts *do* foreground is the dissemination of white ideology into black culture by blacks who act as its conduit. In *Jazz* Golden Gray as a mixed-race negrophobe is no better than a white racist, but in abjection he sees the falsehoods of this frame of reference, realising that because white ideology and familial identification will not co-exist together he must 'choose' one or the other. The text indicates that Gray chooses to give up white ideology, despite the material privileges it has offered him, in order to resolve his abjection, revivify his identity and become whole. The narrative indicates that rather than return to Baltimore, Gray remains with Wild on the margins of Vienna.

Morrison's visions of black cultural history and identity in *Jazz* are innovative, then, for two reasons. Firstly, by Signifyin(g) on black abjection in this text Morrison enables us to see the deconstructive force of abjection and its potential to empower

African-American people and liberate them from an oppressive history of white power, and from the oppressive frame of white ideology. Secondly, the novel's improvisational narrator positions readers of *Jazz* in such a way that they are forced to consider, alongside those of a racist character and unreliable narrator, their *own* conceptions and prejudices in relation to contemporary conceptions of the hybrid African-American identity. Behind this strategy is an attempt to reintegrate the mixed-race figure into the cultural corpus of black America, for reasons of ethnic pragmatism not hegemonic assimilation. The increasing hybridity of black America means that many African-Americans' only genetic affiliation to the originary cultures of Africa remains as a genetic 'trace'. By reason of genetic drift the bodily semiotics of black America are changing. However, its politics of identity are not changing as quickly.

In many respects *Jazz* exposes this anomaly. Whilst Golden Gray is compelled to learn to 'recognise' his affiliation with the black community, the community must also learn to recognise *him.* Neither the white community of Baltimore nor the black community in Vienna initially 'recognises' him as 'belonging' to them. In Baltimore, his white mother and black nurse collude in deceiving Gray about his origins by telling him he was an orphan and therefore a child who did not 'belong' to his mother (p. 139). In Vienna, no one (including his father) initially 'recognises' his blackness (pp. 155, 168). Significantly, it is only after Lestory's 'recognition' of his son, when he 'could not say it wasn't possible. That he needed a midwife or locket portrait to convince him' (p. 170), that Gray's abjection begins to be resolved. Thus the text places great import on the fact that not only must Golden Gray revision himself, but that communities as 'readers' of mixed-race figures, must also reconfigure the way they 'read' hybridity. Morrison's implication of the reader in her artistic and cognitive revisioning of the mixed-race figure brings me to my concluding observation.

Toni Morrison has said she wants to be a political writer 'in the best sense, writing about the world we live in'.[35] Elsewhere, she describes her use of language as parabolic,[36] asserting that through characterisation she seeks to create 'a person who *is* a simile, a metaphor'.[37] Morrison's comments indicate that although *Jazz* is set in 1920s Harlem, and tells us a story set in that period, it can *also* be read as a parable of contemporary black America. The parabolic nature of *Jazz* is hinted at by Morrison's attempts to implicate the contemporary reader in her artistic process of 'realising' the reconfiguring of the mixed-race figure. It also unfolds through parallels between the decades of the novel's setting (the period of the Harlem Renaissance and the Jazz Age) and the decades of its production (the post-Civil Rights epoch). Each era saw the most radical changes in American history to the lives of African-Americans in consequence of massive social changes, firstly in demography and latterly in legislation. Each period witnessed crucial formulations in the social and civil status of black Americans and each witnessed debates leading to the development of new collective myths of identity on a national scale – such as the ideology of the 'New Negro' in the 1920s and the 'Black Power' ideologies of the 1960s and 1970s.

For these reasons Golden Gray can be read as 'a person who is a simile, a metaphor' for the body politic of contemporary black America. Since the major Civil Rights' Acts of the 1960s black America has been torn by ongoing debates as to what should constitute the culturally dominant conception of African-American identity.[38] It has also been engaged in the invention of myths of identity.[39] Gray's hybridity and quest for not only a myth of origins but also a current myth of identity, and the agonistic identity crisis he figures, are all paralleled in the national body politic of black America.

NOTES

[Morrison's fiction has always been concerned with deconstructing the frames of reference within which African-American identity has been, and is, constructed. Angela Burton makes a significant contribution to our understanding of this aspect of her work, and African-American literature generally, by focusing on the mixed-race figure who transgresses the discrete boundaries by which racial identity is maintained and who has received relatively little close attention in Morrison criticism. The way in which Burton links the mixed-race figure, through a fear of 'pollution' of one racial group by another, to cultural hybridity is pertinent for Morrison's writings and to twentieth-century America. Each of Morrison's novels is anchored in an ever-increasing social complexity and embraces a new cultural and ethnic pluralism of which the City in *Jazz* becomes a symbol. Indeed, Morrison's novels can be seen as a search for a collective way of dealing with differentiated identities, themselves the products of racial, gender and geographical differences, rather than absolute binaries which even the concept of hyphenated identities such as African-American privileges. Kristeva's theory of the abject has been frequently invoked by critics, but usually in an attempt to theorise horror or the grotesque in literary fiction and film. Burton points out that Kristeva sees the body as analogous of the psyche and argues that her theory of the abject is ultimately a means of theorising an aspect of race.

Both Burton and Rodrigues are puzzled by the inclusion in the novel of figures whose mysteries are never solved and who disappear from the narrative. Both critics turn to the novel's jazz aesthetic for an explanation; for Rodriques the novel 'jazzifies' the fragmentariness of black history while for Burton the jazz aesthetic is appropriate for a novel concerned with racial hybridity. Ed.]

1. In *The Bluest Eye* (1970) Cholly Breedlove is instrumental in causing his eleven-year-old daughter's insanity by raping her; in *Sula* (1973) Eva Peace burns her adult son to death in his bed; and in *Beloved* (1987) Sethe murders her infant daughter by attempting decapitation. Both Sula and Eva Peace resort to self-amputation as a way of resolving a crisis.

2. Toni Morrison, *Jazz* (London, 1993). First published in Great Britain by Chatto & Windus (1992). All further references are to this edition and are given in parenthesis in the text.

3. Henry Louis Gates, Jr, *The Signifying Monkey. A Theory of African-American Literary Criticism* (New York and Oxford, 1988). See also Henry Louis Gates, Jr, 'The Blackness of Blackness: a Critique of the Sign and the Signifying Monkey', in Henry Louis Gates Jr (ed.) *Black Literature and Literary Theory* (New York and London, 1984), pp. 285–321.

4. Roger D. Abrahams, 'The Changing Concept of the Negro Hero' in Mody C. Boatright, Wilson M. Hudson, and Allen Maxwell (eds), *The Golden Log* (Dallas, TX, 1962), pp. 119–34; p. 125. Cited in H. L. Gates Jr, *The Signifying Monkey*, p. 74.

5. Clarence Major (ed.) *Juba to Jive. A Dictionary of African-American Slang* (New York and London, 1994), p. 416.

6. Ibid., p. 15.

7. Julia Kristeva, *Powers of Horror: An Essay On Abjection*, trans. Leon S. Roudiez (New York, 1982). First published as *Pouvoirs de l'horreur* (Paris, 1980).

8. In my understanding, Kristeva's use of the word 'desire' in relation to abjection is that this word means something nearer to an *involuntary* 'compulsion' or 'obsession', in the sense of being *involuntarily* drawn to look at, think about, remain obsessed by, unpleasant and undesir-

able things which we certainly do not 'want', rather than the kind of pleasurable desire, or *voluntary* obsession, we experience towards things that we do 'want'. So the 'desire' she writes of in relation to horror can be distinguished, for example, from the 'desire' we experience when we are in love. The former is the sense of the word 'desire' as I use it throughout this essay.

9. Barbara Christian, *Black Women Novelists: The Development of a Tradition 1892–1976* (Westport, CT, 1980), p. 16.

10. Frederick Douglass in Christopher Bigsby (ed.), *Narrative of the Life of Frederick Douglass, an American Slave* (London, 1993), pp. 490–1.

11. Ibid., p. 491.

12. James Lincoln Collier, 'Black Consciousness and the White Jazz Fan' in James Campbell (ed.), *The Picador Book of Blues and Jazz* (London, 1995), pp. 332–6, p. 332.

13. Nelson George, *The Death of Rhythm and Blues* (London and New York, 1988), p. 9.

14. Beverley Smith, 'West Indian and Southern Negroes Adjust Rivalries', in *The New York Herald Tribune* (10 February 1930). Reproduced in Allon Schoener (ed.), *Harlem On My Mind* (New York, 1995), p. 129.

15. In their discussions of black musical traditions both Nelson George and Houston A. Baker omit any serious discussion of the mode of jazz. Whilst each discusses a broad range of musical genres, which were developed antecedent to, or parallel with, what each sees as the quintessential black musical aesthetic, rhythm and blues, neither discusses jazz as a dominant mode of black music. See Nelson George, *The Death of Rhythm and Blues*, and Houston A. Baker, Jr, *Blues, Ideology, and Afro-American Literature: A Vernacular Theory* (Chicago and London, 1984; Paperback edn, 1987).

16. Ibid., p. 333.

17. This claim was made by Carl Cons in the Chicago-based jazz magazine, *Down Beat* (December 1937). Reproduced in Campbell (ed.), *The Picador Book of Blues* (1995), p. 127.

18. Frank Dolan, *Daily News* 31 October 1929). Reproduced in Schoener (ed.), *Harlem*, pp. 81–2; p. 82.

19. Houston A. Baker, Jr, *Modernism and the Harlem Renaissance* (Chicago and London, 1987; Paperback edn, 1989), p. 12.

20. In *Tar Baby* Valerian is a modern version of a plantation owner and patriarch, his wealth comes from sugar – he is a candy manufacturer,

and he owns property in the Caribbean, the spatial epicentre of the sugar plantations and slave-labour economy of sugar production. A candy motif is also used as an extended metaphor throughout *The Bluest Eye*.

21. Toni Morrison studied Classics and comments on the significance of classical tragedy in her work in Toni Morrison, 'Unspeakable Things Unspoken: The Afro-American Presence in American Literature', in Harold Bloom (ed.) *Modern Critical Views: Toni Morrison* (New York and Philadelphia, 1990), pp. 202–30; pp. 202–3.

22. Many black women writers note that part of their education included Western canonical texts including the Classics. Biblical discourses have historically played an important part in black culture, as both education and polemic, and have informed arguments in favour of both assimilation and resistance to white culture in the works of key black intellectuals and black political movements. Both Martin Luther King and James Baldwin came from religious backgrounds and were, in the first instance, preachers themselves. Martin Bernal's thesis on the relationship between Classical Greece and African culture offers an interesting argument as to why the two may be cor-related. See Martin Bernal, *Black Athena: The Afroasiatic Roots of Classical Civilisation* (London, 1991). By her own account Morrison felt Bernal had a persuasive thesis. See Morrison in Bloom (ed), *Modern Critical View*, pp. 206–7.

23. Constance M. Carroll, 'Three's a Crowd: the Dilemma of the Black Woman in Higher Education', in Gloria T. Hull, Patricia Bell Scott and Barbara Smith (eds), *All The Women Are White, All The Blacks Are Men, But Some Of Us Are Brave: Black Women's Studies* (New York, 1982), pp. 115–28; p. 123.

24. In the classical story of Oedipus, in order to try and avoid the fulfilment of a prophecy that he would eventually kill his father, Oedipus's father has him exiled and pinned to a rock. Rescued by a shepherd, Oedipus is then raised by surrogate parents. Later, as a young man, he encounters each of his parents consecutively, and, not realising they are his parents, kills his father and eventually marries his mother, who bears his children. When it is eventually revealed to each of them that the prophecy has been fulfilled because Oedipus *was*, in fact, the long lost son of Laios (the man he killed) and Jocasta (the woman he has married), Jocasta hangs herself and Oedipus blinds himself with his dead wife's/mother's brooch, in an act of repentance which is also a metaphor for his own lack of insight, or knowledge, of his origins. He spends the rest of his days as a pariah in the wilderness.

25. Lucilla Burn, *Greek Myths* (London, 1990), p. 69.

26. Ibid., p. 72.

27. In *Jazz* Vera Louise meets with Lestory in secret over some months. Given the racial politics of the American South in the nineteenth century, we can assume that had she not desired her liaison with him, she could have had him punished or killed. Whilst this incident may be seen, at one level, as a parody of the white cultural fantasy that black men are attractive to white women, the narrative consequences of this foundational act of genesis are such that it holds more complex significations.

28. See James Baldwin in Campbell (ed.), *The Picadar Book of Blues*, p. 327; see also Major (ed.), *Juba to Jive*, p. 255.

29. Kristeva, *Powers of Horror*, p. 1.

30. Morrison in Bloom (ed.), *Modern Critical Views*, p. 214.

31. Frantz Fanon, *Black Skin, White Masks*, trans. Charles Lam Markmann, 1967 (London, 1991), p. 112. Originally published as *Peau Noire, Masques Blancs* (Paris 1952).

32. Houston A. Baker Jr, *Modernism and the Harlem Renaissance* (1987; 1989).

33. Joseph Conrad, *Heart of Darkness* (London, 1985), p. 57.

34. Toni Morrison in Bloom (ed.), *Modern Critical Views*, p. 214.

35. Toni Morrison in Olga Kenyon, *The Writer's Imagination: Interviews with Major International Women Writers* (Bradford, UK, 1992), pp. 99–107; p. 107.

36. Morrison has asserted this in 'Toni Morrison', in Claudia Tate (ed.), *Black Women Writers At Work* (Harpenden, UK, 1985), pp. 117–31; p. 126; and also in Morrison in Bloom (ed.), *Modern Critical Views*, p. 225.

37. Morrison, in Tate (ed.), *Black Women*, p. 127.

38. For an example of a heated debate published in the decade Morrison was writing *Jazz* regarding what constitutes African-American ethnicity, see the exchanges between Joyce A. Joyce and Henry Louis Gates, Jr, refereed by Houston A. Baker in *New Literary History*, 8: 2 (Winter 1987).

39. For a critique of certain contemporaneous African-American 'myths' of identity, see Sidney J. Lemelle, 'The Politics of Cultural Identity: Pan-Africanism, Historical Materialism and Afrocentricity' in *Race and Class: A Journal For Black And Third World Liberation*, 5: 1 (July–September 1993), 93–112; p. 98.

Further Reading

A full bibliography of criticism of Toni Morrison's work, let alone African-American writing, is beyond the scope of this book. There are two published bibliographies:

David Middleton, *Toni Morrison: An Annotated Bibliography* (New York: Garland, 1987).
Debbie Mix, '*Toni Morrison: A Selected Bibliography*', *Modern Fiction Studies*, 39, 3&4 (1993), 795–817.

PRIMARY SOURCES

To date, Toni Morrison's novels are: *The Bluest Eye* (1970); *Sula* (1973); *Song of Solomon* (1977); *Tar Baby* (1981); *Beloved* (1987); *Jazz* (1992).

In addition, Morrison has written *Dreaming Emmett*, the play referred to in the Introduction to this volume, and two important books of non-fiction: *Playing in the Dark: Whiteness and the Literary Imagination* (Cambridge, MA: Harvard University Press, 1992); *Race-ing Justice, En-gendering Power* (London: Chatto & Windus, 1993). There are also a number of minor works of non-fiction. Many of these are listed in David Middleton, *Toni Morrison: An Annotated Bibliography* (New York: Garland, 1987).

An essay which provides insights into her thinking about African-American identity and her notions of community is 'Rootedness: The Ancestor as Foundation', in Mari Evans (ed.), *Black Women Writers, 1950–1980: A Critical Evaluation* (New York: Anchor Books, 1984). Reprinted in Dennis Walder (ed.), *Literature in the Modern World: Critical Essays and Documents* (London: Oxford University Press, 1990).

A context in which to place the innovative nature of Toni Morrison's early work is provided by her scathing review of stereotypical assumptions of black people in 'To Be A Black Woman', *New York Times Magazine*, 7 (28 March 1971), 8. Of particular significance is *The Black Book*, 198 pages of scrapbook-like material related to the history of African-American people in the United States, compiled by Middleton Harris and which Toni Morrison edited (New York: Random House, 1974).

There are a number of published interviews with Toni Morrison. They are sometimes contradictory; for example, over the readership for which

Morrison sees herself writing. Interviews providing the most useful insights into her work for the student are:

Jane Bakerman, '"The Seams Can't Show": An Interview with Toni Morrison', *Black American Literature Forum*, 12 (1978), 556–60.
Thomas LeClair, 'The Language Must Not Sweat', *New Republic*, 21 (March, 1981), 25–9.
Judith Wilson, 'A Conversation with Toni Morrison', *Essence*, 12 (July 1981), 84, 86, 128, 130, 133, 134.
Nellie McKay, 'An Interview with Toni Morrison', *Contemporary Literature*, 24: 4 (1983), 413–29.
Claudia Tate, 'A Conversation with Toni Morrison', in Claudia Tate (ed.), *Black Women Writers At Work* (New York: Continuum, 1983), pp. 117–31.
Gloria Naylor, 'A Conversation, Gloria Naylor and Toni Morrison', *The Southern Review*, 21 (1985), 567–93.
Christopher Bigsby, 'Jazz Queen', *The Independent*, 26 April 1992, 28–9.
Olga Kenyon, 'Interview with Toni Morrison', *Baetyl*, 2 (1993), 11–23.

CRITICISM

There are three sections to this select bibliography of critical works. Since this book is concerned with new critical approaches to Toni Morrison's fiction, the first section is devoted to contemporary critical theory. The selected works should enable the student or general reader to discover the different avenues and debates within critical frameworks which for reasons of space have been described only briefly in this book.

The select bibliography of African-American literary criticism is organised as a general list followed by key works in feminist criticism of black literature. These books provide more detailed discussions of some of the key issues and debates in African-American aesthetics and scholarship to which the critics, whose work has been included or referred to in this volume, have contributed.

The select bibliography of criticism on Toni Morrison's work itself lists book-length studies and collections of critical essays. Studies which share a particular critical approach are grouped together chronologically – continuing the volume's discussion of the changing foci within criticism of Morrison's work.

Contemporary Critical Theory

Two useful introductions to contemporary critical theory are:

Madan Sarup, *An Introductory Guide to Post-Structuralism and Post-modernism* (Hemel Hempstead: Harvester Wheatsheaf, 1993).
Raman Selden and Peter Widdowson, *A Reader's Guide to Contemporary Literary Theory* (London and New York: Harvester Weatsheaf, 1993).

Much published work is now available in the area of contemporary theory. There are a number of compilations, a recent trend, intended to provide important essays and/or extracts from key works which students may find useful:

Thomas Docherty (ed.), *Postmodernism: A Reader* (Hemel Hempstead: Harvester Wheatsheaf, 1992).

Maggie Humm (ed.), *Feminisms: A Reader* (Hemel Hempstead: Harvester Wheatsheaf, 1992).

Patricia Waugh (ed.), *Postmodernism: A Reader* (London: Arnold, 1992).

The following, listed in their order of publication, are useful introductory works containing quite detailed discussions and bibliographies:

Terry Eagleton, *Marxism and Literary Criticism* (London and New York: Methuen, 1976).

Jean-François Lyotard, *The Postmodern Condition: A Report on Knowledge* (1979), trans. G. Bennington and B. Massumi (Manchester: Manchester University Press, 1984).

Terry Eagleton, *Literary Theory: An Introduction* (Oxford: Blackwell, 1983).

Patricia Waugh, *Metafiction: The Theory and Practice of Self-Conscious Fiction* (London and New York: Routledge, 1984).

Elizabeth Wright, *Psychoanalytic Criticism: Theory in Practice* (London and New York: Methuen, 1984).

Juliet Mitchell (ed.), *The Selected Melanie Klein* (1986; rpt, Harmondsworth: Penguin Books, 1991).

Elizabeth Freund, *The Return of the Reader: Reader-Response Criticism* (London and New York: Methuen, 1987).

Chris Weedon, *Feminist Practice and Poststructuralist Theory* (Oxford: Blackwell, 1987).

Elizabeth V. Spelman, *Inessential Woman: Problems of Exclusion in Feminist Thought* (1988; rpt London: Women's Press, 1990).

Cary Nelson and Lawrence Grossberg, *Marxism and the Interpretation of Culture* (London: Macmillan, 1988).

Linda Hutcheon, *A Poetics of Postmodernism: History, Theory, Fiction* (London and New York: Routledge, 1989).

Hugh Silverman, *Derrida and Deconstruction* (London and New York: Routledge, 1989).

Nancy Chodorow, *Feminism and Psycho-Analytic Theory* (New Haven, CT: Yale University Press, 1989).

H. Aram Veeser, *The New Historicism* (London and New York: Routledge, 1989).

Patricia Waugh, *Feminine Fictions: Revisiting the Modern* (London and New York: Routledge, 1989).

Thomas Docherty, *After Theory: Postmodernism/Postmarxism* (London and New York: Routledge, 1990).

Mary Eagleton, *Feminist Literary Criticism* (London: Longman, 1991).

Susan Sellers (ed.), *Feminist Criticism: Theory and Practice* (Hemel Hempstead: Harvester Wheatsheaf, 1991).

Francis Mulhern (ed.), *Contemporary Marxist Literary Criticism* (London and New York: Longman, 1992).

Critical Approaches to African-American Writing

Two influential studies published in the 1980s which approach black literature as a manifestation of vernacular traditions should not be ignored:

Houston A. Baker, Jr, *Blues, Ideology, and Afro-American Literature: A
    Vernacular Theory* (Chicago and London: University of Chicago Press,
    1984).
Henry Louis Gates, Jr, *The Signifying Monkey: A Theory of African-
    American Literary Criticism* (London and New York: Oxford University
    Press, 1988).

Baker approaches African-American literature from the twin perspectives
of the blues and slavery, two manifestations of black, cultural vernacular.
Gates explores the influence of the complex, often intra-communal, verbal
games which constitute an important aspect of the black vernacular.

There are a number of accessible introductions to black literary criticism
which do not sacrifice consideration of complex issues. Two of the most
influential of these are:

Henry Louis Gates, Jr (ed.), *Black Literature and Literary Theory* (New
    York and London: Methuen, 1984).
Houston A. Baker and Patricia Redmond (eds), *Afro-American Literary
    Study in the 1990s* (Chicago: University of Chicago Press, 1989).

Gates offers an introduction to black literary theory and to the nature and
function of black writing, primarily fiction. The seven critiques demonstrate a range of critical approaches – cultural, feminist, deconstructionist
and Marxist. Both books are discussed in an important review article:

Joe Weixlmann, 'Black Literary Criticism at the Juncture', *Contemporary
    Literature*, 27: 1 (1986), 48–62.

Weixlmann identifies 1979 as a watershed in African-American literary
criticism after which a shift from rigid black aesthetic and sociopolitical
criticism to more text-centred modes of interpretation becomes clearly dis-
cernible. But theory-based approaches to African-American literature have
created some disquiet. A brief summary of reservations about theory –
poststructuralism, French feminism and the Black Arts Movement – which
seem to be shared by a number of critics of African-American writing is
offered in:

Barbara Christian, 'The Race For Theory', *Cultural Critique*, 6 (1987), 74–5.

Christian's main anxieties are that an over-reliance on literary theory might
encourage monolithic perspectives, devalue the radical political content of
much black writing, and remove criticism from the practice of writing as
black writers perceive it. The difficulty of theorising black culture is the
subject of a collection of provocative essays by hooks who advocates
transforming stereotypical images of black people and culture through
creating alternatives to them:

bell hooks, *Black Looks: Race and Representation* (Boston: South End
    Press, 1992).

Christine MacLeod, 'Black American Literature and the Postcolonial Debate', *The Yearbook of English Studies* (1997), 51–65.
Angelyn Mitchell (ed.), *Within the Circle: An Anthology of African-American Literary Criticism* (Durham, NC: Duke University Press, 1994).

Feminist Criticism(s) on African-American Writing

The ground-breaking study in black feminist criticism was:

Barbara Smith, *Toward a Black Feminist Criticism* (New York: Out and Out Books, 1977).

Black feminist criticism in the first half of the 1980s was generally concerned with reclaiming a 'history' or 'tradition' of black women writers. The best work in this area is:

Barbara Christian, *Black Women Novelists: The Development of a Tradition, 1892–1976* (Westport, CT: Greenwood Press, 1980).
Barbara Christian, *Black Feminist Criticism: Perspectives on Black Women Writers* (New York: Pergamon Press, 1985).

In the latter, Christian highlights how community norms are often in tension with individual desires and do not always work in the interests of black women. This argument has been taken up by Deborah McDowell, Madhu Dubey and Elliott Butler-Evans in works listed below. In the course of the 1980s, there was an increasing concern with the figuration of black feminism. In the 1990s, we tend to think in terms of 'black feminisms' rather than 'black feminist' and this changing emphasis is evident in black feminist criticism from the mid-1980s onward. In this respect, two important works were:

Mari Evans (ed.), *Black Women Writers, 1950–1980: A Critical Evaluation* (New York: Anchor Books, 1984).
Hazel V. Carby, *Reconstructing Womanhood: The Emergence of the Afro-American Woman Novelist* (New York and Oxford: Oxford University Press, 1987).

Some of the major trends, together with the twists and turns, in African-American literary criticism are usefully reviewed in:

Houston A. Baker, Jr, and Joe Weixlmann (eds), *Black Feminist Criticism and Critical Theory* (Penkevill, CT: Greenwood, 1988).
Deborah E. McDowell, 'Boundaries: Or Distant Relations and Close Kin', in Houston A. Baker, Jr, and Patricia Redmond (eds), *Afro-American Literary Study in the 1990s* (Chicago: University of Chicago Press, 1989), pp. 51–70.
Deborah E. McDowell, *The Changing Scene: Black Women's Literature, Criticism, and Theory* (Bloomington and Indianapolis: Indiana University Press, 1995).

The scope and diversity within feminist criticism of African-American writing is evident in:

Valerie Smith, 'Black Feminist Theory and Representations of the "Other"', in Cheryl A. Wall (ed.), *Changing Our Own Words* (New Brunswick: Rutgers University Press, 1989), pp. 38–57.

Elliott Butler-Evans, *Race, Gender and Desire: Narrative Strategies in the Fiction of Toni Cade Bambara, Toni Morrison, and Alice Walker* (Philadelphia: Temple University Press, 1989).

Joanne M. Braxton and Andre Nicola McLaughlin (eds), *Wild Women in the Whirlwind: Afro-American Culture and the Contemporary Literary Renaissance* (New Brunswick: Rutgers University Press, 1990).

Henry Louis Gates, Jr (ed.), *Reading Black, Reading Feminist: A Critical Anthology* (New York: Meridian, 1990).

Susan Willis, *Specifying: Black Women Writing the American Experience* (London and New York: Routledge, 1990).

Houston A. Baker, *Workings of the Spirit: The Poetics of Afro-American Women's Writing* (Chicago: University of Chicago Press, 1991). A discussion of imagistic fields through which Baker finds poetical adherence among texts written by Morrison, Hurston and Shange.

Karla F. C. Holloway, *Moorings and Metaphors: Figures of Culture and Gender in Black Women's Literature* (New Brunswick: Rutgers University Press, 1992).

Jacqueline de Weever, *Mythmaking and Metaphor in Black Women's Fiction* (New York: St. Martin's Press, 1992).

Madhu Dubey, *Black Women Novelists and the Nationalist Aesthetic* (Bloomington: Indiana University Press, 1994). A study of how black women's fiction in the 1970s was written, published and received within a cultural context shaped by black nationalist ideology. Apart from Morrison, Madhu highlights the work of Gayl Jones and Alice Walker.

BOOK-LENGTH STUDIES OF TONI MORRISON'S WORK

Terry Otten, *The Crime of Innocence in the Fiction of Toni Morrison* (Columbia: University of Missouri Press, 1989).

Wilfred D. Samuels and Clenora Hudson-Weems, *Toni Morrison* (Boston: Twayne, 1990).

Trudier Harris, *Fiction and Folklore: The Novels of Toni Morrison* (Knoxville: University of Tennessee Press, 1991).

Doreatha Drummond Mbalia, *Toni Morrison's Developing Class Consciousness* (Selinsgrove: Susquehanna University Press, 1991).

Barbara Hill Rigney, *The Voices of Toni Morrison* (Columbus: Ohio State University Press, 1991).

Patrick Bryce Bjork, *The Novels of Toni Morrison: The Search For Self and Place Within The Community* (New York: Peter Lang, 1992).

Karen Carmean, *Toni Morrison's World of Fiction* (Troy, NY: Whitston, 1993).

Denise Heinz, *The Dilemma of 'Double-Consciousness': Toni Morrison's Novels* (Athens, GA: University of Georgia Press, 1993).

Linden Peach, *Toni Morrison* (London: Macmillan, 1995).

Jan Furman, *Toni Morrison's Fiction* (Columbia, South Carolina: University of South Carolina Press, 1996).

COLLECTIONS OF CRITICAL ESSAYS

Nellie Y. McKay (ed.), *Critical Essays on Toni Morrison* (Boston, MA: G. K. Hall, 1988).

Harold Bloom (ed.), *Toni Morrison: Modern Critical Views* (New York and Philadelphia: Chelsea House Publishers, 1990).

Henry Louis Gates, Jr and K. A. Appiah (eds), *Toni Morrison: Critical Perspectives Past and Present* (New York: Amistad, 1993).

Nancy J. Peterson (ed.), *Toni Morrison, Modern Fiction Studies*, double issue, 39: 3–4 (1993).

CRITICAL APPROACHES TO TONI MORRISON'S WORK

Feminist Criticism(s)

Two of the best examples of feminist criticism on Toni Morrison's fiction written in the late 1970s and early 1980s are:

Jacqueline de Weever, 'The Inverted World of Toni Morrison's *The Bluest Eye* and *Sula*', *CLA Journal*, 22 (1979), 402–14.

Jane S. Bakerman, 'Failures of Love, Female Initiations in the Novels of Toni Morrison', *American Literature*, 52 (1981), 541–63.

Their concerns with inversion and the disruption of the traditional symbolic order are combined with a more overt feminist/deconstructionist framework in:

Susan Willis, 'Eruptions of Funk: Historicising Toni Morrison', *Black American Literature Forum*, 16 (1982), 34–41.

For further development of this notion of disruption within a French feminist literary framework, along the lines suggested by Barbara Rigney in her essay (3) in this volume, see:

Katherine B. Payant, *Becoming and Bonding: Contemporary Feminism and Popular Fiction by American Women Writers* (London and Westport, CT: Greenwood Press, 1993).

In the late 1980s, especially, feminist criticism of African-American literature sought to apply observations which were commonplace in feminist discourse to the study of race. See, for example:

Deborah E. McDowell, '"The Self and the Other": Reading Toni Morrison's *Sula* and the Black Female Text', in Nellie Y. McKay (ed.), *Critical Essays on Toni Morrison* (Boston, MA: G. K. Hall, 1988).

McDowell's essay challenges the notion of race as the sole determinant of identity and the way in which black women have generally been rendered invisible in discourses about blackness. The scope of feminist readings of Morrison's novels over recent years is reflected in the following essays:

Karla Alwes, '"The Evil of Fulfilment": Women and Violence in *The Bluest Eye*' in Katherine Anne Ackley (ed.), *Women and Violence in Literature: An Essay Collection* (New York: Garland, 1990), pp. 89–104.

Kate Cummings, 'Reclaiming the Mother('s) Tongue: *Beloved*, Ceremony, Mothers and Shadows', *College English*, 52 (1990), pp. 552–69.

Paula Bennett, 'The Mother's Part: Incest and Maternal Deprivation in Woolf and Morrison', in Brenda O'Daly and Maureen T. Reddy (eds),

Narrating Mothers: Theorizing Maternal Subjectivities (Knoxville: University of Tennessee Press, 1991), pp. 125–38.

Rebecca Ferguson, 'History, Rememory and Language in Toni Morrison's *Beloved*', in Susan Sellers and Linda Hutcheon (eds), *Feminist Criticism: Theory and Practice* (Toronto: University of Toronto Press, 1991), pp. 109–27.

Feminist-based critical approaches have also informed wider discussions of gender in Morrison's fiction. See, for example:

Carolyn A. Naylor, 'Cross-Gender Significance of the Journey Motif in Selected Afro-American Fiction', *Colby Library Quarterly*, 18: 1 (1982), 26–38.

Vanessa D. Dickerson, 'The Naked Father in Toni Morrison's *The Bluest Eye*', in Patricia Yaeger and Beth Kowalski-Wallace (eds), *Refiguring the Father: New Feminist Readings of Patriarchy* (Carbondale, IL: University of Illinois Press, 1989), pp. 108–27.

Generally speaking, discussions of masculinity in Morrison's work seem indebted to the development of feminist critical approaches. An important issue has been the emphasis on maleness in African-American literary discourse, particularly the way in which this has created an orthodoxy of victimage that unifies and homogenises black men while ignoring the extent to which they share in the ideologies and practices of male privilege. See also:

John N. Duvall, 'Doe Hunting and Masculinity: *Song of Solomon* and *Go Down Moses*', *Arizona Quarterly*, 47 (1991), 95–115.

ANTHROPOLOGICAL/CULTURAL CRITICISM

Preoccupations of anthropological and cultural critical approaches to Morrison's work have been her use of community, myth and a jazz and/or blues aesthetic.

An important discussion of the central place of community in Morrison's first three novels is:

Barbara Christian, 'Community and Nature: the Novels of Toni Morrison', *Journal of Ethnic Studies*, 7 (1980), 65–78.

More recent studies have placed a greater emphasis on the cultural dimension of community. See, for example, Gay Wilentz's essay which argues that Morrison evokes African culture to help maintain African-American culture:

Gay Wilentz, *Binding Cultures: Black Women Writers in Africa and the Diaspora* (Bloomington and Indianapolis: Indiana University Press, 1992), pp. 81–98.

Not surprisingly, *Song of Solomon* spawned numerous essays on Morrison's use of myth. See, for example:

Susan L. Blake, 'Folklore and Community in *Song of Solomon*', *Melus*, 7 (1980), 71–82.

Harris A. Leslie, 'Myth as Structure in Toni Morrison's *Song of Solomon*', *Melus*, 7 (1980), 69–76.

Wilfred D. Samuels, 'Originality and the Search For Self in Toni Morrison's *Song of Solomon*', *Minority Voices*, 5 (1981), 59–68.

The latter links Milkman's quest for selfhood with Western myths employing an anthropological framework from Van Gennep. Key mythic elements in *Song of Solomon* – initiation, renunciation, atonement and relief – are discussed by:

Dorothy H. Lee, '*Song of Solomon*: To Ride The Air', *Black American Literature Forum*, 16 (1982), 64–70.

An overview of the use of traditional African mythology in Morrison's early fiction is provided in:

Grace Ann Hovet and Barbara Lounsberry, 'Flying as symbol and legend in Toni Morrison's *The Bluest Eye, Sula* and *Song of Solomon*', *CLA Journal*, 27 (1983), 119–40.

Criticism in the 1980s showed an increasing scepticism as to the place of the folk tradition in modern black society. See, for example:

James Coleman, 'The Quest for Wholeness in Morrison's *Tar Baby*', *Black American Literature Forum*, 20 (1986), 62–73.

Morrison's use of Western, classical myths – Ulysses, Oedipus, Mother-Earth, Daedalus and Orpheus – is discussed in:

William K. Freiert, 'Classical Themes in Toni Morrison's *Song of Solomon*', *Helios*, 10 (1983), 161–70.

The Fall myth in Morrison's work is the subject of:

Bessie W. Jones, 'Garden Metaphor and Christian Symbolism in *Tar Baby*', in Bessie W. Jones and Audrey L. Vinson (eds), *The World of Toni Morrison* (Dubuque, IA: Kendall/Hunt, 1985), 116–17.

Deconstruction is frequently a tool used by critics of Morrison's work in tandem with feminist and/or anthropological/cultural critical approaches. See, for example, the following essay which discusses Morrison's use of the 'landscape' of New and Old World Western culture, history and cosmological beliefs:

Angelita Reyes, 'Ancient Properties in the New World: The Paradox of the "Other" in Toni Morrison's *Tar Baby*', *Black Scholar*, 17 (1986), 19–25.

An interesting development in anthropological/cultural criticism of Morrison's work came with an increasing focus on her characters as standing at the interface of two or more cultures. See, especially:

Barbara Christian, 'The Contemporary Fables of Toni Morrison', in Barbara Christian (ed.), *Black Women Novelists: The Development of a Tradition, 1892–1976* (London and Westport, CT: Greenwood Press, 1980), pp. 111–79.

More recent work has sought to explore Morrison's concern with the commodification of identity and consumer culture:

Susan Willis, 'I Shop Therefore I Am: Is There A Place For Afro-American culture in Commodity Culture?', in Cheryl A. Walker (ed.), *Changing Our Own Words: Essays on Criticism, Theory and Writing by Black Women* (New Brunswick, NJ: Rutgers University Press, 1989).

Narratology and anthropological/cultural criticism have been brought together in discussions of Morrison's fiction in relation to jazz and blues music. The blues as a vehicle for handing down historical concepts and cultural values is discussed in:

Joyce M. Wegs, 'Toni Morrison's *Song of Solomon*: A Blues Song', *Essays in Literature*, 9 (1982), 211–23.

An interesting comparison of the cultural significance of pain in the blues tradition and in *Beloved*, which sees Morrison as challenging Western intellectual and religious traditions which valorise suffering, is offered by:

Kristin Boudreau, 'Pain and the Unmaking of Self in Toni Morrison's *Beloved*', *Contemporary Literature*, 26, 3 (1995), 447–65.

Not surprisingly, the influence of the jazz aesthetic on the nature and content of Morrison's novels has received some attention, but still awaits a full exploration. A number of studies have professed to find the non-formal techniques of jazz employed in Morrison's fiction. Rice identifies three aesthetic strategies which Morrison's novels and black music share – antiphons, riffing and signifying – the latter being also a feature of African-American oral expression:

Alan J. Rice, 'Finger-Snapping to Train-Dancing and Back Again: The Development of a Jazz Style in African American Prose', *The Yearbook of English Studies: Ethnicity and Representation in American Literature*, 24 (1994), 105–16.

A further possibly jazz-influenced feature of Morrison's fiction is the way in which duets, short pieces of dialogue which are at times harmonious and at times dissonant, are interspersed throughout the text. This is discussed perfunctorily in:

Robin Small-McCarthy, 'The *Jazz* Aesthetic in the Novels of Toni Morrison', *Cultural Studies*, 9: 2 (1995), 293–300.

Small-McCarthy finds evidence in Morrison's fiction of polyrhymic structures, dissonance, harmony, bebop lyricism, and improvisation. The emphasis of his paper is on antiphony which in *Beloved* reaches its peak when Sethe acknowledges Beloved as her daughter and Beloved sings the response. The narrative of *Jazz*, Small-McCarthy argues, is shaped by call-and-response: the unnamed narrator soloist calls and the other players respond.

Jazz as image and metaphor in *Jazz* is explored in:

Eusebio L. Rodrigues, 'Experiencing *Jazz*', *Modern Fiction Studies*, 39 (1993), 733–54. [The extract in this volume is from this essay – Ed.]

Rodrigues is interested in the way in which the novel 'jazzifies the history of a people' which is where Morrison herself apparently sought to place the emphasis (see her interview with Bigsby, 1992).

MARXIST CRITICISM

Although Doreatha Mbalia provides the most sustained Marxist discussion of Morrison's work, a number of critics have employed a Marxist approach as part of a complex theoretical base. An important discussion of women in Morrison's work in relation to class and class assumptions is:

Barbara Christian, 'The Concept of Class in the Novels of Toni Morrison', in Barbara Christian, *Black Feminist Criticism: Perspectives on Black Women Writers* (New York: Pergamon Press, 1985), pp. 71–86.

For a Marxist-feminist reading of *Jazz*, see:

Doreatha Drummond Mbalia, 'Women Who Run Wild: The Need for Sisterhoods in *Jazz*', *Modern Fiction Studies*, 39: 3–4 (1983), 623–46.

Like Rodrigues, Mbalia stresses the 'jazziness' of the jazz era. However, its rebelliousness, defiance, aggressiveness and selfishness are seen as caused by class exploitation and race/gender oppression.

HISTORICIST APPROACHES

The first important study of how Morrison's work re-visions history is Barbara Christian's exploration of African-American women writers' reclamation of history through the memory of their mothers:

Barbara Christian, 'From the Inside Out: Afro-American Women, Literary Theory and the state', *Center for Humanistic Studies Occasional Papers* (University of Minnesota Press, 1986).

This approach is linked to Morrison's apparent 'magic realism' in:

Gabrielle P. Foreman, 'Past-On Stories: History and the Magically Real, Morrison and Allende on Call', *Feminist Studies*, 18 (1992), 369–88.

Houston A. Baker has pointed out that even modern historiography in an ahistorical, postmodern world is the equivalent to having faith in Brer Fox's court. However, he suggests that contemporary Euro-American new historicism might lead us back to painful histories:

Houston A. Baker, Jr, *The Workings of the Spirit: The Poetics of Afro-American Women's Writing* (Chicago and London: University of Chicago Press, 1991), pp. 136–61.

Cynthia S. Hamilton, 'Revisions, Rememories and Exorcisms: Toni Morrison and the Slave Narrative', *Journal of American Studies*, 30: 3 (December 1996), 429–445.

PSYCHOANALYTIC APPROACHES

There are a number of papers which complement Jennifer FitzGerald's essay (7) in this volume and illustrate the scope and range of the different psychoanalytic approaches which may be taken to Morrison's work. Psychoanalytic perspectives on Morrison's fiction developed in the mid-1980s, but some of the initial studies did not have an especially strong theoretical base. See, for example:

Richard K. Barksdale, 'Castration Symbolism in Recent *Black* American Fiction', *College Language Association Journal*, 29: 4 (June, 1986), 400–13.

The majority of psychoanalytic approaches have focused, like the extract from Houston Baker's book in this volume (essay 6), on Morrison's black women characters as in:

Marco Portales, 'Toni Morrison's *The Bluest Eye*: Shirley Temple and Cholly', *The Centennial Review*, 30 (1986), 496–506.
Hortense J. Spillers, 'A Hateful Passion, A Love Lost', in Shari Bernstock (ed.), *Feminist Issues in Literary Scholarship* (Bloomington and Indianapolis: Indiana University Press, 1987), pp. 293–323.

While Portales focuses on the 'demented personality' in *The Bluest Eye*, Hortense Spillers widens the frame of reference and compares the psychologic progression of black women in *Sula* and two other novels by black women novelists. Although Morrison's first two novels seemed to have lent themselves to a psychoanalytic approach, it is only more recently that critics have pursued their psychoanalytic criticism within a poststructuralist framework. See:

Alisha R. Coleman, 'One and One Make One: A Metacritical and Psychoanalytical Reading of Friendship in Toni Morrison's *Sula*', *CLA Journal*, 37: 8 (1993), 145–55.

A Freudian approach to Morrison's fiction, including *Beloved*, is taken in:

Ashraf H. A. Rushdy, '"Rememory": Primal Scenes and Constructions in Toni Morrison's Novels', *Contemporary Literature*, 31 (1988), 300–23.

Barbara Schapiro's essay, which is discussed in the Introduction, like Jennifer FitzGerald's paper, offers an object relations approach:

Barbara Schapiro, 'The Bonds of Love and the Boundaries of Self in Toni Morrison's *Beloved*', *Contemporary Literature*, 32: 2 (1991), 194–210.

Beloved has stimulated papers with a complex theoretical base combining psychoanalysis and feminism and focusing on the black mother:

Barbara Offutt Mathieson, 'Memory and Mother Love in Morrison's *Beloved*', *American Imago*, 47 (1990), 1–21.
Stephanie A. Demetrakopoulos, 'Maternal Bonds as Devourers of Women's Individuation in Toni Morrison's *Beloved*', *African American Review*, 26 (1992), 51–9.

Jean Wyatt, 'Giving Body to the Word: The Maternal Symbolic in Toni Morrison's *Beloved*', *PMLA*, 108 (1993), 474–88.

POSTMODERN APPROACHES

Not surprisingly, *Beloved* has attracted discussion within a postmodern framework. Readers who would like to develop the approach taken by Pérez-Torres in this volume (essay 8) should see:

Patricia Clough, *The End(s) of Ethnography: From Realism to Social Criticism* (London and New Delhi: Sage, 1992), pp. 113–30.

Clough's reading of Morrison's fiction is implicitly postmodern. But her deconstruction of 'realist narrativity' is clearly informed by postmodern assumptions, especially her application of Fredric Jameson's work on 'magic realism' to *Beloved*. For a more explicit postmodern reading of *Beloved*, see:

Brenda K. Marshall, *Teaching the Postmodern: Fiction and Theory* (London and New York: Routledge, 1992), pp. 179–93.

READER-RESPONSE APPROACHES

There have been few attempts to approach Morrison's work using reader-response theories, concerned with the relationship between the activities of reading and interpretation. For a discussion of what is perceived to be a gap between the experience of reading *Beloved* and the explanations offered by interpreters, see:

James Phelan, 'Towards a Rhetorical Reader-response Criticism: the Difficult, the Stubborn, and the Ending of *Beloved*', *Modern Fiction Studies*, 39: 3–4 (1993), 709–28.

Notes on Contributors

Houston A. Baker, Jr, is Professor of English and the Albert M. Greenfield Professor of Human Relations at the University of Pennsylvania where he also directs the Centre for the Study of Black Literature and Culture. He has published extensively on theory and, particularly, on African-American women's writing; canon formation; and Blues and the representation of culture. His recent works include *Blues, Ideology, and Afro-American Literature: A Vernacular Theory* (Chicago, 1984); *Modernism and the Harlem Renaissance* (Chicago, 1987) and *Workings of the Spirit: The Poetics of Afro-American Women's Writing* (Chicago, 1991). Among the numerous books to which he has contributed or edited is (with Patricia Redmond), *Afro-American Literary Study in the 1990s* (Chicago, 1989).

Angela Burton is completing a doctorate in the School of English at the University of Leeds where she has also taught. She is the author (with Linden Peach) of *English as a Creative Art: Literary Concepts Linked to Creative Writing* (London, 1995) and has published on postcolonial writers of the black diaspora.

Cynthia A. Davis received her doctorate from the University of Wisconsin-Madison. She is best known for her work on Stanley Kunitz, on Margaret Drabble and on feminist scholarship, particularly in the area of archetype and myth on which she has contributed to *Courage and Tools: The Florence Howe Award for Feminist Scholarship 1974–1989* (1990), having in 1981 received the Florence Howe award. She is currently executive director of the Partnership Education Fund in Washington, DC.

Madhu Dubey is an assistant professor in African-American literature at Northwestern University, Illinois. She is the author of *Black Women Novelists and the Nationalist Aesthetic* (Bloomington, IN, 1994) and of essays on recent fiction by African-American women writers.

Jennifer FitzGerald is a Senior Lecturer in English at the Queen's University, Belfast, where she also teaches on the Women's Studies programme. Originally a Romantics scholar, she is undertaking further work on Toni Morrison and is currently writing a critical study of Helen Waddell.

Terry Otten is Professor of English at Wittenberg University. He has written on the theatre, Ibsen, Lewis Carroll and Toni Morrison. His publications include *After Innocence: Visions of the Fall in Modern Literature* (Pittsburgh, 1982) and *The Crime of Innocence in the Fiction of Toni Morrison* (Columbia, 1989).

Doreatha Drummond Mbalia is currently an associate professor in the Department of Africology at the University of Wisconsin, Milwaukee. She completed her MA and PhD at the University of Illinois-Urbana in English. In addition to *Toni Morrison's Developing Class Consciousness* (Selinsgrove, 1991), her publications include a study of John Edgar Wideman, and a novel entitled, *My Revolution is Like Honey: She Gets Sweeter All The Time*. She is currently working on *Toni Morrison: Her Life in Her Works* and a biography of Kwame Nkrumah.

Rafael Pérez-Torres is an assistant professor of English at the University of Pennsylvania. His main interests are in Chicano culture and poetry, the cultural significance of the Mexican/United States border, and multi-cultural postmodernism. He is the author of *Movements in Chicano Poetry – Against Myths, Against Margins* (Cambridge, 1995).

Barbara Hill Rigney is Professor of English at The Ohio State University. She is the author of four books including *Madness and Sexual Politics in the Feminist Novel* (Madison, WI, 1978), *Margaret Atwood* (Basingstoke, UK, 1987) and *The Voices of Toni Morrison* (Columbus, OH, 1991), and of numerous articles on feminist theory.

Eusebio L. Rodrigues is Professor of English at Georgetown University. He has published papers on a wide range of English and American twenti-eth-century authors including Saul Bellow, William Faulkner, Graham Greene, E. M. Forster and Toni Morrison. He is the author of *Quest For The Human: An Exploration of Saul Bellow's Fiction* (London, 1981).

Ashraf H. A. Rushdy is an Associate Professor of English and African-American Studies at Wesleyan University. He has published numerous articles on African-American literature and culture, literary theory, and renaissance literature. He is the author of *The Empty Garden: The Subject of Late Milton* (1992) and is currently working on a book-length study of African-American modes of representation in contemporary narratives of slavery, to be entitled *NeoSlave Narratives: Studies in the Social Logic of a Contemporary Form*.

Index